WOMEN OF DESIGN

HOW
BOOKS
Cincinnati, Ohio
www.howdesign.com

WOMEN OF DESIGN

INFLUENCE and **INSPIRATION**
from the **ORIGINAL TRAILBLAZERS** to the **NEW GROUNDBREAKERS**

Bryony Gomez-Palacio **AND** Armin Vit

For more resources for designers, visit www.howdesign.com.

12 11 10 09 08   5 4 3 2 1

Distributed in Canada
by Fraser Direct
100 Armstrong Avenue
Georgetown, Ontario, Canada L7G 5S4
Tel: (905) 877-4411

Distributed in the U.K. and Europe
by David & Charles
Brunel House, Newton Abbot, Devon, TQ12 4PU, England
Tel: (+44) 1626-323200, Fax: (+44) 1626-323319
E-mail: postmaster@davidandcharles.co.uk

Distributed In Australia
by Capricorn Link
P.O. Box 704, Windsor, NSW 2756 Australia
Tel: (02) 4577-3555

Library of Congress Cataloging-in-Publication Data
Gomez-Palacio, Bryony.
  Women of design : influence and inspiration from the original trailblazers
to the new groundbreakers / Bryony Gomez-Palacio and Armin Vit. -- 1st ed.
      p. cm.
  Includes bibliographical references and index.
  ISBN 978-1-60061-085-1 (pbk. with flaps : alk. paper)
  1. Women commercial artists. I. Vit, Armin. II. Title.
  NC998.4.G63 2008
  741.6082--dc22   2008031495

Cover illustration by Marian Bantjes

UNDERCONSIDERATION

Designed by Bryony Gomez-Palacio and Armin Vit

F+W PUBLICATIONS, INC.

Edited by Amy Schell
Art directed by Grace Ring
Production coordinated by Greg Nock

ACKNOWLEDGMENTS

Above all, we want to thank the women featured in this book who set aside time to contribute by answering our seemingly endless barrage of e-mails and requests, dusting off archived projects, photographing new projects, and painstakingly ensuring that everyone involved in each project was properly credited. Without their patience, energy, and commitment, this book would not have been possible.

When we first started this project we inquired with some of our acquaintances about possible women to include—especially as we tried to look beyond the U.S.—and while we may not have included all of their recommendations, their input was invaluable: Patrick Burgoyne, Oded Ezer, Steven Heller, Dado Queiroz, Stefan Sagmeister and Erik Spiekermann.

Despite living in an age where the world's information is a Google search away, we are lucky to know a few well-connected people in the industry that aided us along the way with helpful contact information: Michael Bierut, Phil Hamlett, Steven Heller (yes, again) and Debbie Millman.

In more ways than one, this book would not be in your hands without the support from the wonderful staff at HOW Books who saw the potential in our idea, beginning with Megan Patrick, who championed it, editor Amy Schell, who helped us see it from concept to completion, and Grace Ring, who kept our creative whims within reason.

At the risk of sentimentality, we can't thank our parents, brothers, cousins and extended family enough. Their continued support in all of our ventures keeps us focused and confident. And, as first-time parents, we would be remiss if we didn't deeply thank our lovely daughter Maya, who has provided the necessary amount of silliness and unbridled curiosity necessary to energize us through busy times.

To all, many thanks.

Bryony and Armin

A DIAGRAM OF INFLUENCE AND INSPIRATION

Just as we may find inspiration within the pages of this book and be influenced by the stories and work that these designers, teachers, and writers have shared, they, in turn, provide us with a glimpse of the women they have been influenced by or the ones whose work or persona they admire. While limited in scope to those included in the book—and to three choices, as otherwise a book could be filled with these associations alone—each choice amounts to a broader network of women defining the graphic design profession.

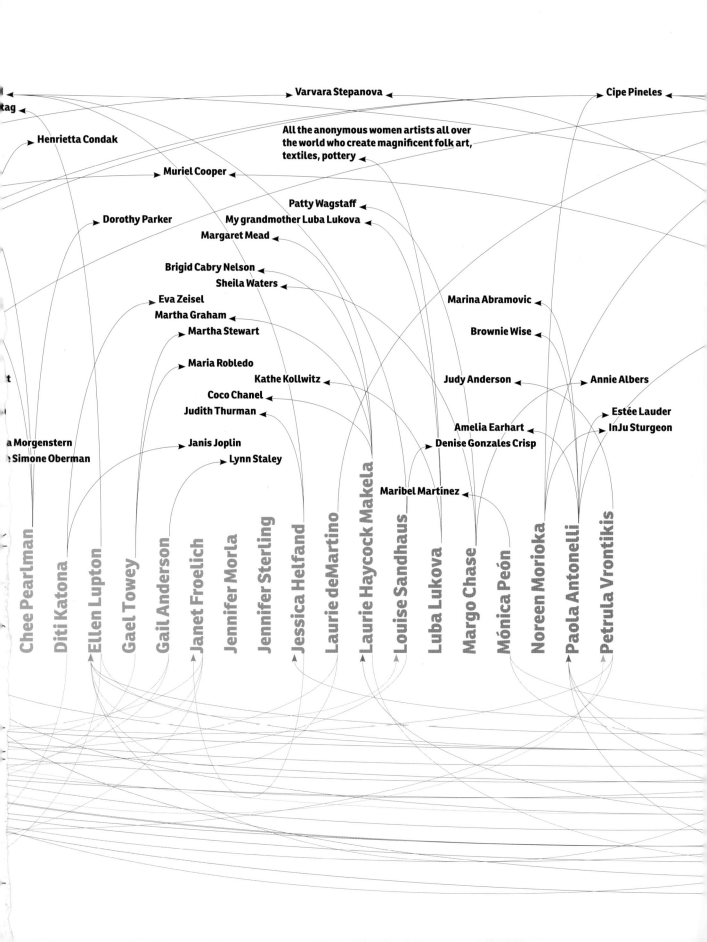

Varvara Stepanova

Cipe Pineles

tag

Henrietta Condak

All the anonymous women artists all over
the world who create magnificent folk art,
textiles, pottery

Muriel Cooper

Patty Wagstaff

Dorothy Parker

My grandmother Luba Lukova

Margaret Mead

Brigid Cabry Nelson

Sheila Waters

Marina Abramovic

Eva Zeisel

Martha Graham

Brownie Wise

Martha Stewart

Maria Robledo

Kathe Kollwitz

Judy Anderson

Annie Albers

Coco Chanel

Judith Thurman

Estée Lauder

InJu Sturgeon

a Morgenstern

Amelia Earhart

e Simone Oberman

Janis Joplin

Denise Gonzales Crisp

Lynn Staley

Maribel Martínez

Chee Pearlman

Diti Katona

Ellen Lupton

Gael Towey

Gail Anderson

Janet Froelich

Jennifer Morla

Jennifer Sterling

Jessica Helfand

Laurie deMartino

Laurie Haycock Makela

Louise Sandhaus

Luba Lukova

Margo Chase

Mónica Peón

Noreen Morioka

Paola Antonelli

Petrula Vrontikis

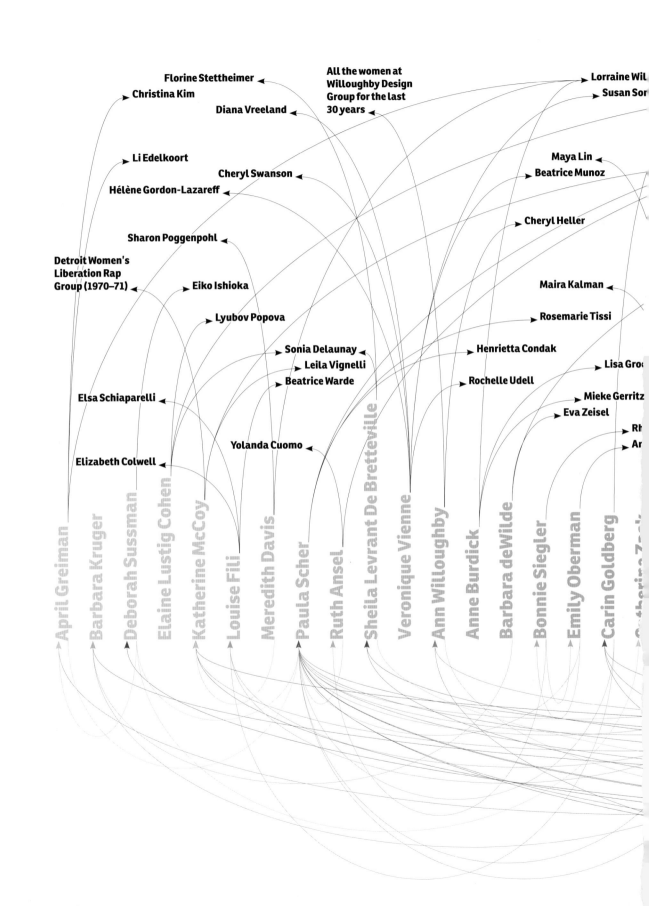

Florine Stettheimer

Christina Kim

All the women at
Willoughby Design
Group for the last
30 years

Lorraine Wil

Susan Sor

Diana Vreeland

Li Edelkoort

Maya Lin

Beatrice Munoz

Cheryl Swanson

Hélène Gordon-Lazareff

Cheryl Heller

Sharon Poggenpohl

Detroit Women's
Liberation Rap
Group (1970–71)

Maira Kalman

Eiko Ishioka

Rosemarie Tissi

Lyubov Popova

Sonia Delaunay

Henrietta Condak

Leila Vignelli

Lisa Gro

Beatrice Warde

Rochelle Udell

Elsa Schiaparelli

Mieke Gerritz

Eva Zeisel

Rh

Yolanda Cuomo

Ar

Elizabeth Colwell

April Greiman
Barbara Kruger
Deborah Sussman
Elaine Lustig Cohen
Katherine McCoy
Louise Fili
Meredith Davis
Paula Scher
Ruth Ansel
Sheila Levrant De Bretteville
Veronique Vienne
Ann Willoughby
Anne Burdick
Barbara deWilde
Bonnie Siegler
Emily Oberman
Carin Goldberg

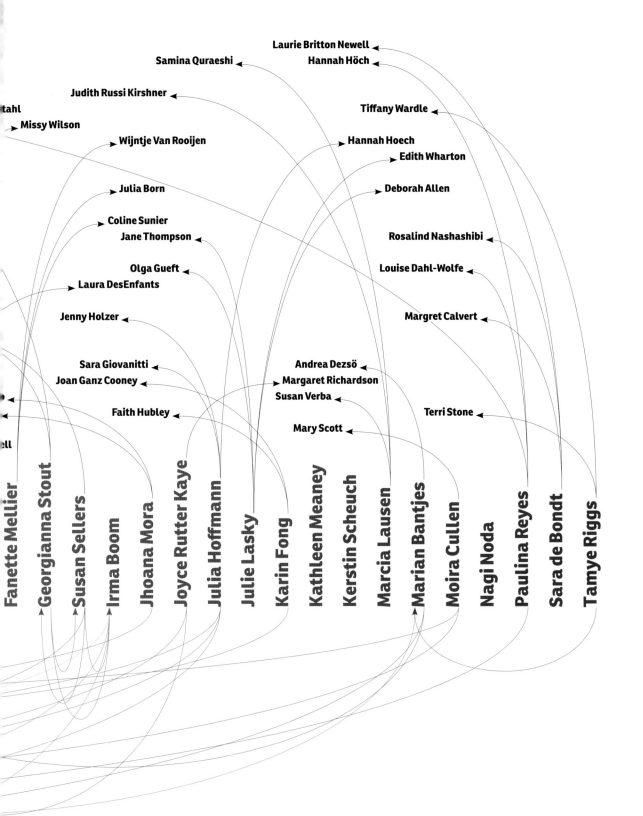

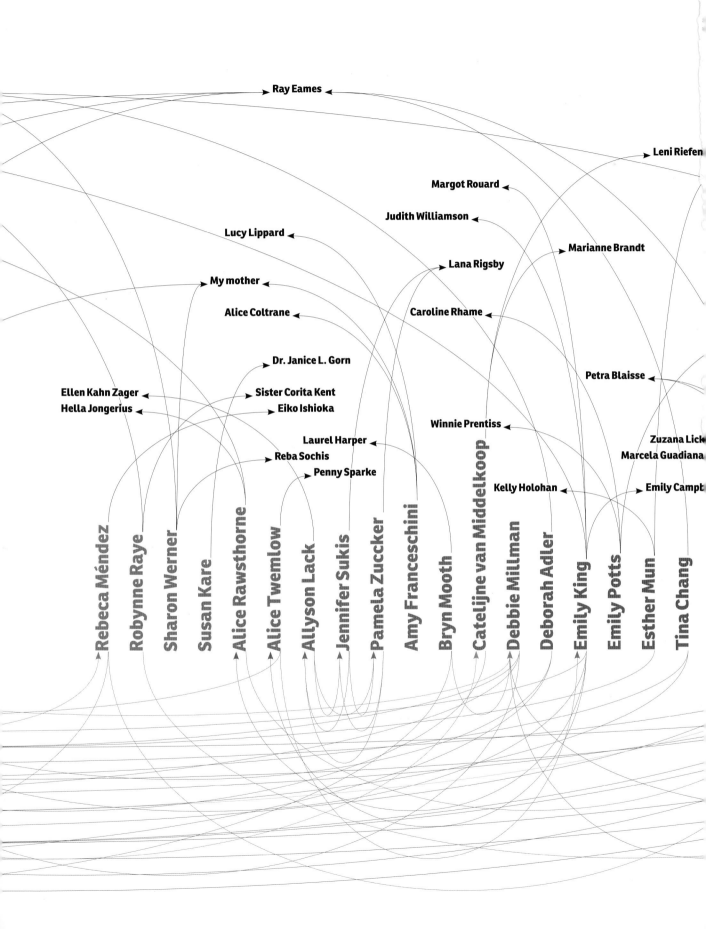

WOMEN OF DESIGN:
A BOOK OF PERIL AND JOY

On more than one occasion, when inviting someone for inclusion in this book, we were met with a resounding "Why?" with varying implications, queries and concerns about the relatively exclusive title and focus of our endeavor. Why would a design book need to be defined by the gender of those that created the work? Shouldn't the work alone be the focus of the book? Will there be a *Men of Design* book? Questions that made us explain our motives succinctly and even convincingly. The genesis of this book was rather mundane, so we could not use that as justification: During the holiday season of 2006, while sitting in a taxi on our way to New York's JFK airport, we must have been talking about a related subject and we both had the same, instant impetus, "Wouldn't it be great if we did a book on women graphic designers?" and upon landing in our destination immediately drafted a quick proposal which, two years later, resulted in the book you are holding now. Clearly, this would not be a satisfying response to anyone questioning the need for this book.

Even clearer but trickier—and one of the perils of not just writing the book, but this very introduction—is the real motivation and circumstance behind our decision in the taxi ride that cloudy day. It's equal parts question, conversation, argument, concern, and point of polemic that extracts some of the thornier aspects of our twenty-first century society: Why aren't there more women represented in conferences, boards of directors, judging panels and other public-facing situations, where men always seem to outnumber them? And, if this general assumption is indeed correct, the follow-up is typically: Why isn't anyone doing anything about it? Having participated in conference and event programming, we've seen firsthand whiteboards with higher ratios of names of men, only to be left head-scratching at the challenge of finding other women that could be invited to balance the scenario. While we would never attempt to discern why or how decisions are made on these matters, nor would we ever advocate some utopian 50/50 regulation that ensures equal gender representation, we can contribute in one way that feels honest to our motives and capabilities: By creating a book that gathers some of the most influential women engaged in the field of graphic design, celebrating their work, history and achievements—serving as a repository of inspiration and a resource of talent, personalities, and success stories.

Peril: Selection Criteria

Originally, we had envisioned a book that would include the "top thirty" women of design. That number instantly grew to forty. Then fifty. Until we realized it was unproductive to put such an aleatory limit on our selection and shifted our energy to producing an open-ended list of women and then define the organization. We drafted numerous lists, making revisions constantly as we explored, extended and limited the edges of potential scopes of inclusion. One of our first limitations was to only include living women that were still practicing as well as those that may have veered slightly away from the profession. This decision was not made to exempt us from exploring (or worse, ignoring) the invaluable contributions of women like Sister Mary Corita Kent, Cipe Pineles, or Muriel Cooper— whose influences linger quite palpably, even years after their passing—but it directed us to making a book that would serve as a snapshot of the graphic design profession at a specific time in its history.

While the book's majority focus is on the actual work produced by designers, it was very important for us to acknowledge that graphic design cannot solely revolve around celebrating the end product—it must comprise the disciplines that support, enrich, define, and enable its understanding and appreciation. Writers, educators, editors and curators that are shaping the community and industry from different angles were included for consideration. Within the practice of graphic design, we considered almost every specialization, from book and editorial design, to packaging, posters, corporate and brand identity, as well as environmental design, motion graphics and, to a limited extent, interaction design and illustration. One exception we made that falls outside of this design-specific range, which may be quite evident, was the inclusion of an artist, Barbara Kruger—as we wanted to highlight her use of type and image that is representative of the imminent power of the very same elements that we work with day to day.

Although not one of our primary goals, an effort was made to extend the representatives of this book to be more international and avoid a completely United States-based selection. With no more than a dozen international women selected, we can't claim global breadth but we hope this could inspire interested authors to explore the potential of a truly international book on the same subject. Establishing these (semi-) objective criteria allowed us to make the final, risky and inevitably subjective selections—a peril that only intensified as we tried to diffuse it by continually asking ourselves a set of questions, which irrevocably led to even more subjective answers. Is the work good? Memorable? Unique? Does it stand the test of time? Or does it just signify a specific time? Are the women well known within the industry or beyond? Does it matter? In the end, however, it all hinged on a simple question: Would *we* want to know and learn more about these women and their work, inspirations, processes and stories?

Joy: Organization

With a satisfactory initial list of women, the structure of the book was more difficult to define than we had originally thought. Initially we considered an organization defined by discipline or specialty (poster designers, book designers, writers, teachers, etc.), but that proved impossible as many of the women did a little bit of everything. Our next idea was to arrange it by age, but... well, that would not be polite. However, this did lead us to decide that we could divide the book in broader chronological chapters and we shifted our focus to assigning women to the moment in time when their influence was most heartily felt and was more resonant, despite the fact that some of them have sustained an enviable length of relevance or that their careers had been in effect for years prior to their moment in the spotlight. For example, Deborah Sussman, whose work has continually evolved over four decades and today leads a vibrant practice, but whose work in the field of environmental design during the 1970s and 1980s was groundbreaking; or Debbie Millman, who has been in the brand and packaging business for more than twenty years, but it has only been in recent years that her contributions have been most evident.

The benefit of making this book in 2008 is that we can easily look back and determine what have been key landmark moments in the history of graphic design. This allowed us to easily divide the book in three chapters that very broadly represent a timeline of our profession. The Groundbreakers are women that made an impact and established a growing legacy before and up to the introduction of the Macintosh computer in 1984, and certainly beyond; the Pathfinders include the women that hit a stride in the late 1980s and into the late 1990s, by defining a path for what a graphic design practice could be and the impact it could have on business and culture; and the Trailblazers are the women in the first decade of the twenty-first century who have built upon this legacy since the late 1990s and taken the expectations of what graphic design is in unexpected directions.

For the Groundbreakers and Pathfinders the last thing we would want to signal is that their contributions ended at the turn of the century or before, as nothing could be further from the truth. Instead we would like to affirm that without the early days of their careers, the foundation of our profession would not be as strong as it is today. And for the Trailblazers (and some Pathfinders), we are not ignoring or dismissing earlier efforts—instead we would like to assert that right now, our eyes are on them, and the potential of defining the direction of graphic design in the near future is excitingly in their hands. While not perfect or bulletproof, this organization allows us to look proudly at our past and eagerly at our future.

Peril and Joy: The Selections

When the dust has settled—or, in this case, when the ink has dried, the pages bound and the shelves stocked—the women included in this book are only a fraction of hundreds of deserving designers, writers and teachers around the world that continually define our profession. Our selection cannot be seen as a dictum. First, because in its tone and presentation, it is not packaged as one; and, second, because these are our selections—simply: Bryony's and Armin's selections—and unavoidably represent our preconceptions, education, knowledge and ability to choose and edit. This empowers us. And scares us to death.

In our final selection we present women whose work, talent, contribution, process, and story we admire and feel represents different sides of our profession that point to both the ampli-tudes and singularities that can be found within graphic design. As tempting as it was to continually question our selections—usually because of worry that someone would be left out—our deadlines luckily forced us to commit, move forward and accept that we just could not include everyone or, much less, that our selections would satisfy every reader. At this point it is imperative to recognize that the omissions are as important as the inclusions: This book could have been 512 pages and still someone would have been omitted, but we take full responsibility of any major oversights and, if given the chance, would be eager to correct them in a future edition; however, we need to be adamant that before critics berate our omissions they consult us, since many of the women were probably approached but for a variety of reasons did not reach this publication.

Despite all the perils, producing this book has been a joy. We have been able to spend endless hours staring at amazing work, attempting to make it all fit in 256 pages; we have learned more about these women by leaving no stone unturned in our research, giving us an opportunity to learn about the history of our profession, as these women have played integral roles in its evolution; and we have deepened our appreciation for the amassed time all of them have invested in the community, their careers, and their lives.

We hope you enjoy the final product as much as we enjoyed the process.

Bryony Gomez-Palacio and Armin Vit
UnderConsideration

TRAILBLAZERS

Detail of: "ABC" giclee print; design by Elain Lustig Cohen (2006).

Surging within the unsympathetic, male-inclined business and academic environments of the 1960s, '70s and '80s, these designers defined their own berths in a fledgling graphic design profession and cultivated an instrumental body of work that would influence future generations. Now, with decades of experience, through a sustained practice and career that have lent them firsthand accounts—even leading roles—of the numerous changes in the profession, their contributions are incisive, authoritative and salient as they continue to exemplify the creativity and business acumen that represents the best graphic designers today.

APRIL
GREIMAN

NATIONALITY
American

YEAR BORN
1948

CURRENTLY RESIDING IN
Los Angeles, California, United States

YEARS IN THE BUSINESS
29

CURRENT POSITION/FIRM
Owner and principal, Made in Space, Inc.

DESIGN EDUCATION
BFA, Kansas City Art Institute (1970)
Graduate studies, Allgemeine Kunstgewerbeschule, Basel, Switzerland (1971)

As imperative as the new digital tools were in triggering change in the graphic design profession, their relevance is minute without taking into account the designers that were willing to embrace them—significantly, April Greiman. Born and raised in New York, Greiman crossed the nation to settle in Los Angeles, the city whose design scene she would come to symbolize. With a typographic, color and spatial sensibility that challenged the existing tenets of Modernism, Greiman's work possessed—and still does—a controlled exuberance that helped define the New Wave movement associated with the West Coast and that, more importantly, has allowed her to do work across a variety of disciplines while continuing to explore the boundaries of design, space and technology.

Since the 1980s, starting with the advent of the Macintosh, you have embraced design as a medium that can mutate, change and break its own boundaries. What keeps you moving ahead? Looking for different methods?

My varied and "transmedia" interests.

It feels as if there hasn't been a singular change, like the introduction of the Mac, that has polarized designers in a significant way. Are we in need of a shake-up?

I think our world is shaken enough, frankly, so to impose something artificial or superficial just doesn't seem appropriate. I think, as a teacher/practitioner, that design education has to be more focused on content and idea-based at the core. I find that with the ease of the current tools, it is easy to perpetuate what I call the look

"I find that with the ease of the current tools, it is easy to perpetuate what I call the look of meaning. I am all for true meaning, where it can be excavated or found."

of meaning. I am all for true meaning, where it can be excavated or found.

With the current pressures of bottom-line economies and professions, it is very easy to make something look good, without any substance.

When you first moved to L.A. in 1976, the design community did not enjoy the success of its East Coast counterpart in New York, where you are originally from. How has the city's design aesthetic and philosophy changed in the last three decades?

L.A. has come of age. It is now the capital, not only of the entertainment business, but also of fashion and art.

You can get a great cup of coffee now in L.A. It is a super fantastic town to dine in—from the ethnic influences of its neighborhoods to the very upscale, special cuisine, which is uniquely L.A.

There is a complete renaissance in the downtown area. Besides the wonderful MOCA (Museum of Contemporary Art) and The Geffen Contemporary, there is the Japanese American National Museum, Japanese American Cultural and

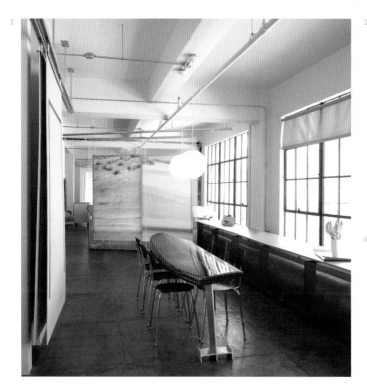

[1] Made in Space lunchroom in collaboration with RoTo Architects; surfboard table design in collaboration with Sean Fell (2003). Photo by Ron Hill.
[2] Identity for Dosa 818 (2002). [3] Identity for RoTo Architects (1999). [4] Color, surfaces and materials palettes for Prairie View School of Architecture, Texas A+M University, by RoTo Architects (2004). Photo by Assassi Productions. [5] "Drive-by Shooting: April Greiman" digital photography exhibition, Pasadena Museum of California Art (2006). [6] 19th Amendment Commemorative Stamp for Women's Voting Rights for the U.S. Postal Service (1995).

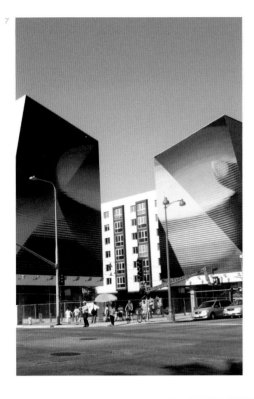

Community Center, Gallery Row Downtown, the fabulous Walt Disney Concert Hall and the new Cathedral of Our Lady of the Angels.

I don't really know how to describe the philosophy of a city...but I would say that the continual openness, unique physical access to the natural environment, and hotbed of creativity it lives and thrives on, is perhaps better here than in any other U.S. city.

L.A. is, and always will remain, funky!

In exploring your portfolio it is surprising, at least to us, to see so much identity and branding work, from restaurants to motels. What attracts you to this facet of design?

We also see identity in the color, surface, materials and palettes we do for archi-

tects and architecture. We enjoy taking an identity element or concept and seeing it change in scale and material. We have a body of work in the environmental area as well.

I also have a foot in the fine art world and, in particular, take on technology and concept challenges in defining our own projects and pursuits.

You recently had an exhibition of digital photography called "Drive-by Shooting" that blurrily focused on your surrounding environments. How has design influenced what you see through the lens?

"Drive-by Shooting" has been going on for about twenty-five years, and all over the world—not just in my surrounding environments. I particularly chose an image or two from all the different countries in

an effort to demonstrate that somehow innate in these is a special, often recognizable color palette.

I have always been interested in the sciences, particularly physics (for laymen). Developing the work and the awareness of things like motion, time and, of course, the impact of technology has been a natural evolution.

Coincidentally, I am also a naturalist. So, put these all together, and there you have my teaching and my learning.

Our shortest question: Where to from here?

Where is here? A short answer.

[7,8] Mural commissioned as public art for the Wilshire/Vermont Metro Station (2007). [9,10] Brand work for the Southern California Institute of Architecture (2003).

BARBARA
KRUGER

NATIONALITY

American

YEAR BORN

1945

CURRENTLY RESIDING IN

New York, New York and
Los Angeles, California, United States

YEARS IN THE BUSINESS

30+

CURRENT POSITION/FIRM

Artist
Professor at the University of California, Los Angeles

PREVIOUS EMPLOYMENT

Designer, *House & Garden, Aperture,*
and *Mademoiselle* magazines
Professor, California Institute of the Arts,
and The School of the Art Institute of Chicago

DESIGN EDUCATION

Syracuse University (1965)
Parson's School of Design in New York (1966)

While there are many influential artists in the world, designers have long gravitated towards the work of Barbara Kruger, specifically to her iconic work that poignantly blended image and typography through black-and-white photography contrasted with red and white Futura Bold Oblique—ingredients we have all toiled with. Before being a globally celebrated artist, Kruger worked for Condé Nast Publications, first at Mademoiselle where she eventually became the lead designer, and then as designer, art director and picture editor of House & Garden and Aperture. Kruger's approach and body of work, which extends from prints to installations, alludes to the power and influence that image and typography can have.

Unlike other artists, graphic designers have a certain affinity to your work, with an instant connection based on our shared use of commercial imagery and typography. You probably don't want to outcast anyone, but is this reciprocal? Do you find a different connection with commercial artists than fine artists?

The graphic design subculture is full of incredibly "creative" people, and by that I mean there is a necessity to be fluent in a million different styles and visual overtures. The reason for this is that, in many ways, the assignment is to construct someone else's image of perfection alongside your own. The difference to me between a so-called artist and a so-called designer is a client relation. For artists who basically deal with their own limitations and not a client's, we don't have to have such a varied menu of solutions because we are trying to solve things that we have laid out for ourselves. I do feel that the kind of cleverness, beauty and economy that I see in many graphic design solutions is incredibly admirable, and it takes a lot of visual and mental gifts.

So from your experience at Condé Nast, do you sympathize with the challenges that designers face when working with clients?

Having experience in editorial design, where it's so much about seriality, about repetition, and about a consistent style, helps me to understand those frustra-tions of trying to negotiate between what you see as effective and beautiful and what a client demands.

We have to admit, though, you've really killed Futura Bold Oblique for all of us. We can't use it without someone saying, "That looks like Barbara Kruger"...

My goodness, you know, I never thought anyone would know my name. It's just funny the way historical circumstances, social relations and historical reckonings are constructed... It's so weird. But, anyways, I interrupted the question...

"The difference to me between a so-called artist and a so-called designer is a client relation."

Images courtesy of Mary Boone Gallery, New York. **[1]** *"Untitled" (We don't need another hero) photographic silkscreen/vinyl (1987).* **[2]** *Installation for Mary Boone Gallery, New York (January 1991).* **[3]** *"Untitled" (I shop therefore I am) photographic silkscreen/vinyl (1987).* **[4]** *"Untitled" (When I hear the word culture I take out my checkbook) photograph (1985).*

"All art is about the creation of a kind of commentary, about what it means to be alive, to live another day, to breathe another breath."

Why did you choose this typeface?

I used to use it a lot at the magazine, definitely Helvetica, Franklin Gothic and sans serifs a lot too, but there was also Century Schoolbook and Bodoni. *Mademoiselle* was a young woman's magazine, and it had a young, trendy, artsy reputation as opposed to *Glamour*, so sans serif type equated with the kind of modernism that seemed to go hand in hand with that demographic. So I used a lot of Futura then.

Having spent time as a designer for Condé Nast working on magazines like Mademoiselle, House & Garden and Aperture, do you ever think that you could have made a career out of graphic design?

Oh, no. No, no. When I first started there, it was a job. I didn't know if I wanted to be an artist... I didn't know anything. I had no college degree. I was drawn to art as a way to objectify the world, which is a large part of what artists have to do in order to function at all. I'm not saying that was true with me, but when I first started all I wanted to be was the Designer or Art Director of the World! I loved magazines like *Domus* and *Nova* (an incredibly hip magazine out of London), and they were great, but after a while I realized that other people functioned so much better at this than I, and I had to figure out a way to define myself through my own work, being an artist. So the idea of being an art director or designer consistently and forever soon left me. I just wasn't cut out for it.

And, as you well know, so much of it and so many of the demands are just about power and hierarchy within a corporation or group, and because all of that was so apparent to me, I didn't want to be a dancing bear in that sort of vaudeville act.

It's tempting to simplify your work to Futura Bold Oblique + Black-and-White Photography + Red since it is your most iconic work as it relates to graphic design. Yet it's obviously only a part of it. What connects this and the rest of your work?

One of the things that threads through my work constantly is direct address. It can be used in any number of mediums, whether it's type, an image, a moving image or sound, and I continue to use it in most, but not all my work. Direct address became especially more powerful and effective to me once I started working in installations, where you can really address the viewer and create more immersive work, rather than just an "objet d'art" on a wall.

Is there any new medium or type of project that you are looking to tackle or engage in?

The idea of using film and video is something I've been doing for a while to bring up the scale of my work a little. Now I'm doing a 3,000-square-foot piece for a new student center being built at the University of California, San Diego, using large images and LEDs running a Reuters news feed. I'm also doing some video projects, one in Beverly Hills on two sides of a large, vacant Robinsons-May building that can be seen from afar.

On a recent interview with Debbie Millman on her radio show, Design Matters, you emphasized that your work revolves around the notion of how we treat each other. Could you expand on this?

All art is about the creation of a kind of commentary, about what it means to be alive, to live another day, to breathe another breath. Whether it's about pleasure or rage, those emotional states are what I think a lot of art takes as its focus. So whether it's about conflict or happiness or whatever, at the dinner table, in the bedroom, in the boardroom, in the military barrack, that's the stuff to make art about. And that can come out as an installation, or as the video I have been shooting for the past twelve years, or it can come out as a novel, or a movie—art can be a million things. It's not just the stuff that comes out of the so-called art world.

Is there anything in your current work that relates more directly to graphic design?

Unlike many artists, especially painters, I design all my exhibitions. So it's not like I show up at an exhibition and the work is up. Where the work is located on the wall and how it is hung has always been a concern of mine, even in my early shows. For all my shows, the installations, the film aspect of them, how the sound comes out—I design all that. To me this is the biggest design component in my work right now. It's not whether I'm using Futura or Helvetica. So this, to me, is how design continues to live in my work. Since I've been doing installations for the past twelve or fourteen years, the design component has been spatialized.

5  6  7

8

Images courtesy of Mary Boone Gallery, New York. **[5]** *"Untitled" (Your gaze hits the side of my face) photograph (1981).* **[6]** *"Untitled" (Buy me I'll change your life) photograph (1984).* **[7]** *"Untitled" (We have received orders not to move) photograph (1982).* **[8]** *"Twelve"; Four-channel digital video installation for Mary Boone Gallery, New York (March 2004).*

"The first lesson I learned in starting my own studio was to never depend on any one client or type of business. Though I had all of the book jacket work I needed, I chose to diversify—and had I not done so, I probably would have soon been out of business."

Louise
Fili

Detail of: *Oil packaging for Williams-Sonoma (2000).*

DEBORAH
SUSSMAN

NATIONALITY

American

YEAR BORN

1931

CURRENTLY RESIDING IN

Los Angeles, California, United States

YEARS IN THE BUSINESS

40

CURRENT POSITION/FIRM

Founder, creative leader, Sussman/Prejza & Company, Inc.

PREVIOUS EMPLOYMENT

Office of Charles and Ray Eames (1953-57 and 1961-67)
Studio Boggein, Milan (1958-59)
Les Galeries Lafayette, Paris (1959-60)

DESIGN EDUCATION

Doctorate of Humane Letters, Bard College (1998)
Institute of Design, Chicago (1950-53)
Hochschule für Gestaltung, Ulm, Germany (1957-58)
BFA, visual arts and acting, Bard College (1948-50)
Black Mountain College (Summer 1948)

Few designers can boast of having worked with the legendary Charles and Ray Eames—Deborah Sussman can. She did so for ten years and is quick to note their influence. Yet it's unnecessary. Her interdisciplinary approach, curiosity and unpredictable output since 1968 is evidence enough. In the years since establishing her design firm—joined by husband and partner Paul Prejza in 1980—Sussman has created built environments, from the iconic look of the 1984 Olympic Games in Los Angeles to the graphics of Hasbro's corporate headquarters, that defy common conventions by bringing a unique sensibility of color and graphic imagery that enhance the experience.

Let's start with one of your landmark projects, designing and applying the visual identity of the 1984 Olympic Games in Los Angeles. Looking back more than twenty years, how do you feel this project reflects your design approach? And how does it measure up, based on what you've learned?

The Olympics in Los Angeles was as exciting to design as it was to watch and experience.

These games were the first privately funded Olympiad in history. Before we became involved, a logo had been designed—the red, white and blue "star-in-motion." However, it was deemed inappropriate to express a national United States patriotic presence. It was agreed by the Los Angeles Olympic Organizing Committee and us designers that the Olympics should express the culture of the Los Angeles/Southern California area rather than that of the Federal Government. Mainly, our inspiration came from Mexico, Japan, Indonesia and India—predominant cultures found in Southern California. Therefore, we reinterpreted the language of communal celebration used along and near the Pacific Rim.

I had a long-term love affair stemming from work, photography, personal relationships and travel in most of these countries—much of my work and that of Sussman/Prejza were already impacted by these experiences. From the start, our concepts, forms, color and the overall visual language developed spontaneously, intuitively and naturally. Architect Jon Jerde called the "look" that we were developing "Festive Federalism" because it combined elements of the flag (stars and bars) with a totally new palette of colors and forms.

There was a limited budget and very little time, which in some ways added to the excitement. I was inspired by the challenges, and by the intensity, energy and sense of purpose in the design team and our clients. At the peak period there were 150 designers racing together for gold.

Myself, and many others, were possessed by the same fever that the athletes brought to the Games. For me, it was—and remains—the ultimate expression of everything I had learned and loved in my career.

The Olympics must have been a huge undertaking, but so is the majority of the work you do. What do you enjoy about

Interiors and branding of the Gund Arena, home of the Cleveland Cavaliers, Ohio.

the endlessly complex practice of environmental design?

I've always liked interaction with creative people and discourse with open-minded, risk-taking clients. When the intent of our mission is to benefit peoples' lives, one can handle the stress inherent in all environmental work.

My imagination plays a big part in even the most complex of programs. Frequently I get ahead of myself (and the team) by synthesizing before analyzing. So that can mean back-pedaling for me. It's tough for intuitive people to digest all the logical factors that ultimately play a large role in the solution. Perhaps my non-linear way of thinking helps me to handle the multiple constraints innate in most projects.

Happiness is when what's in my head gets built. Great happiness comes from seeing people use and interact positively with our designs.

It came as a surprise to us that you designed the identity for the NBA's Cleveland Cavaliers in 1993, a task usually reserved for niche firms. However, this is merely an indication of how varied and rich your clients have been. How have you been able to adapt to and attract different industries?

There are many reasons. Sometimes you develop long-term relationships with clients that attract other clients. After the Olympics we somehow became a hot item in the sports world. In the case of the Cavaliers, the major decision maker was becoming almost blind. To describe a color, I would refer to familiar examples (red, like in tomato soup). We built

physical models of graphics ideas that he could interpret by touching them, using his hands. It was very rewarding.

S/P has been multi-disciplinary from its inception, which enables us to tackle projects ranging from urban branding, exhibits, retail centers, cultural venues and transportation programs.

You worked for more than a decade, albeit interrupted, with Charles and Ray Eames. How has this experience influenced your practice?

[1, 2, 3] *Los Angeles Olympiad environmental and branding program (1984).*

CITY NATIONAL PLAZA

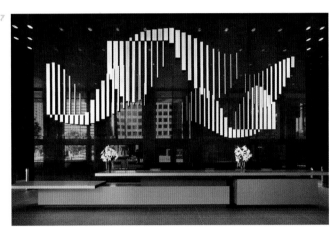

A truly honest answer is beyond the space in this book. Briefly, the person that I am, the work that I've done, and the nature of S/P, is the result of my long-term involvement with the Eames office. Charles and Ray and I became friends. They were also parental figures to me. We all worked pretty much 24/7. We were a family.

Among their many innovations was a new way of seeing the world. Early on, they pointed to many phenomena that were taken for granted and undervalued by most people. They hung that famous tumbleweed in the living space at the "House"—along with paintings by Hans Hoffman (Ray's teacher). Suddenly the ordinary—spools of thread, the smell of bread baking, a bolt of cloth, among countless other humble artifacts of daily life around the world—became significant. My generation of designers was forever influenced by these discoveries and everybody began collecting things that had previously not been anointed.

My predilection for photographing street life around the world and for engaging with environmental design was nurtured and developed while working at the Eames office.

In 1983 (with Saul Bass, among others) you founded the AIGA chapter of L.A. Why was this important for you at the time?

The original AIGA office in midtown New York was tiny, and the design community was as well. But it was a place where one felt honored, somehow, and gratified to access. It had "the best of the best" in publications, posters and books. It was run by the delightful Carolyn Warner Hightower. Since only a percentage of designers could use that resource it made sense to establish a West Coast presence, and when Carolyn and David Brown (of Champion Papers at that time) hoped to expand AIGA into a national organization, they approached me to organize the first chapter in L.A.

On a cold evening in Santa Monica, I invited Saul Bass, April Greiman, Dave Goodman and a few others to our studio. Everyone agreed that it was a good thing to do—but some of the guys wanted it to be like a club, with a spa, bar, pool, etc. That never happened. There was also an Art Directors Club here and they were not happy with this new AIGA kid on the block. It took a while, but eventually the Art Directors Club merged with

[4, 6] Elements of master signing program, Walt Disney World in Orlando, Florida (1987–90). [5, 7] Identity and interior elements for City National Plaza in Los Angeles (ongoing).

8

9

10

11

and actually became an active part of AIGA, L.A.

There had been a lot of innovation and new frontiers and media exploration on the West Coast. People could reach out and connect without having to travel across the country with a West Coast chapter.

You have been active in the environmental design field through four decades. What have been the most significant changes you have experienced?

When I began to do this in the late 1960s, there were two women who practiced and innovated in this field. Both were in San Francisco: Marget Larsen and Barbara Stauffacher. Of course, Ivan Chermayeff

"Happiness is when what's in my head gets built. Great happiness comes from seeing people use and interact positively with our designs."

and a very few others were engaged in big public projects. Daring designs could get built because there were only a few decision makers, and they were in direct contact with the designer.

Now everybody does it—architects, landscape architects, planners, branding and marketing firms (big ones, little ones),

advertising agencies, and innumerable environmental graphic design firms, even fabricators who operate without the annoyance (or fees) of designers. Clients pick and choose among many competitors. RFQ's (Request for Quote) and RFP's (Request for Proposal) often do not even require knowledge of the designer's aesthetic, evaluation of track records, or personal interviews. It is a very different world compared to my earlier years. Today, one frequently deals with layers of management without even meeting the decision maker. And many clients now have internal design staff that alters their consultants' work. But there is always more to do, new challenges and opportunities, in a tougher, wider arena.

[8, 10] Renovation of the Los Angeles Universal City San Francisco AMC Cinema (2007). [9, 11] Identity and exhibition for the Museum of the African Diaspora (MoAD), including a three-story, 2,000-image mosaic (2005).

ELAINE
LUSTIG COHEN

NATIONALITY
American

YEAR BORN
1927

CURRENTLY RESIDING IN
New York, New York, United States

PREVIOUS EMPLOYMENT
Always freelance

DESIGN EDUCATION
BFA, The University of Southern California (1948)

Her graphic design career may not be thoroughly chronicled, but Elaine Lustig Cohen produced a substantial body of work spanning book covers, identity and signage while keeping alive the last name of one of the most celebrated designers in history, Alvin Lustig, her husband of seven years. Cohen first managed his studio as an all-encompassing assistant, but as Lustig, who suffered from diabetes, slowly lost his sight he relied on Cohen to execute his ideas. When Lustig passed away in 1955 at forty years old, Cohen established her own studio. In 1973, with her second husband Arthur A. Cohen, she opened Ex Libris, a gallery and bookstore devoted to avant-garde European printed matter. With brief dabs in design, Cohen has been painting and doing collage work since the mid-1960s.

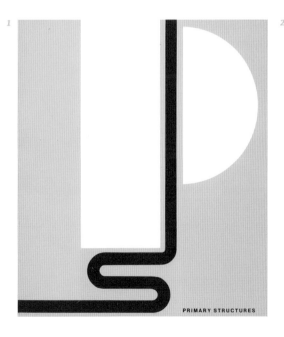

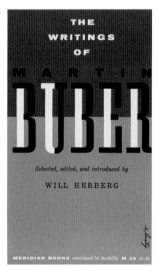

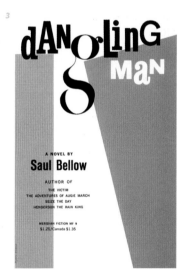

[1] *Catalogue for* The Jewish Museum *(1966).* [2] *Book jacket for* The Writings of Martin Buber *by Will Herberg (1956).* [3] *Book jacket for* Dangling Man *by Saul Bellow (1959).*

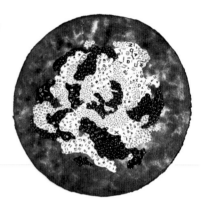

"How do I divide my time? During the 1950s and early 1960s mostly graphic design, interior design and signage. Painting, collage, works on paper from the mid-1960s to the present, with some graphic design from time to time."

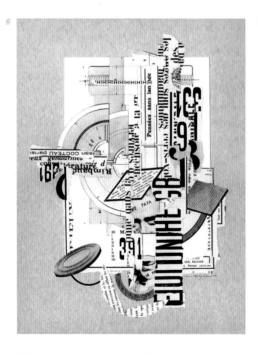

[4] "ABC" Giclee print (2006). [5] "Pangaea" watercolor and collage (2006). [6] "391" Collage (1998). [7] Poster for The Museum of Modern Art in New York (2001).

KATHERINE
MCCOY

As a practitioner, writer, teacher and advocate, Katherine McCoy's career has fluidly evolved along with the last forty years of design history. From her first design position at Unimark International in 1967, where corporate modernism was in full swing, to her role as co-chair of Cranbrook's 2-D Design program, where postmodernism was brewed in the mid-1980s, McCoy's pendulum-like engagements have always been leveled by a critical and analytical view of the profession, represented in her own work and writing. Now perched in the high altitudes of Denver, McCoy runs a design studio and workshop enterprise along with her partner and husband, Michael McCoy. Where will the pendulum swing next?

NATIONALITY	American
YEAR BORN	1945
CURRENTLY RESIDING IN	Buena Vista, Colorado and Denver, Colorado, United States
YEARS IN THE BUSINESS	40 years in the profession of design (not "business" or "industry")
CURRENT POSITION/FIRM	McCoy & McCoy Associates (1971-present) High Ground Tools and Strategies for Design (1995-present)
PREVIOUS EMPLOYMENT	Cranbrook Academy of Art, co-chair, Department of Graduate Design (1971-95) Illinois Institute of Technology, Institute of Design, senior lecturer (1996-2004)
DESIGN EDUCATION	BA, industrial design, Michigan State University (1967)

More than forty years ago you held your first design position at Unimark International, a paragon of the then–new corporate modernism. How formative was this first experience?

I was very excited to join Unimark International as a junior designer after college graduation. It was an exceptional way to begin one's design career. Unimark was like graduate school for me.

The Unimark designers were excellent, and I learned a great deal from them. I had the opportunity to work with two Swiss graphic designers, Harry Boller and Peter Tuebner, who were my first sources of knowledge about the Swiss grid system. I watched their every move! Massimo Vignelli, a Unimark vice president who headed their New York office, flew in periodically to discuss projects.

The Unimark clients and projects were high quality, well-funded and challenging, allowing us the opportunity to do our best work.

The Unimark designers had books that I had never seen before—the Swiss "bibles" by Müller-Brockman, Karl Gerstner, Armin Hofmann and Emil Ruder. In 1967 these books were only available in one bookstore in the United States—George Wittenborn in New York City. I photocopied each entire book after-hours on Unimark's photocopier!

Unimark was very demanding. We all worked very long hours, often over sixty hours a week. But we were highly motivated by a missionary zeal to improve the design quality of the built environment in people's lives. The state of design in the U.S. was pretty awful in

the 1950s and 1960s, and we wanted to clean it up. The highest compliment one could say about a design was, "That is really clean!" *Clean* meant minimalist, modernist form based on an objective and systematic problem-solving process. Sans serif typography (Helvetica and occasionally Univers) on a grid was always a key element. The Unimark office had a bank of flat files filled with Helvetica transfer lettering.

After working at a few other design firms, you and your husband, Michael, an industrial designer, set up your own outpost, McCoy & McCoy. This collaboration has stood, to different extents, since the 1970s. How have you been able to maintain it? Do you separate business from pleasure?

Michael and I met in our university's industrial design studio, so we shared

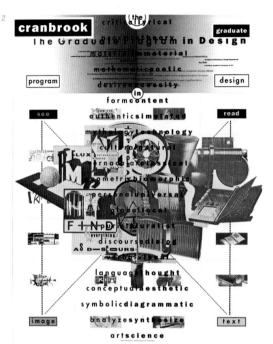

a passion for design from the beginning. We married two weeks after my graduation, and it was natural to continue sharing our design enthusiasm. I brought things home from Unimark constantly and we poured over them. Mike began his own studio at that time, and it was natural that I worked on those projects with him after-hours. When we began at Cranbrook, we formalized our partnership as McCoy & McCoy.

We've always lived and breathed design. We do take time off from design, although not in a formalized or structured way. Design is not just from 9 to 5 with personal life in the evenings. Our work lives and personal lives are more fluid and less formally structured than many people's.

Our individual design interests and abilities seem complementary. Because we each know a lot about the other's work, we are able to support and assist each other, and celebrate each other's accomplishments.

Over the years, we have found that it is healthy for each of us to have our own focus and build our own reputation in that. Then, when we collaborate, we both have the maturity to be equal contributors.

When we were first out of school, it was very important for me to build my own career and establish myself as a designer independent of my husband. This was the late 1960s when there were few women in design. In fact, except for a six-month period, I was the only female designer in each place I worked. And at Cranbrook, I was the only woman on the faculty for almost twenty years. I worked for four different design firms and studios before Cran-

brook, and I gained valuable experience from each. I've always enjoyed working in organizations, whereas Mike has always preferred to work independently. I have also devoted many fruitful years to work and leadership in professional design organizations—the Industrial Designers Society of America, the American Institute of Graphic Arts and the American Center for Design.

For close to twenty-five years, you and Michael were at the head of Cranbrook's 2-D and 3-D programs, where you literally reinvented the school. What was this experience like?

The Design Department had languished in the late 1950s and 1960s, and was waiting to be rebuilt. It was a blank slate, and we invented as we went. The department had been interdisciplinary since its

[1] Radical Graphics/Graphic Radicals *cover for Chronicle Books; design assistance by Erin Smith and Janice Page (1999).* **[2]** *Graduate Design poster for Cranbrook Academy of Art (1989).* **[3]** *McCoy & McCoy brochure (1977).* **[4]** *Identity system and architectural signage for Cranbrook Educational Community (1990-94).* **[5]** Cranbrook Design: The New Discourse, *for Cranbrook Academy of Art Design Department (1990).*

inception under Charles Eames in 1939, including both three-dimensional and two-dimensional design disciplines. The school hoped to continue that tradition, and we believed in that as well. Our early teaching drew on our backgrounds in the modernist, functionalist problem solving of industrial design, combined with the objective methods and minimalist forms of Swiss design. But it was 1971, and we were also involved in the social ideals of the counterculture. Lorraine Wild once characterized us in an essay as "hippie modernists." But we weren't total hippies because we never saw a reason to "drop out." We believed design could be practiced in ways that reflected those late-1960s ideals. In the early 1970s we stressed altruistic team projects and public information about design.

Then in the later 1970s, we began to be influenced by Robert Venturi's ideas about postmodernism and vernacular form in architecture, and we worked to apply those ideas to industrial and graphic design. The advertising designer and illustrator Ed Fella was a good friend and spent a lot of time at Cranbrook. He was experimenting with vernacular forms in his work and brought that into the mix. And Wolfgang Weingart's work started a second wave of Swiss influence in American graphic design. All this combined into a wave of enthusiasm among our graphic design students and me to explore new graphic visual forms. We had largely mastered Swiss minimalism and were ready for new directions. A period of formal experimentation began in the department. We all produced some pretty interesting work that was published widely and became quite influential.

But by 1985, the Cranbrook graphic design students began looking for something beyond new form languages. Jeff Keedy

was one student that began reading communications theories voraciously and focused on post-structuralist language theory, literary theory and deconstruction. We all analyzed and debated how these ideas could be applied to graphic design in many critique sessions, and we gradually found ways to incorporate post-structuralist concepts into design strategies that we all realized in design projects.

Then in the early 1990s, just before we left Cranbrook, interactive and time-based media began to color the Design Department discussions. Several grant-funded projects gave students the opportunity to explore possibilities for new interactive user interfaces.

When we left Cranbrook in 1995, I was very pleased that P. Scott Makela and Laurie Haycock Makela, 1991 graduates of the department, were appointed to head the new Cranbrook department of 2-D Design. Cranbrook realized it was not likely to find another qualified 2-D/3-D couple to share a department/studio/house/salary, so the school created two departments. Today's 2-D and 3-D Cranbrook Design departments share contiguous space and are interdisciplinary via proximity.

An interesting aspect of your time at Cranbrook was that you, the program, and the industry went through a significant evolution from the principles of modernism to those of postmodernism. At the time, how did this change happen?

In 1971 Cranbrook was an obscure design outpost, out of sight from the New York design establishment of those days. That freed us to explore. Our publications and competition awards quickly put the program in the spotlight, earning both praise and condemnation as our work began to challenge accepted

design norms. We never had an "agenda" to challenge the status quo, but Cranbrook's art school values encouraged us to experiment. We always stressed the importance of building a bridge between theory, experiment and practice. We encouraged our students to apply their experiments to real client projects, and our graduates to realize their ideas in high quality studios and firms.

At a point in the early 1980s, our close friend and design collaborator Ed Fella was asked by Chevrolet's advertising agency to design their annual car catalogue "in that Cranbrook style" so it would appeal to the youth market. We were shocked that the mainstream advertising establishment valued this new expression, even if only to encourage a target market to buy cars.

Through all the years you were recognized as an academic, you kept doing design work. How important was it to maintain that aspect of your career?

Cranbrook's department chairs are called Artists in Residence and Designers in Residence, and the school provides each with a studio in which to practice. The school's central concept is that both graduate students and faculty alike should confront the creative process daily, with the faculty acting as role models and mentors. We were expected to devote roughly half of our time to our personal design practice. It was a stimulating creative environment, and we found that the exchange of ideas was a two-way street with our graduate students. I would never want to only teach or only practice—these two modes are complementary, and enrich each other.

In 1992 you started the Living Surfaces conferences for the now–defunct American Center for Design (ACD). Some designers

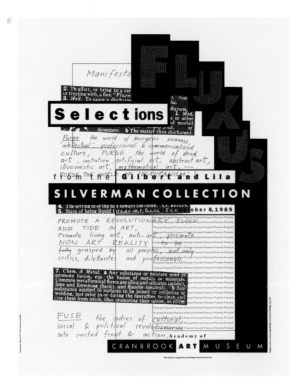

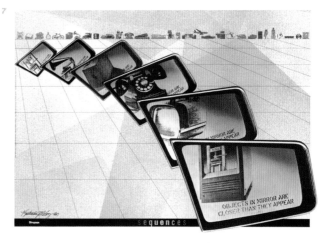

we know claim them to be some of the best events in our industry. What was the driving force behind these conferences?

Around 1990 I felt the need for information on the emerging field of new media and time-based communications design. At an ACD board meeting, I suggested that the organization should initiate a conference in this area, and the other board members said, "Fine. You do it." So I did. As chair of the first conference, I asked P. Scott Makela—who had just graduated from Cranbrook's Design Department in 1991 and was exploring sound and motion—to design the announcement poster and promotional materials. Together we invented the name *Living Surfaces*. That name continues to resonate for me as a description of new media. That first conference drew a very good audience and took

on a life of its own. Every year there was a different chairperson who shaped the conference's focus to reflect the rapidly-emerging trends in new media.

Unfortunately, the 2001 Living Surfaces Conference was scheduled just three weeks after 9/11 when air travel was disrupted, so it had to be canceled. ACD was not able to sustain itself without Living Surfaces' big contribution to its annual budget, so it had to close its doors—another victim of 9/11.

One last tall order... In the four decades that you have been involved with design, what have been the most satisfying shifts that have informed your career path?

Growth. The design disciplines are living things, constantly growing and evolving

from their early twentieth century origins. Each of us should be working daily to contribute to this growth and metamorphosis. We need to push the envelope, and do our best not to settle for the status quo on any project. Design is not in stasis, a fixed perfect thing with timeless rules; it's never "finished," as some modernists have hoped for. And that's a good thing! That is one of the reasons why I am a designer—there's walways something more to discover.

I also firmly believe that any one change or design innovation does not replace or negate all previous design achievements. We stand on the shoulders of giants and build from there. We are building a body of disciplinary knowledge.

That's exciting!

---

[6] *Fluxus Selections poster for Cranbrook Art Museum (1989).* **[7]** *Sequences poster for Simpson Lee Paper Company (1988).* **[8]** *Colorado Geologic Guidebook for United States Bureau of Land Management (2004).* **[9]** *Academic catalogue for Cranbrook Academy of Art (1982).*

> **"I would be more unhappy and frustrated being silent than opening myself up for attacks. Most of my clients appreciate the direct honesty. It's who I am."**

Paula
Scher

"Design tells interesting stories—stories that are not told in words, but are just as complex and revealing as reportages or works of fiction."

Véronique
Vienne

Detail of: NEWS Beauty, Self magazine (1990).

LOUISE
FILI

NATIONALITY

American

YEAR BORN

1951

CURRENTLY RESIDING IN

New York, New York, United States

YEARS IN THE BUSINESS

33

CURRENT POSITION/FIRM

Principal, Louise Fili Ltd

PREVIOUS EMPLOYMENT

Art director, Pantheon Books (1978–89)

DESIGN EDUCATION

BS, studio art, Skidmore College (1973)

School of Visual Arts (1973)

From book covers and book design to packaging and identity, Louise Fili has generated a stunning body of work with a consistently beautiful typographic enthusiasm that has not dimmed since the late 1970s. After spending two years with Herb Lubalin, Fili designed a gasp-inducing 2,000 book covers over the course of a decade as art director of Pantheon Books. Through her own studio, established in 1989, Fili extended her reach beyond book covers and into identity design for restaurants as well as food packaging. Her interest in book design is now prevalent through her authorial work with husband Steven Heller.

Let's take it from the top. Beginning in 1976 you worked for Herb Lubalin for two years. In retrospect, how important and relevant was this experience?

The opportunity to work for my long-time design hero, Herb Lubalin, in an environment where type was given the utmost respect and in a studio that was small enough for me to be able to witness Herb's process, was invaluable.

After that, you designed over 2,000 book jackets for Pantheon Books in ten years. You probably could have retired after that output. What were some of the highs and lows of this time?

My start at Pantheon coincided with my developing interest in design history. The wonderful thing about designing book jackets, especially for Pantheon's Euro-centric titles, was that every day I was able to explore another period of typographic history. When the letterforms I wanted to use didn't exist as typefaces, I would find a way to create them. (Memory is mercifully selective, so I don't seem to recall any lows.)

Then, you opened your own studio in 1989, which today is known for the blissful work you have done for restaurants and food packaging. How did you transition from the publishing world to this new industry?

The first lesson I learned in starting my own studio was to never depend on any one client or type of business. Though I had all of the book jacket work I needed, I chose to diversify—and had I not done so, I probably would have soon been out of business. The restaurant and specialty food worlds were not easy to tap into, but I made a concerted effort to make contacts through architects, trade shows, etc. Eventually, after the first few projects and some James Beard nominations (these are like the Oscars, but for the culinary world), it got a lot easier.

As fellow New Yorkers we must admit that we sometimes choose restaurants to dine in if you have designed their identity. What are some of the peculiarities of working with restaurateurs, who face one of the most competitive markets?

In New York City, a restaurant is the number one business most likely to fail. Some restaurateurs exhibit behavior that barely falls short of that of a gangster. These particular clients have no understanding or respect for what a designer does, and therefore do not value the work. That said, while I love this industry, I have learned

to be very careful about who I choose to work with.

Could you tell us a little about how you run your business? At times it seems you have an army of designers working feverishly on package designs with dozens of SKUs (stock-keeping unit), but the work never loses its handcrafted sensibility.

I have kept my business virtually the same size since the beginning—two assistants. It is not possible for me to grow beyond that number and still maintain the personal, handcrafted look that I strive for. I prefer to work with clients who have small businesses, where I have a better chance of creative control. Larger businesses mean larger budgets and larger headaches. I also prefer to work

with clients who I personally like, and whose product I believe in.

Your work displays a wonderful mix of "old world" graphics with an undeniable modern sensibility. First, how much is this a reflection of your own personality? And, second, what kind of resources do you mine for such references?

My style is hopelessly personal, which is why I limit my work to subjects that I am interested in. My trips to flea markets in France and Italy, collections of package designs (both vintage and modern), photographs of shop signs, type and alphabet books, among other things, are all important sources of inspiration to me.

Time according to Louise Fili:

Work
Family
Cook
Sleep

You have also published numerous books, some in collaboration with your husband and über-prolific writer, Steven Heller. What is your personal impetus in this?

Since my background is in publishing, these projects have been a good way to combine my love of making books with my passion for collecting for my own personal design inspiration.

---

[1] *Wine labels for Matt Brothers (1999).* **[2]** *Identity for Mermaid Inn Restaurant (2004).* **[3]** *Oil packaging for Williams-Sonoma (2000).* **[4]** *Identity for Le Monde Restaurant (2000).*

[5] Book jacket for The Lover *by Marguerite Duras (1998). [6] Identity for Sfoglia Restaurant (2006). [7] Identity for Tiffany & Co. (2007). [8] Margarita mix packaging for El Paso Chile Company (1998). [9] Identity for Belli (2007). [10] Sauce packaging for Bella Cucina (2000). [11] Biscotti packaging for Bella Cucina (2000). [12] Identity for Picholine Restaurant (1999).*

MEREDITH DAVIS

NATIONALITY	American
YEAR BORN	1948
CURRENTLY RESIDING IN	Raleigh, North Carolina, United States
YEARS IN THE BUSINESS	Teacher, 37 years; practicing designer, 1978-89
CURRENT POSITION/FIRM	Director of Graduate Programs, Department of Graphic Design and Director of the Ph.D. in Design Program for the College of Design, North Carolina State University
PREVIOUS EMPLOYMENT	Teacher and assistant chair at Virginia Commonwealth University (1976-89) Principal, Communication Design Inc. (1978-89) Curator, Hunter Museum of American Art (1975-76)
DESIGN EDUCATION	MFA, design, Cranbrook Academy of Art (1975) MEd (1974), BS (1970), art education, The Pennsylvania State University

Advocating for a more comprehensive, critical, and challenging design education spanning the extremes between high school and doctoral studies may not match every designer's professional ambitions—making Meredith Davis's contributions and efforts over the course of thirty years ever more important and palpable. Along with other students at Cranbrook, she developed a curriculum for use in 500 Michigan public schools; in an initiative with AIGA, she helped establish a set of criteria for design programs through the National Association of Schools of Art and Design; and, most recently she is Director of the Ph.D. program at NCSU. Davis also led a design practice for well over a decade in the 1980s, creating an energetic body of work that would have been a joy to see evolve into the twenty-first century.

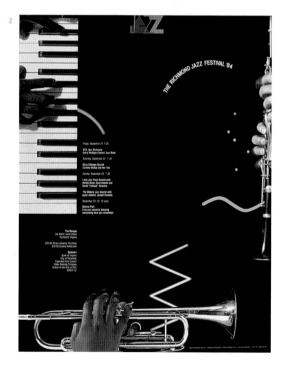

[1] *Poster for the Richmond Jazz Festival (1984).* **[2]** *Poster for the Five Sundays in August Jazz Festival (1985).*

You've headed the Ph.D. in Design Program for three years now and have been involved in shaping it for the past eight. How has the program evolved?

Ours was only the second doctoral design program in the U.S. It is an interdisciplinary collaboration among architecture, landscape architecture, graphic design and industrial design. We've graduated more than twenty students since 1999 and have another fifteen in the pipeline.

We started with two tracks: one in community design and another in something loosely defined as information design. The interdisciplinary framework at the beginning was one of convenience and was not well matched to faculty or student research interests. When I became the head of the program, I mapped faculty research and really studied student inquiries. I felt if we were to make an impact on the interdisciplinary agenda for design research, we needed to focus less on our affiliations and more on where design could have influence.

So we redefined the framework for the curriculum. Students now work in: design for learning; design for sustainability; design for health and well-being; design for the urban context; design for technology; and history/criticism. The faculty teams that support this research are truly interdisciplinary, often including non-designers from psychology, anthropology, rhetoric, philosophy, environmental sciences and planning.

What will your upcoming books for Thames & Hudson address? How do they tackle any issues about current design education?

The books share in common the issue of context. I think graphic design education has spent too long focusing only on the fit between form and content. Past strategies for teaching design have encouraged simplification; I believe what is called for today is making it clear and managing its complexity, not pretending that we can reduce it to something less messy. You don't get to these issues by talking only about the relationship between form and the subject matter of the communication. So the approach of the books is to promote the importance of understanding context.

Also, these are textbooks designed for classroom use. In setting a pedagogical approach, I questioned the continuing relevance of longstanding assumptions about how students learn in design—for example, that they learn best through a progression of concepts from simple to complex. The simple-to-complex teaching model dictates that we begin foundation instruction with the arrangement of abstract form before any content is introduced, implying that form is not content. This is a kind of trickle-down Bauhaus pedagogy. Students learn the "rules" of composition by detecting a pattern in what makes their teachers smile. So the purpose of the series is to re-examine and challenge such assumptions about how to teach design for their relevance in the twenty-first century.

With all this academic work, it might be easy to overlook your decade-long brush with a graphic design practice in the 1980s. Do you miss doing design work for clients?

Most of my years in professional practice were concurrent with full-time teaching and academic administration. From 1978–89 I ran a rather demanding design office that did work for Fortune 500 companies, government and cultural organizations. Our office also did an enormous amount of pro bono work for local nonprofits with which we shared common interests. I also taught full time and ran the graduate program at Virginia Commonwealth University while practicing. These diverse activities were very complementary in terms of the issues and interactions with people; I saw little difference between helping a student to understand a design problem and helping a client to understand a design solution. But wearing three hats was exhausting and I found that my outlook on practice suffered from too little time for reflection in the later years.

In the mid-1980s I was also pulled into more work nationally with professional associations (AIGA, American Center for Design, Graphic Design Education Association) and was asked to do more writing. And I became increasingly interested in the necessity to build a research culture in the field. Something had to give, and I decided to sell my share of the practice to my partner and move to the College of Design at North Carolina State University, where research was a higher priority. The focus of my work shifted to writing and research, allowing schedules that were more flexible in accommodating full-time teaching. I haven't regretted that decision. I actually feel I have a deeper connection with design now than I had through my practice.

How do you divide your time?

Today, I am a teacher, researcher, writer and reluctant administrator. Writing is my way of processing what I'm thinking about, of organizing ideas into arguments or structures that give order to their complexity; it allows me to see patterns and a path for moving forward. The research work arises from the need to understand something more fully and to add to the bank of ideas that support my teaching and writing.

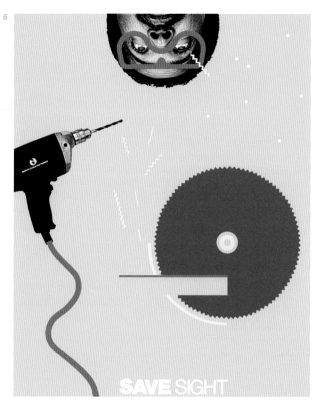

[3, 4] Annual report for Best Products Company (1981). [5, 7] Portfolio catalogue for artist/illustrator Sue Coe (1980s). [6] Safety poster for Virginia Electric and Power Company (1987).

PAULA
SCHER

NATIONALITY

American

YEAR BORN

1948

CURRENTLY RESIDING IN

New York, New York and
Salisbury, Connecticut, United States

YEARS IN THE BUSINESS

37

CURRENT POSITION/FIRM

Partner, Pentagram Design

PREVIOUS EMPLOYMENT

Partner, Koppel and Scher (1984-90)
Art director, CBS Records (1972-82)

DESIGN EDUCATION

BFA, Tyler School of Art, Temple University (1970)
DFA Honoris Causa,
Corcoran College of Art + Design (2001)
DFA Honoris Causa,
Maryland Institute College of Art (2008)

With an unparalleled typographic approach that can adapt and thrive in a perplexing number of applications—record covers, staircases, air-conditioning ducts—and for an enviable range of clients—Citibank, Tiffany & Co., and The Public Theater, to name a few—the work of Paula Scher has surfaced to the top of the profession for more than three decades. She started in the music industry at CBS Records and also briefly at Atlantic Records, then broadened her scope of work in the mid-1980s through her own studio, Koppel and Scher. She has been a partner at Pentagram since 1991, where her energetic design has fully developed into a multidisciplinary portfolio.

Let's talk first about an overlooked, perhaps simply implicit, aspect of your career. You have done everything from album covers, to packaging, to environmental graphics, to posters, to major corporate identities. Did you ever picture this as the outcome of your career? How have you swayed from one discipline to the next?

I never thought I would have the opportunity to do all that I've done. When I was a record cover art director and I wanted to design magazines, I was told that I couldn't because I only had experience being a record cover art director. I thought that was incredibly dumb. I want to be able to design anything and everything that I find interesting.

May we suggest the opening titles of a feature film as a future challenge? Any other secret design ambitions?

I'd like to design a typographic stage set.

Typography, in all its forms, shapes and sizes, has been integral to your body of work. If you would indulge us in a little allegory... What do you expect typography to do in your hands? What do you see in letterforms?

Letterforms are abstractions. Words have meanings. Designing with typography can be a form of abstract expressionism.

You have been part of the New York design community since the 1970s. How has the landscape changed since then? Socially, economically, creatively...?

There used to be a core group of powerful men—I'm married to one of them, Seymour Chwast—who ruled the design community. I always called them the *machers* (Yiddish for "big shots"). They were united by their generation, and by Paul Rand. They were very loyal to each other and dismissive of young designers outside their circle. That changed. There isn't central power in the community anymore. It's more dispersed.

You are outspoken and not afraid to say what you think. Whether it's about politics, culture or design, you have an opinion that you want to have heard. There must be pluses and minuses to this when dealing with clients and designers. Thoughts?

I would be more unhappy and frustrated being silent than opening myself up for attacks. Most of my clients appreciate the direct honesty. It's who I am.

Teaching has been a big part of your career as well. You spent over two decades at the School of Visual Arts alone. What has kept

1

2

3

4

5

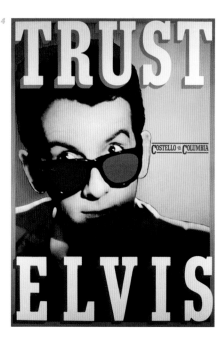 

[1] *Citi brand identity for Citibank (2000).* [2] *Poster for the 1995-96 season campaign for The Public Theater (1995).* [3] *Brand identity and packaging for Tiffany & Co. (2003); Photo by Nick Turner.* [4] *"Trust Elvis" poster for Columbia Records (1981).* [5] *"Changes One" and "Changes Two" LP covers for Atlantic Records (1974).*

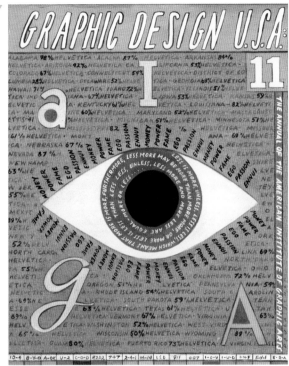

> **"My partners at Pentagram teach me daily. I learn simply by being around their work. I owe the breadth (and length) of my career to this partnership. I compete with them and measure myself against them and continually learn from them. I don't know what they get from me—hopefully, the same thing."**

you involved in, and coming back to, this realm for all these years?

Teaching helps me to think. If I can articulate how to make something better, I can apply it to my own work. It keeps me young.

You have been a partner at Pentagram since 1991. How has the organization informed your work and, in turn, how do you feel you have influenced it?

My partners at Pentagram teach me daily. I learn simply by being around their work. I owe the breadth (and length) of my career to this partnership. I compete with them and measure myself against them and continually learn from them. I don't know what they get from me—hopefully, the same thing.

[6] *Environmental graphics for New Jersey Performing Arts Center (NJPAC) Lucent Technologies Center for Arts Education (2001); Photo by Peter Mauss/Esto.*
[7] *Book jacket design for* Graphic Design USA: 11, *AIGA (1990).*

⁸ The Metropolitan Opera

The Met
ropolitan
Opera

[8] *Identity for the Metropolitan Opera (2006).* **[9]** *Signage and environmental graphics for Bloomberg L.P. corporate headquarters (2005); Photo by Peter Mauss/Esto.* **[10]** *Environmental graphics for New 42nd Street Studios / The Duke Theater (2000); Photo by Peter Mauss/Esto.* **[11]** *Great Beginnings promotion for Koppel & Scher (1984).*

"We've always lived and breathed design. We do take time off from design, although not in a formalized or structured way. Design is not just from 9 to 5 with personal life in the evenings. Our work lives and personal lives are more fluid and less formally structured than many people's."

Katherine
McCoy

Detail of: Poster for "Architecture, Symbol & Interpretation" for Cranbrook (1980).

Photo by Sheila Metzner

RUTH ANSEL

For a designer that has shaped the field of editorial design, Ruth Ansel's entry into the field is nothing short of unconventional. Without an education in design, Ansel held brief positions at Columbia Records and apprenticed for Erik Nitsche, was briefly married to Pentagram founder Bob Gill, then traveled across Europe for, as she puts it, "work and adventure," and, finally, got her first position as art director of Harper's Bazaar in 1961 with the aid of a competent fine arts portfolio. After Harper's Bazaar, Ansel took on The New York Times Magazine and later Vanity Fair, continually breaking ground in the field of editorial design. Since 1992, Ansel runs her own studio that carries on her tradition of arresting imagery and beautiful typography.

NATIONALITY	American
YEAR BORN	Late 1930s
CURRENTLY RESIDING IN	New York, New York, United States
YEARS IN THE BUSINESS	50+
CURRENT POSITION/FIRM	Ruth Ansel Design
PREVIOUS EMPLOYMENT	Art director of *Harper's Bazaar* (1960s)
	Art director of *The New York Times Magazine* (1970s)
	Art director of *Vanity Fair* (1980s)
DESIGN EDUCATION	BFA, Alfred University (1957)

Early in your career you went in search of work and adventure in various European cities. Looking back, how did this experience influence your future relationship with design?

When my then-husband Bob Gill and I suddenly divorced, I left for Europe looking for three things—to escape the hurt, to find work and to confront the unfamiliar. I was interested in learning film title design and thought I'd work my way down from London to Cinecittà near Rome. In Paris I met the celebrated art director/photographer Peter Knapp of *ELLE Magazine*. *ELLE* was the most influential fashion magazine of its time because it encouraged its innovative stylists to be free of designer constraints and to mix high fashion with street fashion. In Milan I was hired as an assistant at Studio Boggieri, working on Olivetti ads.

Unfortunately I was never taken seriously at Cinecittà. (All they wanted to do was pinch my bottom.) I finally ran out of money and knew it was time to come home. It was an eight-month adventure filled with discovery. The art, churches, architecture, streets and gardens I came across for the first time in my life left an indelible impression. Traveling through Europe, where history lives on in the present, was a rite of passage that fully engaged my senses and has continued to inform and inspire me over the years.

Much of your work has been in collaboration with photographers, illustrators, writers and directors. What would you say were key factors to these successful partnerships?

The key factors to these successful partnerships would have to be responsiveness to change. The subject of fashion is change. Change of attitude, change of what is socially acceptable, change of definitions of beauty, change of lifestyles. You have to be a catalyst for change. Working with an editor or illustrator is, in effect, no different in principle than working with a photographer. In the case of photographers, they are fully responsible for creating good photographs, but most importantly, you, as the art director, must cast the right photographer with the right assignment. The development of this relationship involves first familiarizing yourself with their work then knowing when to challenge their comfort level. Know when to say, "Shoot this in black and white, try this location, find a new model, shoot close-ups..." anything that will turn them onto a new path of discovery. The

[1] Vanity Fair magazine spread "Making Whoopi"; art direction and design by Ruth Ansel; photography by Annie Leibovitz (1984). [2] Harper's Bazaar magazine spread "The Galactic Beauty to the Rescue"; art direction Ruth Ansel/Bea Feitler; design and collage by Ruth Ansel; photography by Richard Avedon (April 1965). [3] Harper's Bazaar magazine spread "Blowing Fashion Through the Heart of Paris"; art direction Marvin Israel; design by Ruth Ansel; photography by Mel Sokolsky (1963).

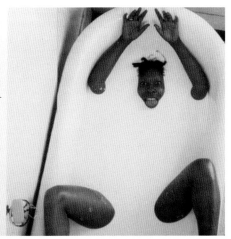

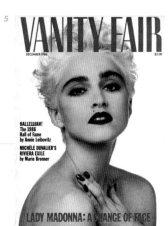

[4] Harper's Bazaar *magazine cover; art direction Ruth Ansel/Bea Feitler; design by Ruth Ansel; photography by Richard Avedon (April 1965). This cover sported a lenticular blinking eye in its worldwide distribution.* **[5]** Vanity Fair *magazine cover; art direction and design by Ruth Ansel; photography by Herb Ritts (1986).* **[6]** Peter Beard, Collector's Edition, Fayel Tall *opening page; art direction and design by Ruth Ansel; photography by Peter Beard; published by Taschen (2006).* **[7]** Harper's Bazaar *magazine spread "Night Flowers"; art direction Ruth Ansel/Bea Feitler; design by Ruth Ansel; photography by Hiro (circa 1960s).*

8

FALL 2000

9

The New York Times Magazine

DECEMBER 5, 1976/SECTION 6

Judith Jamison:
'Don't call me a star.
Call me a dancer.'

STOPPING
THE DEADLY TRADE
IN PLUTONIUM

CONTENTS: PAGE 32

10

ultimate responsibility you have is to help them stretch their talent. That involves having a critical eye and letting them know what you think when they turn in something disappointing. Every artist wants to collaborate with another artist so they both can heighten each other's experience.

You art directed several publications for three decades. How has the role of the art director evolved?

You have to trust your instincts. Work with the best. Celebrate talent and provide a place for these talents to flourish. I think predictability in magazines has become the rule, and I'm completely for the opposite. I like readers to be disturbed. Obviously you are responsible for the layout and look of all the visual elements on the page. You put it all together. Always

hire people smarter than you, and always be the student, not the teacher.

In the early 1990s you founded your own firm, Ruth Ansel Design. Was there a significant transition?

There really is no difference. The principle is the same. Find the best people—in this case the most enlightened clients—and recognize that you have a common goal.

With projects for Gianni Versace and Club Monaco, or the upcoming book on Elsa Peretti, do you foresee a step away from the fashion world in the future?

I've discovered that most of the work that has been significant in my life before I launched my own design studio has had a natural connection to my past. Culture in all its various forms has always been my main muse, a never ending source of

inspiration and pleasure. I love fashion, film, art, architecture, interior design, poetry, music, theater, dance and all printed matter, publications of all sorts. Out of that comes the book, a perfectly designed, self-contained universe. It allows for a personal dialogue between the reader and the creator. It is portable and private. Nothing so far that I have seen has come along to replace its simplicity of design. Creating a beautiful visual book, an object that will live long after me, is quite enough of a challenge. Basically, if I can continue to do what I love, then that is a dream project for me.

"Always hire people smarter than you, and always be the student, not the teacher."

[8, 10] *Advertising campaign for Club Monaco; art direction and design by Ruth Ansel; photography by Richard Avedon (2000). Includes actor Justin Chambers from* Grey's Anatomy, *just before he became famous.* [9] The New York Times Magazine *cover; art direction and design by Ruth Ansel; photography by Bill King (December 5, 1976).*

SHEILA
LEVRANT
DE BRETTEVILLE

NATIONALITY
American

YEAR BORN
1940

CURRENTLY RESIDING IN
Hamden, Connecticut, United States

YEARS IN THE BUSINESS
40

CURRENT POSITION/FIRM
The Sheila Studio
Professor and director of studies in graphic design
at Yale University School of Art

PREVIOUS EMPLOYMENT
Yale University Press (1965–67)
Olivetti, Milan (1968–70)
Los Angeles Times (1979–80)

For the last three decades Sheila Levrant de Bretteville has been cementing her legacy in design education: First in the 1970s as the founder of the Women's Design Program at the California Institute of the Arts; then in 1981 as initiator of the communication design program at the Otis Art Institute of the Parsons School of Design; and since 1990 as professor and director of graduate studies in graphic design at Yale. During her academic career, de Bretteville has produced work that embraces user participation and the effect the work has on local communities—her celebrated work in the public art realm reflects this sensibility by weaving itself into the neighborhoods it inhabits.

"How do I divide my time? In a zillion pieces that include: visual/library/online research; conversations with my husband, Peter, our son, his wife, my grandchildren, friends, students, colleagues and people at the sites where I work; designing permanent public installations; staring into space; feeling lucky to be alive and engaged; railing against our government; and responding to too much e-mail!"

Your legacy, as a designer and educator, has been continually framed through your commitment to feminism. How much do you think your accomplishments have been the result of this?

When I think of myself and my work I do not frame it by my feminism. That reframing is the result of the current reengagement with 1970s feminism. My work is influenced by my earliest memories of my father—his sense of community and commitment to his fellow workers in the garment factory, his re-creation of family

through the "Levrant Family Circle" and the meetings we had in our home. It is influenced by listening to Paul Robeson sing "Ballad for Americans," voicing his concern that in going to an elite college he risks becoming a snob and forgetting the group of people who are always forgotten—women, a group that is often forgotten, undervalued, and overlooked. Whether I am at Yale with our students, or in the streets, parks and libraries where my work is permanently installed, I have found ways to make my profession

be connected and committed to listening, asking, and having conversations. The resultant physical form it intended to be was an invitation to participate, to listen to the variety of voices—it is this vitality that is a marker of what democracy means that I find exciting.

Since 1990 you have been the director of the Yale University Graduate Program in Graphic Design. How have you maintained, as well as helped evolve, the relevance of this program?

This program continues to be exceptional and vital because both faculty and students are committed to their practice, are critically engaged in making their own work evolve, and are relevant to their time and who they are in the world within which they live and work. None of us is interested in simply repeating what we did last year.

The working faculty members who teach here are developing their own work—pushing the profession by developing their practice, thereby redefining the profession. They push at its edges to make it become what it has yet to be, and that makes it possible for us to ask the students to do the same.

Robert Storr, our new dean, has asked that this generation create new language and new metaphors that mirror the spirit of the program. This summer Susan Sellers, Dan Michaelson and I have rewritten our thesis requirements, changing what we say and do instead of replicating what we did last year. Each semester for the past seventeen years here I have met with the students to discuss what is working and what is not from their perspective.

And, of course, the wide range and quality of lectures, conferences, library resources and faculty here at Yale University nourish and inspire our students both intellectually and creatively, enhancing their sense of personal and professional agency as well.

I have said this before, but it bears repeating: Neglected areas of inquiry abound. Lack of imagination has designers teaching the same education they themselves received, rather than

"Neglected areas of inquiry abound. Lack of imagination has designers teaching the same education they themselves received, rather than re-imagining different kinds of programs and projects."

re-imagining different kinds of programs and projects.

From the West Coast during the 1970s at CalArts and the 1980s at Otis, to the East Coast during the 1990s and 2000s at Yale... Would you mind sharing a few notes on this odyssey?

[1] *"ShrinkWrap" poster for the California Institute of the Arts (1970).* [2] *A new threshold step for the Old Water Tower in Yekaterinburg, Siberia for CEC ArtsLink (2006).* [3] *"Lazy Susan Table," 10,000 possible open-ended sentences on organizing, working—and not... for the Rhode Island Department of Labor and Training, in collaboration with Henk van Assen (2000).*

Although I love having verdant springs, crisp, cool autumns and snowy winters, I still long for and enjoy the smell of the California hills, the sense of open possibility without reason that Los Angeles offers, and my in-depth participation in the women's movement, all of which contributed to the ease with which I switched from designing a sequence of images and texts in print materials to designing the permanent visual and verbal gestures in the public spaces through which a wide variety of people move.

And the shift from east to west to east has meant much more literal movement on my part as well. In the past six months I have done work and/or given talks in Siberia, China, and Qatar. This is true for my faculty as well, those who come here from China and Holland and Switzerland and do work in Japan, Korea, China, Holland, and so on.

How important is it to have a practice that complements your academic efforts?

Essential! None of us in the program I direct are buried in academia or just make projects for a tiny audience of friends, or do what we did last year. I—and those I know and cherish here at Yale and in New York, Boston and Amsterdam—not only juggle a private and professional life, but I am also completely committed to engaging critically with that harsh, greedy and difficult public sphere of professional life!

You have been a proponent of graphic design being less about corporate services and more about inclusion of different voices and consideration for the community the

work affects. Have you seen any changes in this regard within our profession in the last thirty years?

I am still trying to provide what is missing, pushing to open up the world around me to positive change. I am eager for both public art and graphic design to be less literal and more thought provoking. I hope that our profession defines social issues and engages with social issues less narrowly. Class, race, gender, religion and the power structures we are too often stuck within are very complex and variegated areas of study and engagement, yet the profession still defines political work as angry railing. I would like to see a bit more humility, less greed, and more efficiency in deriving the best effect from the least of means.

[4] *"Take a break... Out to Lunch... Back to work..." in the courtyard of the Rhode Island Department of Labor and Training, in collaboration with Henk vanAssen (2000).* [5, 6] *New York City subway station "At the start... At long last...", for the Metropolitan Transportation Authority of New York City (1998).* [7] *One of six panels honoring individual women who worked for change in the show "HEAR US" at the Boston State House + Massachusetts Foundation for the Humanities, in collaboration with Susan Sellers (1999).*

VÉRONIQUE VIENNE

NATIONALITY	French and American
YEAR BORN	1942
CURRENTLY RESIDING IN	Paris, France
YEARS IN THE BUSINESS	40
CURRENT POSITION/FIRM	Writer, teacher, lecturer
PREVIOUS EMPLOYMENT	Graphic designer, exhibit designer, art director, branding & marketing consultant, spokesperson, magazine editor, copywriter, ghost writer
DESIGN EDUCATION	École des Beaux-Arts, Paris and Besançon

To say that the career of Véronique Vienne has been diverse would be an understatement. As a writer, she has penned numerous articles on a broad range of topics as well as a short monograph on Chip Kidd, yet she is more broadly recognized for her best-selling The Art of *series, sparked by the inaugural* The Art of Doing Nothing: Simple Ways to Make Time for Yourself. *As an editor she has gathered provocative essays for books like* Citizen Designer: Perspectives on Design Responsibility *and edited mainstream magazines like* House & Garden. *Vienne has also acted as editorial designer, creative director and branding consultant for a variety of clients. She teaches at the School of Visual Arts' graduate program, and she splits her time between Paris and New York. C'est la vie for designers, right?*

Your career has been mesmerizingly broad, from editorial designer, to branding agency creative director, to teacher, to writer. Over the years, what has kept you moving from one discipline to the next?

Recently I heard Maira Kalman describe her work process as "running around in an alert stupor." I thought, Wow! That's me too!

Currently, as a writer for the most part, you have stayed connected to design and even explored some of its less glamorous ramifications like social responsibility and ethics. What is it about design that keeps you plugged in?

Design tells interesting stories—stories that are not told in words but are just as complex and revealing as reportages or works of fiction.

In the design industry we know you from your writings about our profession, but the topics you explore reach far beyond it. You are also quite recognized for The Art of Doing Nothing, a book that doesn't even mention Milton Glaser or Helvetica or branding. How do you nurture this curiosity and ability to articulate such subjects?

For me, writing is first and foremost about designing words on a page—words that will make readers feel more alive, the same way design can make viewers feel more intelligent.

As a writer, how do you see your role at the School of Visual Arts' MFA Design program?

I teach my students how to think of their work as part of a larger conversation. I coach them to see the big picture. I want each of them to be the smartest person in the room.

Is there a stone left unturned so far in your design-centric career?

Oh yes!!! I wish I had had the time to become a better designer. But as a single mother, I had to make choices. One of them was to put my career on the back burner while my daughter was growing up. It was a tough decision to come to, but once I had made up my mind, it was pure joy.

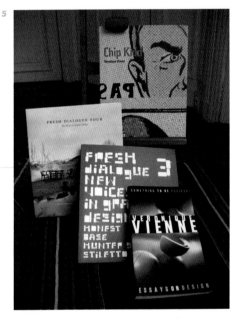

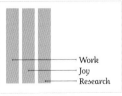

How Véronique Vienne uses up her time:

Work
Joy
Research

[1] *"Love,"* Self *magazine (1990).* **[2]** *"Legs & Arms,"* Self *magazine; photography by Jim Varriale (1990).* **[3]** *"How to Keep Your Body Young,"* Self *magazine; photography by Antoine Verglas (1990).* **[4]** *Books in which Véronique Vienne has been involved.* **[5]** *Design books authored by Véronique Vienne.* **[6]** *"Seduced,"* Self *magazine (1990).* **[7]** *Translations of a series of books authored by Véronique Vienne.*

PATHFINDERS

Detail of: *Martha Stewart Everyday at Kmart seed packaging; design by Gael Towey (1999).*

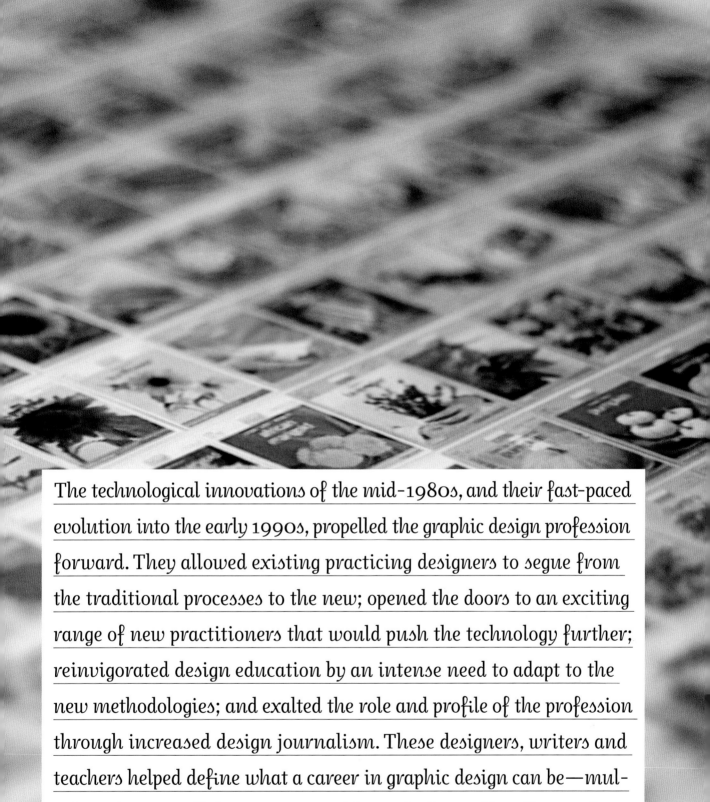

The technological innovations of the mid-1980s, and their fast-paced evolution into the early 1990s, propelled the graphic design profession forward. They allowed existing practicing designers to segue from the traditional processes to the new; opened the doors to an exciting range of new practitioners that would push the technology further; reinvigorated design education by an intense need to adapt to the new methodologies; and exalted the role and profile of the profession through increased design journalism. These designers, writers and teachers helped define what a career in graphic design can be—multidisciplinary, collaborative, mutable, and, above all, influential.

ANN
WILLOUGHBY

It is hard to imagine an independent design firm—with overhead sometimes amounting to twenty staff members and the upkeep of one of the most beautiful barns you've ever seen—running for thirty years straight, but Willoughby Design Group, established in 1978 by Ann Willoughby, has been producing strong work and has maintained its presence in the design community ever since. Willoughby—whose design career started as an intern at Belk Department Store in Mississippi for seventy-five cents an hour— was an advocate of branding long before it became a business catchphrase, with work that extended beyond isolated design solutions. As a teacher and avid member of AIGA, Willoughby's commitment to the profession extends, too, beyond the norm.

NATIONALITY

American

YEAR BORN

1946

CURRENTLY RESIDING IN

Kansas City, Missouri, United States

YEARS IN THE BUSINESS

30

CURRENT POSITION/FIRM

Founder and CEO, Willoughby Design Group

DESIGN EDUCATION

BFA, fine art and design,
University of Southern Mississippi (1968)

By the time this book is published you will have achieved a commendable milestone: thirty years in the business. This may be a tall order, but could you sum up how your design practice has changed in the last three decades?

From day one I instinctively believed design was about making life better and more meaningful. The process of creating something of beauty, value and usefulness thrills me today as much as it did thirty years ago. The tools and media we used to shape and distribute experiences have changed drastically in the last thirty years, yet design is much more understood today in our culture. I was first introduced to designers, writers and architects at the Aspen Design Conference in the 1970s, when design was less understood and visible, at least in the U.S. Fortunately my company was inspired from the beginning by an international vision of the value of design.

In the early days of my career a lot of designers worked in "commercial art studios" or advertising agencies. In those days agencies and companies contracted out to studios and freelancers. This studio structure never appealed to me, especially when I was brought in as part of the execution process without the ability to shape the overall idea. During the late 1980s and throughout the 1990s design studios were finally recognized for their fresh thinking and creativity. During this period we began to attract world-class clients and designers.

Today, there is another shift. As the computer became a ubiquitous design enabler, companies began shifting the work of studios to their in-house agencies, and design firms began to specialize in new media.

This shift has allowed us to refocus our business on something I have always believed: Design, leveraged to its full potential, represents an untapped opportunity to reshape a more sustainable world. Over the past couple of years we have been fortunate to work with leading companies and organizations on initiatives that support economic, social and environmental innovation. Willoughby is now engaged in some of our most meaningful and successful work in our thirty-year history.

Over the course of your career you have been heavily involved with AIGA as a member of the national board, a founder of the AIGA Center for Brand Experience and an

AIGA Fellow. What keeps you involved in this organization?

AIGA is both a community of friends and a professional organization that has been instrumental in helping our company grow. Recently, I felt it was important to give back to AIGA and to help a younger generation of designers in the same way I was so generously supported in my youth.

Over the past twenty years I have joined other communities (TED and POP!Tech) that have expanded my understanding of the world.

You've been an advocate for branding for a few years now, even when it was fashionable to despise the word. How has the notion of branding evolved in the last decade?

If you want to see a room full of designers throw a tizzy fit, mention the word *brand*. For example, my friend and mentor Milton Glaser literally hates the word. (Substitute the word with *reputation*, and everyone calms down.)

I believe the noun *brand*, when turned into a verb as in *branding*, is inherently neutral. It became a dirty word a few years back because some people associated the word *branding* with all things negative about our modern system of unchecked mass consumerism, shoddy products and corporate greed. While it is true that many companies lost their way, not all companies and brands are bad. This was, and is still, a problem. But our culture is evolving along with the thinking about brands. Smart companies got the message and realized that the financial and cultural value of their brands depends on giving their

stakeholders and customers meaningful, well-designed, sustainable products and experiences. The demand for transparency fueled by the power of social networks and industry watchdogs is making it impossible for a brand to say one thing and do another. There is no place to hide, so companies are remaking their brands to reflect the values of society.

Some may not know this, but your first job was, literally, as a window dresser—a phrase that is sometimes used as a pejorative for design that lacks substance—for a department store. That is quite a non-traditional start in this business. How important was it to have a different perspective on the principles of design?

During college I worked for a man who adored Stanley Marcus, so he challenged me to transform his exclusive, newly-

---

[1] *Identity for Kevin Carroll, Katalyst (2004).* **[2]** *Paper promotion,* Sustainability/Designability: Strathmore Sustainability Portfolio, *for Mohawk Fine Papers Inc. (2006).* **[3]** *Shopping bags and gift packaging for Feng (2006).*

> **"How do I divide my time? Most of the time design, life, and work blend together in a rather pleasant way. I work a lot and I travel often for both work and pleasure. I am very lucky."**

built department store into a brand that would compete with Neiman Marcus. I was given a fantastic opportunity to design and manage all of his advertising and merchandising while still in school. I was only eighteen when I started my career, but I learned more in those four years at the department store than I did in the classroom. To compete with Neiman Marcus and New York retail was a tall order in those days when fashion and creativity was at its pinnacle. This was before TV and malls replaced the fine art of fashion illustration and window design. I actually won a few national awards for my work.

Looking back, this was a perfect way to start a design career. I learned how marketing, merchandising, design and storytelling helped attract and build a loyal customer base.

[4] Brand identity and storefront for Sheridan's Lattés & Frozen Custard (2005). [5] Rules of the Red Rubber Ball: Find and Sustain Your Life's Work by Kevin Carroll (2004). [6] The Willoughby Design Barn, envisioned by Ann Willoughby and designed by el dorado inc. (2000). [7] Letterpress and illustration layered wall and open kitchen of SPIN! Neapolitan Pizza—the newest fast-casual restaurant from the Gail Lozoff +Willoughby partnership, from which Einstein Bros. Bagels also spawned (2004).

"A great designer is a good listener."

Jennifer
Morla

ANNE
BURDICK

For most designers separating interactive from print work, or writing from design is common, but for Anne Burdick the complete opposite applies. A truly immersive designer, Burdick blends all the principles of writing and designing (regardless of medium) into a practice that is equally adept at producing beautiful books—like the complex Wörterbuch der Redensarten, winner of the coveted "Most Beautiful Book in the World" prize at the Leipzig Book Fair—and constructing groundbreaking web sites—like the electronic book review, an online literary review and journal that is miles away from the typical web site. Burdick is a devoted teacher, currently heading the Media Design Program at the Art Center College of Design.

NATIONALITY
American

YEAR BORN
1962

CURRENTLY RESIDING IN
Los Angeles, California, United States

YEARS IN THE BUSINESS
23

CURRENT POSITION/FIRM
Chair, Graduate Media Design Program,
Art Center College of Design
Principal, The Offices of Anne Burdick

DESIGN EDUCATION
MFA and BFA, California Institute of the Arts (1992/1991)
Undergraduate work, Art Center College of Design,
San Diego State University (1985)

Design and writing are at the core of your practice. How do you integrate them?

As I've written elsewhere, both my writing and my design are informed by Jay David Bolter's notion of a "writing space," from his book of the same name. I am interested in the relationship between the space for writing—the physical container and cultural context—and the writing itself. While I'm definitely more of a designer who writes rather than the other way around, I move back and forth between the two so frequently that I'm no longer aware of it. Now I'm most interested in the structure and representation of ideas.

Lately, I've been producing a lot of "talks"—keynote presentations, Pecha Kuchas, and the like. Talks demand an interplay between showing and telling.

They are time-based and image-driven like film, but they carry the rhetorical expectations of an essay. It's a fun challenge to create a visual-verbal performance that clarifies a complex idea without being too pedagogical. I'm not saying I've accomplished that yet... I'm merely saying that for me, putting together a talk—particulary one in which I'm crafting a new argument—requires the tightest integration of writing and design that I've experienced to date.

In 1995 you guest-edited two issues of Emigre, where you posed the question, "What happens when the worlds of writing and design coincide, overlap and collide?" Have you seen this question addressed in the design profession in the last decade?

Yes, absolutely. Stuart Bailey, Denise Gonzales Crisp, William Drenttel and

Mieke Gerritzen are four very different designers whose work is an integration of written language and design. But the larger change has taken place within the writing community where writers such as Mark Danielewski use the graphical arrangement and typography of their writing to write differently.

There are some obstacles that keep the design profession from fully understanding the implications of this work. To me, a key culprit is the way in which typography is taught. Designers who learn the "typographic principles of good design" may be ready to further a tradition (consciously or otherwise), but their focus on rules and form may leave them disengaged from the words they design and, worse, from an awareness of their role in the circulation and generation of culture. A

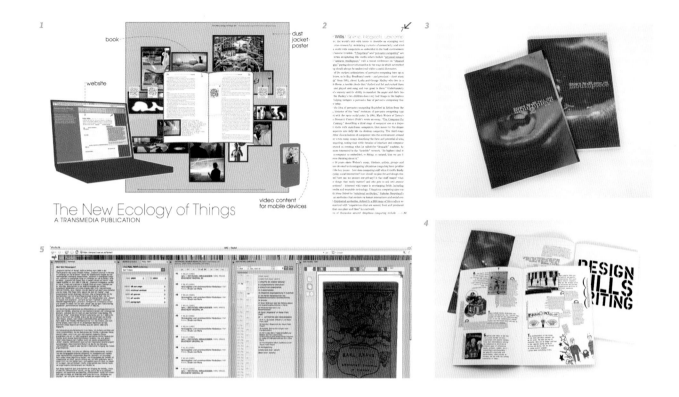

The New Ecology of Things
A TRANSMEDIA PUBLICATION

more useful approach—and timely, given the rise of new communication environments—would be something along the lines of language design or writing design in which visible language is addressed as a fluid combination of writing, technology and culture.

You have been involved with electronic book review, the online literary review and journal, since the mid-1990s as an editor, designer and contributor. What have these relationship meant to you?

At a time when we were all feeling tremendous pressure to get digital, electronic book review (ebr) allowed me to enter the digital arena by following my interest in the materiality of writing. I found myself collaborating with key members of the electronic literature community at a very exciting moment. From ebr 3.0

forward (we're now on 4.1), the nature of the project changed considerably from the treatment of individual essays to the design of an application for reading and writing. While our work was once aligned with the net.art movement of the 1990s, we now find ourselves participating in the emerging field of the Digital Humanities. The project continues to evolve but, most importantly, the collaboration with editor Joe Tabbi and database and application designer Ewan Branda remains engaging. The collaboration challenges me to consider the impact of my design decisions on literary practice.

As an example—and this is going to sound incredibly geeky—one of my favorite debates revolved around how to display icons that allow readers to com-

ment in the margins of an essay. The questions went something like this: "What kind of textual unit comprises a complete thought? How can we automate activities that are extricably tied to content? Are the comments parasitic, disruptive, or additive?" In the end our decision was equal parts programming, editing and interface design.

Apart from your current position you have also taught at North Carolina State University, CalArts, and Otis College of Art and Design. Why the interest in teaching?

The short answer is that I am more interested in design as a discipline than as a profession. I would like to see graduate education inform the practice in the way that research does for, say, medicine. I believe that those of us working in graduate education have the responsibility to do

[1, 2] Book and web site for New Ecology of Things transmedia publication for Art Center College of Design, Media Design Program (2007-08). [3, 4] Guest editor for Emigre magazine, issues 35 and 36 (1995-96). [5] Austrian Academy Corpus web site for the Austrian Academy of Sciences (2007).

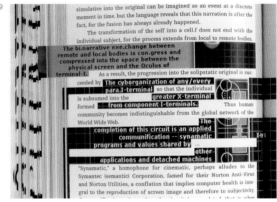

the work that can only be done within a research-like environment. The graduate studio can be a testing ground where students and faculty can invent, tinker, take risks, challenge assumptions, and generate new theories, methods, and form. My current challenge is to frame this work in a way that makes its value apparent.

On a more personal level, the easy answer is that I learn more about design from teaching than I do from designing (a cliché, but true). Working one-on-one with young designers and seeing them come into their own is tremendously satisfying. But I also value education as a context for faculty to make work that is exploratory, speculative or exceedingly theoretical.

You work across print and web mediums, do you see any differences between the two, or is it all one big, happy canvas?

In the Media Design Program, we teach students to design in a media-specific way, meaning with a full awareness of the possibilities and limitations of different media forms. I believe that to design well, one should exploit the unique affordances of the medium they work in. When designing books, for instance, I see my work as an extension of a set of traditions called "book design," but I also look at the book as yet another interface for reading with its own distinct navigational capabilities, organizational logics, and ergonomics of use that are built into its physical form, the codex. By the same token, a screen (and its hardware and software) not only has a different materiality and operational capacity, it engages an entirely different set of traditions than the book does.

Now that almost anything can become a communication medium (your sleeve, your car door), do "principles" derived from print have any relevance whatsoever? The issues are interesting to me, but they're hardly new; visual communication has a long and varied history entwined with new technologies, shifting values, and emergent practices. While we will continue to use inherited aesthetics and metaphors to orient us in unfamiliar environments, I'm wary of hard and fast rules based on experience elsewhere. Instead, we need to engage with whatever medium we're using—play around with it, see what works. I believe that specific responses—rather than generalities—and openness to discovery are the best guiding principles for design in any medium.

[6, 7, 8, 9] Writing Machines *book and web supplement for Peter Lunenfeld, Mediawork Project, MIT Press (2002-03).* **[10]** *electronic book review 4.1 web site (2007).*

BARBARA
DEWILDE

NATIONALITY

American

YEAR BORN

1962

CURRENTLY RESIDING IN

Montclair, New Jersey, United States

YEARS IN THE BUSINESS

21

CURRENT POSITION/FIRM

Associate art director, Knopf Publishing Group

PREVIOUS EMPLOYMENT

Design director, Martha Stewart
Living Omnimedia (2000–04)
Principal, deWilde Design Office (2004–07)

DESIGN EDUCATION

BA, graphic design, Penn State (1985)

From books to magazines—from the inside to the outside—Barbara deWilde has designed some of the most endearing layouts and covers to grace newsstands in the last two decades. She first started in 1987 as one of the designers in the small, celebrated, creative in-house department at Knopf that produced a desirable number of book covers. She then became a design director at Martha Stewart Living Omnimedia, where she redesigned Martha Stewart Living and oversaw its sister publications. In 1999 deWilde established her own studio where she maintained a healthy dose of work culminating in the redesign of House Beautiful. And in 2007 she returned to Knopf, to dazzle again from where it all started.

From 1987 to 1999 you were part of the celebrated team-of-four (Chip Kidd, Carol Devine Carson, Archie Ferguson and you) at Knopf Publishing Group, Random House Inc. What was this early experience like?

It felt surprisingly like a start-up venture, a new company with an all-new staff. Our editorial guru, Sonny Mehta, was a newcomer as well, ready to make this Knopf imprint his own. In the office, Chip, Carol, Archie, and I were surrounded by superstars of postmodern design—Louise Fili, Carin Goldberg, Lorraine Louie—and I was desperate to distinguish myself. Sonny encouraged it.

Chip and I had been trained to make our own imagery at design school, so we did that at Knopf, too. Anything was fair game: vernacular images, found objects, printers' typographic reference books...

even the stat camera. (That's a flatbed camera, now obsolete, used to enlarge or reduce type. We found that the tonal paper would work like a Polaroid camera, and we made images with it.) I had worked at an ad agency for six months previous to coming to Random House and had been exposed to the practice of using swipe art, usually photography. We began sifting through photo history for images to use on the books, which at the time wasn't done for fiction titles. Now it's ubiquitous, but it wasn't then. It was exciting to see a shift away from the decorative jacket. We were pretty driven and competitive with each other, which propelled the work further.

It was a very lucky and exciting time to be working in jacket design, and every approved sketch felt like something of a

breakthrough. Simultaneously, Barnes & Noble and other book retailers were expanding through the creation of superstores, and conversely, vinyl records were being downsized to CDs. The graphic design for books became more prominently displayed, like in a gallery. I feel very fortunate to have been involved at that moment in publishing design.

After Knopf you became the design director of Martha Stewart Living (MSL), a magazine that you helped evolve into a very recognizable design aesthetic that beautifully emphasized the content. What was this process like?

I have a very vivid memory of Gael Towey taking me out to lunch and telling me that I was expected to redesign *MSL*. It was terrifying. How do you redesign something that's already perfect?

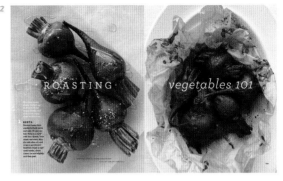

MSL was a model for the design of the woman's magazine, and I was a fan.

Before I describe the redesign, I think it's important to know how the magazine is put together. The content is created by core editors working in teams with stylists and art directors. The stories are not written in advance or reported on from the outside world. If you're working on a story about lamps, someone at *MSL* is making the lamps and the art director is learning, watching, helping. Each art director is deputized to be the editorial storyteller and works in collaboration with the team and a photographer to create the content that you ultimately see printed in the magazine. The more typical model for a magazine involves contributors to create the story, photo editors to arrange for the photography and art directors to lay out

the pictures using a set word count. The art department at *MSL* was sizable. At one point there were twelve staffers putting together the magazine every month, which was very hard to control visually. The simplicity of the design was beautiful, but also very practical... and they wanted me to change it?!

So here goes. There were only three things that readers regularly complained about: (1) the type was too small, (2) the projects looked too hard, (3) the recipes had too many ingredients. My only complaint was that there were too many different typefaces; I think we had six and they came from four different families.

"I have a very vivid memory of Gael Towey taking me out to lunch and telling me that I was expected to redesign MSL."

Jonathan and Tobias are like modern day matchmakers for designers and typefaces. I described seemingly disparate attributes that I wanted the type to have, and they listened and asked questions. Brilliant questions. We talked about the two magazines that most remind me of *MSL*: *Popular Mechanics* from the 1950s and *Harper's Bazaar*... somehow smashed together. I wanted to work with two font families only, but it did grow to three in the end. I wanted a text face that was extremely readable... large lowercase x-height, pretty and not too dark when set as text, but usable for headlines. Jonathan called that the workhorse face. I also wanted a serif font that had a beautiful

[1] Martha Stewart Living *magazine cover (2003).* *[2]* "Roasting Vegetables 101" Martha Stewart Living *spread (2002).* *[3]* "China Asters" Martha Stewart Living *spread (2002).*

italic that could be used like a script in display. When the magazine is teaching you how to do something, it needs to be very readable; when it's rhapsodizing about the most beautiful rose, it needs to be romantic... closer to the type that you'd find on the bottom of a turn-of-the century botanical print.

This was a yearlong process and hard to condense, but the direction we followed came from type designs that both Jonathan and Tobias had a great fondness for—the hand-drawn type on ancient maps. Surveyor was the beautiful font and later Archer, a slab serif, was the workhorse. We did depart from some of our original ideas to come up with Archer. It wasn't as derivative of ancient maps as we had originally thought it would be (Jonathan said it reminded him of an Italian Vespa!), but the two fonts did feel right together and very fresh.

> I wanted a text face
> that was extremely readable...
> large lowercase x-height, pretty
> and not too dark when set as text,
> but usable for headlines.
> **ARCHER BOOK**
>
> *I also wanted a serif font*
> *that had a beautiful italic*
> *that could be used*
> *like a script in display.*
> **SURVEYOR TEXT ITALIC**

The redesign was presented to Martha as a "Before and After" show. We analyzed each page of the magazine, pulling out content—lists for materials, sidebars, charts, caption text, and typesetting—to show how easy the stuff really was to do and make. A material list that asks for three items looks easier than no material list at all. If a column had a theme (like recipes that are all made with buttermilk), we devoted a page to a beautiful picture of buttermilk to show the theme. We came up with five different ways to open a story in the front of the magazine to keep the pacing lively, and we launched some new columns. It was incredibly difficult and would have been impossible without my co-designer, Mary Jane Callister, a goddess of type design. Martha loved it, and we had to roll the whole thing out while we were producing the existing design. I liken it to changing the tires on a moving car. Enough said.

Five years later, you established your own practice in 2004. After seventeen years of working in a group environment, what was it like to be on your own?

It's funny. Even though I'd been working in small and large groups, I still spent much of my design time alone in my office trying to define the problem at hand. It's a pretty solitary experience. I think the thing that I missed most was the friendly face that would be there after I had surfaced from my computer screen. I also missed working with photographers who talk about art and travel and the things that they love. They are so exotic to me because I am someone who is usually either designing or raising kids. Working from home was really a decision that I made for my personal life. I have two kids. My son was a pitcher when I was at *MSL*. I missed every game, and then he stopped pitching. I have never forgiven myself for that. And on the rare occasion when I could pick up my daughter at school, her teacher said that that was all she talked about all day. Her mom was going to show up. So, enough was enough. That time was not a rich design time, but it was great for us. I did get some projects that I wouldn't have been able to take on while at Knopf or at Living. I designed the AIGA annual that simultaneously announced their new online archive. It was an interesting undertaking with half the budget of previous annuals. I made myself typeset every page with no help. For some reason I thought that was an interesting challenge.

You recently returned to Knopf Publishing Group, Random House Inc. What brought you back to book cover design?

I was looking for balance. I want to be a designer, and I want to be a mom. I know what it takes to be a designer and executive in a large company and I loved it, but I couldn't do both. I understand book publishing and I love reading. I love the people who are attracted to this book corner of the world, and I really get a kick out them. I also have gained so many skills from my magazine experience that I wanted to apply to jacket design. I am much more confident with photo art direction, for example. It's also nice to be known. When I came back to Knopf, everyone was still here. It's a special place. People don't leave. Still, my son will go to college next year and my daughter will graduate in five years, so who knows.

For most of your career you have focused on editorial design. What attracts you to this discipline?

I love books, and I love storytelling. I love understanding the text and trying to imagine the way a text could be represented. I'm not academic and cringe at the thought of a serious discussion about the books I've read, but I enjoy taking that leap of faith that is necessary to change words into something visual.

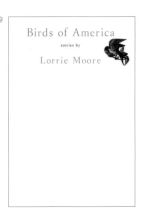

[4] Book jacket for For the Relief of Unbearable Urges by Nathan Englander (1999). [5] Book jacket for The Wife by Meg Wolitzer (2003). [6] Book jacket for Quarrel & Quandary by Cynthia Ozick (2002). [7] Book jacket for Altmann's Tongue by Brian Evenson (1998). [8] Book jacket for The Last Thing He Wanted by Joan Didion (1998). [9] Book jacket for Birds of America by Lorrie Moore (1999).

BONNIE
SIEGLER

NATIONALITY
American

YEAR BORN
1963

CURRENTLY RESIDING IN
Brooklyn, New York, United States

YEARS IN THE BUSINESS
14

CURRENT POSITION/FIRM
Co-founder, Number 17

PREVIOUS EMPLOYMENT
VH1, MTV Networks (1989-93)

DESIGN EDUCATION
BFA, Carnegie Mellon University (1985)

Being married to a filmmaker may be—aside from love, of course—one more way in which Bonnie Siegler is able to bridge the seemingly wide gap between traditional design and design for film and television. Her four-year duty as design director for VH1 did not hurt her expertise, and the numerous identities and animations she developed over the course of the following fifteen years only helped to broaden it. And, still, her work extends into print and branding through Number 17, the design firm she founded with Emily Oberman in 1993. The two women have a relationship and friendship that has rendered them almost inseparable—so much so that they often finish each other's sentences.

You and Emily Oberman have been operating as Number 17 since 1993 and have formed a strong identity through your work together, but you each come from slightly different backgrounds. How does your experience at VH1 manifest in the way you work?

We really benefited from our varying experience. I essentially came from the client side and brought insider knowledge of how corporations work, make decisions, and communicate; Emily came from a successful design studio and brought insider knowledge of how design studios work, make decisions, and communicate. Somehow, we put all this experience together and made our own thing out of it.

Tell us about your dynamic, working as partners, both as designers and representatives of your business in front of clients. Do you get to play good cop/bad cop often?

The good cop/bad cop thing really works! With each client, we get to wear different hats, and we take turns with different responsibilities to keep it even. Also, this way we both get to do a lot of different things every day and we don't get bored.

Whether it's a book for Sex and the City or the opening titles for Will & Grace, you seem to have a finger on the pulse of pop culture. What makes you thrive in this realm?

We like watching TV, going to the movies, reading books, newspapers, blogs, magazines and all that good stuff. We are really just fans of pop culture in general. And nothing is more fun than getting to do a book about one of your favorite TV shows.

> **"The good cop/bad cop thing really works! With each client, we get to wear different hats, and we take turns with different responsibilities to keep it even."**

For the last fourteen years you've been designing the opening credits for Saturday Night Live (SNL), a show that reinvents itself constantly. How do you keep up? And what goes into this project?

It's a different scenario every year. Sometimes we start from scratch (we have designed the logo twice), and sometimes we just revise it a bit, but we always try to maintain that *Saturday Night Live* feeling. Every single year, though,

All work shown developed at Number 17, under creative direction of Bonnie Siegler and Emily Oberman. [1, 2] Book design for Sex and the City: Kiss and Tell, *for Melcher Media; design by Eva Hückmann (2003). [3, 4, 6] Web site for Very Short List; design by Holly Gressley (2007). [5] The New York Times Op-Art; design by Bonnie Siegler and Emily Oberman (2005).*

7

8

POPULAR ARTS TELEVISION

9

NATIONAL SEPTEMBER 11
MEMORIAL & MUSEUM
AT THE WORLD TRADE CENTER

10

we have very limited time, and we end up editing all hours of the night and even do our presentations in the middle of the night. But we always have fun and then get to go to the show and the party afterwards!

The scope of projects you develop is very broad, from motion to editorial to identity design. What does it take to be able to fluctuate between all these mediums?

We try to bring a certain kind of problem solving to every project we work on, and we tend to focus more on the thinking than the medium it gets applied to. This was less true when we started in 1993, but now everything we do ends up existing, in some way or another (and whether we design it or not), in many platforms, and the medium is more and more irrelevant.

You have been highly involved with AIGA, volunteering time and energy. What do you take away from this?

One of our greatest achievements was probably creating, programming, and running DFTV.001 and DFTV.002 (Design for Film and Television), but we have also worked on many other conferences and committees. We have forged great friendships with local and national board members but really just enjoy hanging out with fellow designers. Also, AIGA meant so much to me when I was in college as it helped me understand the world I was getting into, and now I truly enjoy doing the same for the next generation. AIGA is an incredible organization. Everyone should participate.

It's hard to imagine you two apart. What has been the best, and hardest, part of working together?

Best: It can be really hard running a business, and being able to share the burden makes the hard times bearable and the good times more fun. Hardest: Relationships are a lot of work, and we are both, essentially, married to two different people (our husbands and each other). We fight, disagree and cry, but we always make up.

---

[7] *Book jacket for* It's Kind of a Funny Story *by Ned Vizzini, for Benetton; design by Wade Convay and Abigail Smith (2004).* **[8]** *Logo for Trio, TV channel for Universal Television; design by Bonnie Siegler and Emily Oberman (2005).* **[9]** *Logo for the National September 11 Memorial & Museum; design by Jessica Zadnik (2007).* **[10]** *Logo for Orbitz, for TBWA / Chiat / Day; design by William Morrisey (2000).*

EMILY
OBERMAN

NATIONALITY
American

YEAR BORN
1962

CURRENTLY RESIDING IN
Brooklyn, New York, United States

YEARS IN THE BUSINESS
14

CURRENT POSITION/FIRM
Co-founder, Number 17

PREVIOUS EMPLOYMENT
Senior designer, M&Co. (1987-93)

DESIGN EDUCATION
BFA, The Cooper Union (1985)

As a senior designer for Tibor Kalman's influential M&Co., Emily Oberman had a crash course in designing for television in her work for the Talking Heads's acclaimed music video "(Nothing But) Flowers" among other projects in print and identity design before establishing Number 17 with Bonnie Siegler. Together, their work spans every discipline from motion graphics, to identity design, to editorial design for cultural and entertainment focused clients. Both women have been actively involved with AIGA as board members and by directing full conferences like DFTV.001 and .002 (Design for Film and Television), and they are also devoted teachers—Siegler at the graduate program at the School of Visual Arts, and Oberman at The Cooper Union.

You and Bonnie Siegler have been operating as Number 17 since 1993, but you each come from slightly different backgrounds. How does your experience at M&Co. manifest in the way you work?

Funnily enough I feel like Number 17 is structured very similarly to the way M&Co. was (and hopefully Bonnie feels the same way about VH1). Like M&Co., our studio is very open in terms of its layout and the way we work. Bonnie and I like that the designers bring their own ideas and style to each project. Also, life at M&Co. was always a nice mix of hard work and silliness (and snacks), and we try to maintain that balance at Number 17 as well.

Tell us about your dynamic, working as partners, both as designers and representa-tatives of your business in front of clients. Do you get to play good cop/bad cop often?**

Our dynamic is a pretty good one, if I do say so myself. We do get to play good cop/bad cop, as well as buddy cops and good cop/silly cop. We also get to play Burns and Allen, Lucy and Ethel, Lerner and Loewe, Starsky and Hutch, Ernie and Bert and even Bonnie and Clyde. And we switch between them equally. I do believe that most of our clients come to us, in part, because of our dynamic.

Whether it's a book for Sex and the City or the opening titles for Will & Grace, you seem to have a finger in the pulse of pop culture. What makes you thrive in this realm?

Shallowness. Kidding. Honestly, we are just interested in lots of kinds of things, ranging from the logo for the National September 11 Memorial & Museum to titles and parody commercials for *SNL*. To us it is all culture, whether it's pop or not.

For the last fourteen years you've been designing the opening credits for Saturday Night Live (SNL), a show that reinvents itself constantly. How do you keep up? And what goes into this project?

SNL is a brand, a brand that has been around for almost thirty years and actually has a pretty clear brand identity, so there is a world in which the design should fall. That isn't to say that it's the same every year. The challenge is inventing a new way for the brand that is *SNL* to look and feel while keeping it related. It's always a rush, which keeps it feeling lively. They never start working on the opening until there are only about two weeks before the season premiere. So I

1

2

3

4

5

6 SATURDAYNIGHTLIVE

*All work shown developed at Number 17, under creative direction of Emily Oberman and Bonnie Siegler. **[1]** Opening sequence for Saturday Night Live, for NBC; design by Andrew James Capelli (2000). **[2]** Packaging for Homemade Baby, 100% organic baby food; design by Mark Aver and Jessica Zadnik (2005-present). **[3]** Identity for Housing Works Bookstore and Cafe; design by Eric Adolfsen (2005). **[4]** Book cover for Americans in Paris: A Literary Anthology by Adam Gopnik, Library of America; design by Allison Henry (2004). **[5]** Launch campaign of Air America Radio, for Ethan Cohen; design by Emily Oberman and Bonnie Siegler (2004). **[6]** Logo for Saturday Night Live, for NBC; design by Emily Oberman and Bonnie Siegler (2000).*

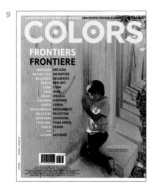

would say a lot of hard work, late nights and panic goes into this project.

The scope of projects you develop is very broad, from motion to editorial to identity design. What does it take to be able to fluctuate between all these mediums?

A short attention span. It also takes a desire to get better at many different things. Each time we take on a new kind of project we get to learn about a new topic as well as a new form of communication. We really do believe that constantly changing the kind of work we do keeps us on our toes, while keeping us from getting too bored.

You have been highly involved with AIGA, volunteering time and energy. What do you take away from this?

There is something very nice about being part of a community. And it so happens that designers, for the most part, are smart and funny and creative and interested in a great variety of things, so being able to connect with your peers is a wonderful thing. It is also very nice to be able to give something back to a community that has been good to us. That sounds like a beauty pageant answer, but it really is true.

It's hard to imagine you two apart. What has been the best, and hardest, part of working together?

The best thing is that you are never alone. You never have to face an angry client alone, or if one of you starts rambling in a meeting or a pitch the other can get you back on track. There is always someone

to laugh with after a meeting has gone horribly wrong or fantastically right, and there is always someone to help make your idea a little better or make a little more sense, and there is always someone to hold your hair if you throw up.

The worst thing is that you are never alone. As much as we love each other, sometimes you just want to run with an idea and not have to explain it. So sometimes we fight and that hurts, but then we make up and we're back to what's good about working together. Collaborating is hard work—even for us, and we get along very well for two people who have sat less than four feet away from each other for fourteen years—you just have to work at it.

[7, 8, 9, 10] Colors *magazine, for Benetton; design by Wade Convay (2004).*

CARIN
GOLDBERG

NATIONALITY	American
YEAR BORN	1953
CURRENTLY RESIDING IN	Brooklyn, New York, United States
YEARS IN THE BUSINESS	34
CURRENT POSITION/FIRM	Principal, Carin Goldberg Design
PREVIOUS EMPLOYMENT	CBS Television Network, CBS Records, Atlantic Records, Condé Nast, mid-1970s-early 1980s
DESIGN EDUCATION	The Cooper Union School of Art (1971-75)

Working under Lou Dorfsman at CBS Television Network and alongside Paula Scher at CBS Records must have prepared Carin Goldberg for her lengthy tenure as an independent designer. With dozens of record covers and hundreds of book covers in the 1980s and 1990s, Goldberg's design sensibility is a mix of sophisticated typography and rich visual awareness of historical design that morphs and evolves… plus, dashes of humor and wit that have always pervaded her work. In 2003, Goldberg took on the task of running the creative department at Time Inc. Custom Publishing as art director. Shortly thereafter, she returned to her own work, stepping away from book covers and into more in-depth projects reflective of her amassed expertise.

You have literally designed hundreds of book covers for many publishing houses including Simon & Schuster, Alfred A. Knopf and Doubleday. You have also worked on dozens of album covers for record labels such as Warner Bros., Motown and EMI. Both areas of design are similar on many levels while remaining very different; can you talk about your experience in handling both? Have you developed a preference over the years?

Well, I haven't designed a record cover for many years. Short of designing The Wallflowers cover and a couple of others, I haven't designed CD covers at all. I pretty much jumped from 12" squares to book jackets and covers.

Like with most projects I try to interpret the content in a unique, timely way. Interpreting music is really no different than interpreting an author's words. The segue from record covers to book jackets was pretty seamless. I can't say I had a preference. I will say that I was truly lucky to be at the right place at the right time for both, and it was fun while it lasted.

You opened your own firm, Carin Goldberg Design (CGD), in 1982. In 2003 you started working at Time Inc. as creative director, mostly working on various publications. How did this impact your work at CGD? What experiences enriched your work, and what did you chose to leave behind?

Yes, it's true that I did somehow find my way into a full-time gig for the first time in years. I left my own practice to take this job because the timing was right. The salary and benefits were excellent and the challenge of taking on a department of twenty-six designers and photo editors and approximately twenty-five projects all at once was exciting. I was given the chance to change the structure of the department, and that allowed me to have the role of visionary, mentor, smarty-pants. It was very much like running an agency. Because it was custom publishing we had clients to consider, keep happy, enlighten and convince in addition to making our numbers each quarter. I was lucky enough to work with a fantastic managing editor who was open to new ideas. We pitched new projects and redesigned projects that were getting stale. We had opportunities to work with companies like Microsoft to whom we pitched some very out-of-the-box ideas that were received quite well. I know I made a big impact on how the department functioned and how the work "looked," and that was gratifying. It was

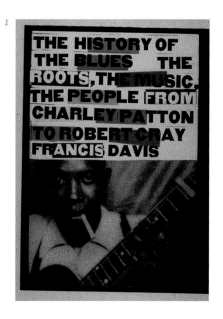

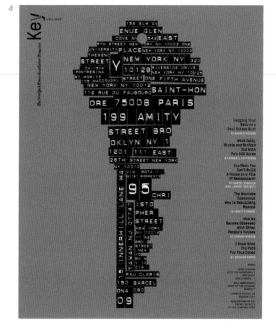

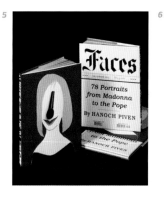

[1] *Book jacket for* The History of the Blues: The Roots, the Music, the People *by Francis Davis (mid-1990s).* [2] The Senior Library 2004, *School of Visual Arts (2004).* [3] *Book jacket for* Blue Jelly: Love Lost and the Lessons of Canning *by Debby Bull (late 1990s).* [4] *Cover for* Key, The New York Times *real estate magazine (Fall 2006).* [5] *Book jacket and interior for* Faces: 78 Portraits from Madonna to the Pope *by Hanoch Piven and Steve Brodner (2002).* [6] *Book collection by Kurt Vonnegut (late 1980s).* [7] *Poster series for the Hong Kong Heritage Museum (2003).*

8

9

10

11

fun for about a year and a half until the work and clients that were coming in to the department were uninspired, and I didn't see it changing. I felt I had done the department a service, cleaned it up and injected it with some good design, but it was time to say goodbye. I believe you should leave the party while you're having a good time. At the time I accepted the job of Creative Director I was pretty sure I didn't want to do book jackets anymore, so taking on a full-time job didn't seem like a risk. It was more like taking a leave of absence and a good way to reinvent myself. It was a good thing to do. No regrets.

For many years you have been involved with the design community, currently as president of the AIGA New York chapter, and serving on the board of Alliance Graphique Internationale (AGI). Why have you chosen to be so deeply involved with these organizations? And what do you hope to achieve?

What I get in return for the countless hours I put into these endeavors is the chance to make change within the design community. I get to work with extraordinary, like-minded people who continually teach me new things. I get to give the design community a reason to care about their profession and to create an environment of inclusion and camaraderie that crosses gender, age, race and disciplines. I won't say that it isn't a total time-sucker, but it is mostly very gratifying and stimulating.

You have been teaching at the School of Visual Arts for over two decades. Have you considered taking a break? What motivates you year-in and year-out?

Actually, I have taken a break for two years and will be returning in September 2008. I teach because I love the discourse. I love the dialogue that happens during the process. I also feel a responsibility to my profession to teach students that what we do is important, thoughtful and a true, meaningful craft. Frankly, there are far too many design students right now and many who do not understand the responsibility of design and designing. I hope that I can impart my belief in the integrity of our profession to my students. And, there is nothing more thrilling than to see students learn, grow, thrive, get better and generally succeed. I also know that when I teach I grow with them and I'm a better designer for it.

[8] *Spread from* The Russian Garbo, Pentagram Papers 38 *(2007).* **[9]** *Book development, design and editing of* Catalog, *for Stewart, Tabori and Chang (2001).* **[10]** *Book jacket for* Sinatra! The Song Is You: A Singer's Art *by Will Friedwald (early 1990s).* **[11]** *Book jacket for* The Queen's Throat: Opera, Homosexuality, and the Mystery of Desire *by Wayne Koestenbaum and Tony Kushner (1994).*

"Books are this great physical thing that you can hang onto forever, and I love the research and tiny details that go into putting one together. I'm a complete sucker for the head-of-a-pin stuff and don't get to do that much anymore in my day-to-day world, so it's a treat."

Gail
Anderson

Detail of: Design Legends rope tricks.

"**Theater is always alive; real people play in front of real people. I guess that obsession I have with accessibility and engaging the viewer comes again from the theater: You need the audience's reaction and understanding to be able to continue with your work.**"

Luba
Lukova

Detail of: Poster for Visual Metaphors (1998).

CATHERINE
ZASK

NATIONALITY
French

YEAR BORN
1961

CURRENTLY RESIDING IN
Paris, France

YEARS IN THE BUSINESS
23

CURRENT POSITION/FIRM
Freelance

DESIGN EDUCATION
ESAG, Paris (1979-84)

Through slicing, repeating, probing, rearranging, and looking where no one tends to look, Catherine Zask has created a unique typographic language born out of exploration that typically finds its way to her client-based work for a multitude of cultural institutions for which she creates posters, identities and collateral materials. From Alfabetempo, a new alphabet based on rearranging individual strokes of each character, to "latent spaces," the white spaces between words and paragraph lines, Zask is continually examining the possibilities of typography and devising unique approaches and concepts that typify her design sensibility. Zask's work has been exhibited in numerous exhibitions around the world.

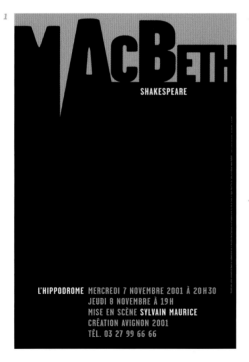

[1] Macbeth *poster for L'Hippodrome (2001).* *[2, 3, 4]* *Identity, web site and animation of Prix Émile Hermès for Hermès International (2007).*

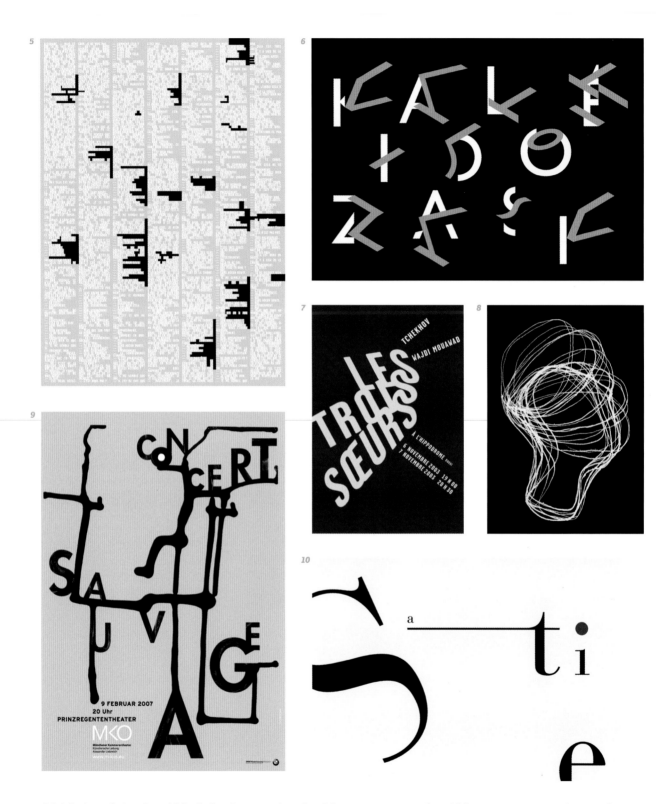

[5] *Alcibiade au téléphone (2000).* [6] Kaléidozask *invitation for Zask's exhibition at Artazart, Paris (2006).* [7] Les Trois Sœurs *poster for L'Hippodrome (2003).* [8] X-Ray of thought *(2000).* [9] Concert Sauvage *poster for Münchener Kammerorchester (2007).* [10] *"Satie" spread in a Scam (Société civile des auteurs multimedia) program (2001).*

CHEE
PEARLMAN

Addressing and coalescing design as a broader concept that encompasses myriad disciplines is a tall order—one that Chee Pearlman has mastered over the years. As the editor of I.D. magazine for fifteen years, Pearlman generated a publication that weaved all aspects of design into an influential source of knowledge. As founder and co-chair of the Chrysler Design Awards for ten years, she brought forward and celebrated the most influential designers of the late twentieth century*. In her role as conference director—most recently of the Art Center Design Conference—Pearlman's programs are cross-disciplinary and slightly ahead of the zeitgeist. And as a writer for Newsweek, Travel + Leisure, Popular Science and The New York Times, she gives designers a voice in the mainstream.

NATIONALITY
Global citizen

CURRENTLY RESIDING IN
New York, New York, United States

YEARS IN THE BUSINESS
It's all business

CURRENT POSITION/FIRM
Director, Chee Company, Inc.

YEARS AT I.D.
15

PREVIOUS EMPLOYMENT
Waitress

DESIGN EDUCATION
On the job

Matte black, plastic, stocky and mean –

DESIGN FOR KILLING

the aesthetic of menace sells guns to the masses.

By William Owen

[1] *"Design for Killing" by William Owen, I.D. magazine (September/October 1996).*

* Including Paula Scher, Gael Towey, Susan Kare, April Greiman, Katherine McCoy and Ellen Lupton among other luminaries like Tibor Kalman, Steve Jobs, and Frank O. Gehry.

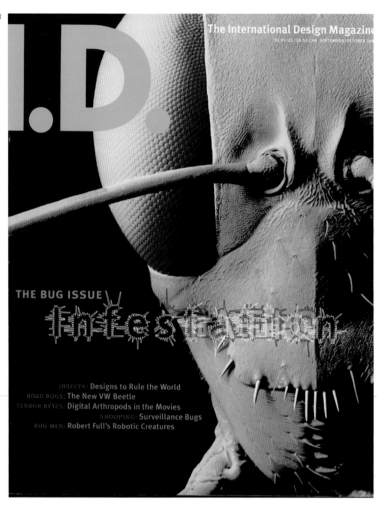

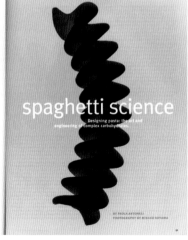

[2] I.D. *magazine cover (March/April 1993).* *[3]* I.D. *magazine cover, "The Bug Issue" (September/October 1997).* *[4]* *"Top This" by Phil Patton,* I.D. *magazine (May/June 1996).* *[5]* I.D. *magazine cover (November 1995).* *[6]* *"Spaghetti Science" by Paola Antonelli,* I.D. *magazine (September/October 1998).*

DITI
KATONA

Over the course of twenty years, the design firm Concrete, founded by Diti Katona and her husband, John Pylypczak, in 1988, has developed a range of work that never settles for any specific style or approach, always shifting to find the most appropriate solution for each client. From playful and colorful to elegant and subdued to contemporary and unexpected, Katona's leadership and design sensibility permeates the work of the firm—which has grown to fifteen employees—across corporate and brand identity, packaging and collateral work.

NATIONALITY
Canadian

YEAR BORN
1961

CURRENTLY RESIDING IN
Toronto, Ontario, Canada

YEARS IN THE BUSINESS
24

CURRENT POSITION/FIRM
Partner/creative director,
Concrete Design Communications Inc.

DESIGN EDUCATION
BFA, York University, Toronto (1984)

1

All projects shown under the creative direction of Diti Katona and John Pylypczak. **[1]** Product packaging for Sula Beauty Inc.; design by Agnes Wong and Natalie Do (2007).

[2] Courier bag from the visual identity program of Masterfile; design by Brian Morgan and Andrew Cloutier (2005). [3] Magazine insert for Holt Renfrew; design by Omar Morson; photography by Chris Nicholls (2003). [4] Shopping Bags for Aritzia; design by Melatan Riden; photography by Kanako Sasaki (2007). [5, 7] Identity for Cava; design by Agnes Wong (2006). [6] Brochure for Lida Baday; design by Natalie Do; photography by Chris Nicholls (2006).

ELLEN
LUPTON

NATIONALITY
American

YEAR BORN
1963

CURRENTLY RESIDING IN
Baltimore, Maryland, United States

YEARS IN THE BUSINESS
22

CURRENT POSITION/FIRM
Director, graphic design MFA program,
Maryland Institute College of Art (MICA)
Curator of Contemporary Design, Cooper-Hewitt,
National Design Museum, Smithsonian Institution

PREVIOUS EMPLOYMENT
Curator, Herb Lubalin Study Center,
The Cooper Union (1985–92)

DESIGN EDUCATION
BFA, The Cooper Union (1985)
Doctorate in communication design,
University of Baltimore (2008)

Designer, writer, teacher, curator, advocate: These may seem like the specialties of five individuals, but they are, instead, the roles Ellen Lupton dexterously plays. As an author, Lupton has written and designed some of the most instrumental books in our profession—from Design Writing Research, *the 1996 book she wrote with husband Abbott Miller, to her 2004 book* Thinking With Type: A Critical Guide for Designers, Writers, Editors, & Students. *In her work at the Cooper-Hewitt National Design Museum, Lupton opens the door to the public at large to experience our work. As a teacher and director of the MFA program at MICA, she empowers students to produce tangible work—2006's* D.I.Y.: Design It Yourself *was co-authored with them—in a learning and explorative environment. And she continually embraces the shifts, both technological and philosophical, in design and culture.*

If there is one impossible thing to do (and this is a compliment), it's to pigeonhole you into any one role or specialty. As an exercise, would you please list all the things you do, and all the design disciplines that are of interest to you and/or that you may have practiced yourself?

My primary roles are as a designer and writer. Most of the design that I do is in the service of my writing projects; for me, design is a tool for shaping and delivering my content. The content of nearly all my work is design, so it's a rather closed loop in which both practices feed each other. My work in the classroom, lecture hall, and museum space are extensions of this loop.

As curator of contemporary design for the Cooper-Hewitt National Design Museum you are able to expose our profession to a broader audience. What do you strive for in the exhibitions you spearhead?

I try to create exhibitions that will include something new or surprising for the expert audience (designers and museum professionals), but that will above all speak to the general viewer. My goal is to make design relevant and understandable to as many people as possible.

You have published (written and designed) numerous and wonderful books about design. Thinking With Type *is perhaps one of the most popular books among designers; it sure is one of our favorites. What process do you go through for this facet of your work?*

The first thing I think about is my readers. Who are my potential readers (students? writers? designers?) and what might they want from a book? What would make this book accessible and useful to them? These questions may seem obvious, but writers don't always work in that direction, thinking first in terms of what they want to say. I created

> "I divide my time into very small pieces in order not to waste any. I have a full-time position as director of the MFA program at MICA. I have a part-time permanent staff position as curator at the Cooper-Hewitt. I'm also a mother and homemaker and an independent writer, curator and lecturer."

1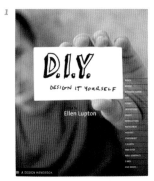

2

3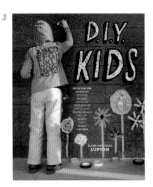

Thinking With Type because I wasn't seeing any other book quite like it on the market. I found the other books to be either excessively detailed for a beginning reader or cutesy and "dumbed down." I created *Thinking With Type* with my own students in mind.

One of your most recent books, D.I.Y.: Design It Yourself, lit a bit of a spark in us designers, who have long fought for the opposite: Let Us Design It For You. But you have fully embraced the D.I.Y. movement. What attracts you to it?

D.I.Y. is a huge cultural movement that is affecting every creative discipline, from music and art to journalism, fashion, filmmaking and beyond. We are living in a period of unprecedented self-education. People want information, and they have the tools to find it. They want skills, and

they have the means to acquire them. The desire to do it yourself is about personal empowerment—it's about the ability to control the details of a project without asking permission, and it's about the pleasure of making things. For designers, D.I.Y. is not an us/them thing (although some designers think of it that way). Graphic designers engage in D.I.Y. every time they touch down into a field that has a specialist core. For example, video editing, animation, typeface design, and web design are all specialized fields that embody enormous amounts of localized expertise; they are also areas that generalist designers engage in rather fearlessly, using their own points of view and experiences. Making a simple animation on the web is a different kind of activity from producing *Monsters, Inc.* I wouldn't want to see either activity go away.

You are the director of the MFA program in graphic design at the Maryland Institute College of Art (MICA). What principles have you instilled in the program? What sets it apart from other programs in the U.S.?

Our program is very practice-oriented. We do real-world projects as a team, such as producing books together that function in the global marketplace. Our first book was *D.I.Y.: Design It Yourself*, mentioned earlier, which was designed, written and produced by students and faculty in the MFA program. We are also releasing a book on basic design (Spring 2008) and a new title on indie publishing, about how to design and publish your own book. These and other public projects make a contribution to the broader design discourse while giving our students opportunities to publish their work and communicate with real audiences.

[1] D.I.Y., Design It Yourself, edited by Ellen Lupton; designed by the Graphic Design MFA program at Maryland Institute College of Art, cover by Mike Weikert with photograph by Nancy Froehlich (1996). [2] Exhibition design for "Mechanical Brides" at the Cooper-Hewitt, National Design Museum by Ellen Lupton, Constantin Boym and Laurene Leon (1993). [3] D.I.Y.: Kids by Ellen and Julia Lupton; designed by Ellen Lupton; cover photograph by Nancy Froehlich (2007).

4  5

6

7  8

Our students also take studio electives in a variety of disciplines, including graphic design, typography, printmaking, video, animation and interaction design, so there's a good mix of group work and individual work. On the spectrum of design programs, there are schools like Cranbrook, which take an independent, fine arts approach, and schools like School of Visual Arts (SVA), which emphasize practical engagement with the social world. We are more like SVA, for sure.

Is there any personally unexplored aspect of design that you would like to tackle further, either as curator, designer or writer?

My big interest now is how design relates to everyday situations, from making your bed to raising your kids. Design is a form of thought and action, as well as an approach to creativity. Design is a tool that can be used by anyone on earth. Design isn't just about making stuff; it's about making stuff happen.

You shared a design studio in the late 1980s with your husband, Abbott Miller, and he currently teaches at MICA. Your personal and professional lives undoubtedly intertwine. How does this relationship influence what you do?

Abbott and I met as students at Cooper Union. I fell in love with him pretty much immediately, but we were "best friends" for a very, very long time. We worked together on many projects as students, and then we started our own freelance gig when we graduated, which we called Design Writing Research. When Design Writing Research became financially viable, Abbott left his day job (working for Richard Saul Wurman) to head it up. I stayed with my curatorial work and contributed when I could to the studio. Soon enough, all that intellectual and creative collaboration blossomed into true love. We've been married now for well over fifteen years and have two beautiful children. I don't know if any scientific studies have been done about "design couples," but our marriage is both delicious and stable. Loving each other intellectually translated into romantic love that has never stopped being hot. And Abbott is a great dad who loves his kids more than anything in the world. He is now a partner at Pentagram, and Design Writing Research lives on as an idea that we could both return to again later in life—together, I hope!

[4, 5] Mechanical Brides: Women and Machines From Home to Office *by Ellen Lupton, designed by Ellen Lupton and Hall Smyth (1993).*
[6] Design, Writing, Research: Writing on Graphic Design, *written and designed by Ellen Lupton and J. Abbott Miller (1999).* **[7, 8]** *Exhibition curated by Ellen Lupton and Elaine Lustig Cohen for "Letters From the Avant-Garde" at the Cooper-Hewitt, National Design Museum (1996).*

"You don't sell design. Like the medical profession, clients—like patients—come to you when they have a problem. Think about your favorite doctor—how they treat you, care for you and advise you— and then think of how you work with your clients."

Noreen
Morioka

Detail of: Poster for The Sundance Film Festival (2007).

NATIONALITY	
American	
YEAR BORN	
1952	
CURRENTLY RESIDING IN	
New York, New York, United States	
YEARS IN THE BUSINESS	
30	
CURRENT POSITION/FIRM	
Chief creative officer, Martha Stewart Living Omnimedia (MSLO)	
PREVIOUS EMPLOYMENT	
House & Garden magazine	
DESIGN EDUCATION	
CFA, Boston University	

GAEL
TOWEY

The photography is beautiful, the typography stunning and the materials tantalizing— whether it's a magazine on the newsstand or a product on the shelf, the offerings from Martha Stewart Living Omnimedia never fail to meet those standards. And Gael Towey, chief creative officer of the vast enterprise, ensures that everything does. Since 1990, when Towey joined MSLO, she has established a visual and tonal branding that permeates existing and new products, unifying them through a flexible sense of quality and dedication instead of a governing set of rules. Approaching two decades of involvement, Towey's design temperament has made each product approachable and satisfying.

1

2

[1] *Martha Stewart Collection at Macy's, cake mix (2007).* **[2]** *Martha Stewart Collection at Macy's, Trousseau luxury bedding (2007).*

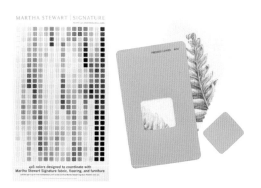

[3] Martha Stewart Living *magazine cover (September 2004).* [4] Martha Stewart Living *magazine spread, "Peach glossary" (July/August 1995).*
[5] Martha Stewart Living *magazine spread, "Hydrangea" (September 1994).* [6] Martha Stewart Weddings *(first issue) magazine spread, "Bouquets"*
(Winter/Spring 1995). [7] *Martha Stewart Furniture with Bernhardt, Kingsland Chinoiserie Secretary from the Katonah line (2007).* [8] *Martha Stewart*
Signature Paint with Sherwin-Williams (2002-04).

Illustration by Robert Risko

NATIONALITY	American
YEAR BORN	1962
CURRENTLY RESIDING IN	New York, New York, United States
YEARS IN THE BUSINESS	24
CURRENT POSITION/FIRM	Creative director, Design at SpotCo Instructor, MFA Designer as Author program, The School of Visual Arts Book collaborator with Steven Heller
PREVIOUS EMPLOYMENT	Senior art director, *Rolling Stone* magazine (1987-02) Designer, *The Boston Globe Sunday Magazine* (1985-87) Assistant designer, Vintage Books (1984-85)
DESIGN EDUCATION	BFA, graphic design, School of Visual Arts (1984)

GAIL ANDERSON

No typographic approach, no matter how far-fetched —bottle caps, SpaghettiOs, mosaic—is off limits to Gail Anderson. Expressive and bold, yet considered and restrained, her editorial spreads as art director of **Rolling Stone** *for fifteen years captured and interpreted the essence of its features and, along with fellow art director Fred Woodward, established it as one of the most celebrated magazines. In 2002, Anderson made a momentous change by joining SpotCo, a firm specializing in design and promotion for the entertainment industry—giving her a completely new range of canvases (from taxi-top signs to Times Square billboards) primed for her unconventional and evocative approach.*

At Rolling Stone *you worked for many years within the same physical format. What was it like to go from that context to the wide array of posters, billboards, bus signs, magazine ads, etc., required for a Broadway/Off-Broadway production now that you are at SpotCo?*

The transition from magazines to the world of clients and the theater was much harder than I'd imagined. I had to start over. My seemingly okay credentials meant little since I was an unfamiliar face in the room at meetings. The theater world is small and insular, and everyone knows everyone else pretty intimately. Here I was with a history limited to the shows I'd seen as a child and the few I'd been able to afford or have time for as an adult. Fortunately for me, my pop culture knowledge base is pretty extensive, and I'm an old soul, so I was

familiar with the traditional shows, film adaptations and stars.

I was used to working with editors and the rhythm of a bi-weekly cycle, with recurring themes and special issues. I knew the characters I had to please, as well as the audience. For the most part, my department was filled with peers, and I had a long-standing relationship with my boss, Fred Woodward, so we knew each other inside out and had similar temperaments. I figured I loved entertainment and typography, so the switch to posters made sense, particularly since our opening spreads in *Rolling Stone* were very much like posters.

I moved over to SpotCo thinking that I was well-equipped to work in a different but, to me at least, somewhat similar arena. When I look back now, I really

have to give my current boss, Drew Hodges, credit for taking a chance on an art director from a different discipline, someone who hadn't really worked with clients before besides the occasional freelance project. I spent at least the first two years flying by the seat of my pants, and Drew's help in getting me up to speed was and is still invaluable.

My audience is different now; it's a little older and wealthier, so the chance for the experimental stuff isn't always there. But within the parameters we're given, I hope that we still do innovative work for Broadway. And believe me, the parameters are unbelievable sometimes— billing is often based on contractual percentages and locations. Big stars are often 100% of title, and above title, too, and that's not negotiable. Sometimes

[1] *"Chris Rock Star" by Fred Schruers,* Rolling Stone *magazine; photography by Mark Seliger; art direction by Fred Woodward (October 2, 1997).* **[2]** New Vintage Type *co-authored with Steven Heller, Thames & Hudson (2007).* **[3]** Harlem Song *poster for George C. Wolfe; art direction by Drew Hodges* (2002).* **[4]** The Good Body *poster for The Araca Group, Harriet Newman Leve, East of Doheny; design with Jessica Disbrow*; illustration by Isabelle Dervaux (2003).*

1

2

3

4
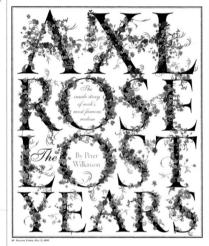

5

6

7

8

[5] *"Axl Rose: The Lost Years" by Peter Wilkinson,* Rolling Stone *magazine; illustration by Alex Ostroy; art direction by Fred Woodward (May 11, 2000).*
[6] *Personal sketchpad, Cardinal Spellman High School (1977).* **[7]** Anna in the Tropics *poster for Daryl Roth, Roger Berlind; lettering by Anthony Bloch* (2003).*
[8] Man of La Mancha *poster for David Stone, Susan Gallin; illustration by Ward Schumaker and James Victore* (2002).*

* Work developed at SpotCo

names have to be stacked, and sometimes they're side-by-side. It can be frustrating, but most of the time I think of it as a big puzzle and it's fun to make all the pieces fit.

It was certainly a blow to the ego to move from the ranks of young gun to old warhorse. While of course, during my last years at *Rolling Stone*, I'd grown out of being part of the youthful demographic and graduated to the parent of the youthful demographic, I was still not the oldest person in the room. Now, I'm the only one who remembers Watergate or the shows on TV Land when they were in first run. One of the designers almost passed out when I said I remembered the first moon landing.

You have co-authored several books with Steven Heller. Graphic Wit: The Art of Humor in Design, Type Play *and most recently* New Vintage Type: Classic Fonts for the Digital Age *among them—these cover wide-ranging subjects. Why the love for publishing? What motivates you to take on a new title? How would you describe your collaboration with Steven?*

I love working with Steve, and that relationship keeps me going. The books help me stay plugged into what designers in the outside world are doing, and it keeps me abreast of trends and changes in the industry. Books are this great physical thing that you can hang onto forever, and I love the research and tiny details that go into putting one together. I'm a complete sucker for the head-of-a-pin stuff and don't get to do that much anymore in my day-to-day world, so it's a treat.

Steve is fast; you need captions and he'll send them over that afternoon. He

> **"Teaching has helped me to learn how to articulate and defend ideas, and it was instrumental in putting me at ease when speaking at conferences. I had no idea that I was actually funny, and when I do talks, I'm surprised that I have a droll side that emerges when I tell stories about what I do."**

responds to e-mail immediately. He's a dynamo, juggling all these crazy projects at once. And he's not possessive of his words. That makes the collaboration fun. Everything's up for discussion. And of course, he knows something about everything, so that makes it easy, too. Steve's such a cheerleader for design and has a great attitude about the books and all the tedious work that goes into each one. I'm filled with complete dread every time around. Am I going to have time to get it done? What if no one sends work? But it always works out in the end, and no lives are lost.

Aside from working and authoring books, you are also on the faculty of the Master of Fine Arts program at the School of Visual Arts, where you teach typography. How do you approach this different discipline? And we hear that in the classrooms and in conferences "students love you." Any inkling as to why that might be?

I really like teaching. I go into that with complete dread each semester, too. What if I have nothing to say and they know it? What if they see me for the fraud that I am? But like the books, once you get started and learn the names, it's all such a pleasant diversion from real life. I encourage the class to have fun. They have the rest of their lives to deal with difficult clients and editors and all the

political stuff. I want them to have a good time working with type, with words, and trying stuff they wouldn't otherwise, or weren't taught in undergrad. There's nothing to lose, and that's important to remember in school. It's all about loosening up and having an open mind.

When I started teaching, I was surprised to learn that I was comfortable speaking in front of a group, though I think I still don't share enough of my own point of view in an effort to make it all about them. But teaching has helped me to learn how to articulate and defend ideas, and it was instrumental in putting me at ease when speaking at conferences. I had no idea that I was actually funny, and when I do talks, I'm surprised that I have a droll side that emerges when I tell stories about what I do. It's helped to reinforce whatever tiny amount of ego is there.

That said, I'm still completely tongue-tied in front of large groups of clients. I get a little intimidated, but that's gotten better as I've gotten more shows under my belt. I get sort of quiet when I'm scared, but fortunately for me, that's often mistaken for introspection. My dirty little secret is that I'm not thinking about the work at all; I'm thinking about what's for lunch.

JANET
FROELICH

NATIONALITY
American

YEAR BORN
1946

CURRENTLY RESIDING IN
New York, New York, United States

YEARS IN THE BUSINESS
30

CURRENT POSITION/FIRM
Creative director, *The New York Times* magazines

DESIGN EDUCATION
BFA, The Cooper Union (1970)
MFA, Yale University (1968)

Within the girth of the Sunday edition of The New York Times *lies one of the most pleasurable design experiences:* The New York Times Magazine. *With art direction by Janet Froelich, the magazine's cover is consistently a surprising delight, complemented by an equally astute interior that is relentlessly well designed, from the front of the book to the feature and beyond. With more than three decades of editorial experience—starting as a designer at the* New York Daily News*—it's no surprise that Froelich can lead her team to deliver an admirable publication in a non-stop, year-long schedule. Froelich's direction extends to other* Times *publications like* Key *(real estate),* Play *(sports) and* T *(style)... All equally distinctive and distinguished in their design.*

You arrived in New York as a fine artist, which you have said before wasn't a great fit for you. Slowly you found your path into design by joining the team at Heresies: A Feminist Publication on Art and Politics, which changed your course. How did you fall in love with design?

I was a serious painter for many years. I had studied fine art at Cooper Union (undergraduate) and Yale (graduate school), and I came to New York to make art. But I found life in the studio lonely and difficult. Looking back I think I did not have the level of self-confidence or self-absorption to pursue that life and that career. But I knew so many wonderful artists, many of them women, and several of my acquaintances had formed a collective to publish *Heresies: A Feminist Publication on Art and Politics*. Through my involvement with this group I grew to love design.

In my school years, design had been denigrated by the term *commercial art*, and no one in the painting department wanted to be associated with it. But at *Heresies,* I gravitated towards the design chores, learning production skills, studying typography, reading manuscripts and looking at photographs. The collective would argue over content, treatment and layout all night long, and then a few of us would remain and design until morning. It was obsessive work, sometimes amateurish, always fascinating. I loved the process. I was still making art, but out of someone else's content. It could be smart, it could tell stories, and it was about anything and everything in the world.

After seeing an ad in the newspaper searching for an art director, you called the Daily News and interviewed with them. Lacking

the necessary experience they offered you an entry-level position, which you eagerly took. What was it like to work on the same thing daily yet create a unique piece day after day?

I loved my job at the *Daily News*. I was hired by Phillip Ritzenberg, a wonderful art director and a real newspaperman. He told me he saw my potential even though I had a meager design portfolio, and no real newspaper experience. He once told me, "You will do 365 of these pages a year, and if five are any good, you're lucky." In the mornings, I would be so excited to get the paper at my local newsstand and see my pages, but then, on my way in to work, I'd find them underfoot on the subway platforms. It was liberating, and completely antithetical to a design school experience.

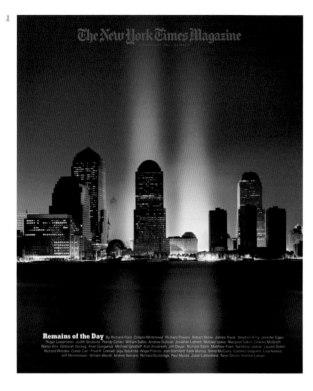

I loved the atmosphere of the city room. The technology was rapidly changing from hot metal to cold type, from scurrying copy boys and metal spikes to the desktop publishing we all now know, and I was able to learn the new skills with everyone else in the throes of this transition.

And there is no one I'd rather spend time with than a good journalist. They are the most curious people in the world.

A few years later you were working on the launch of the **Tonight Newspaper,** *a new magazine for the* **Daily News** *inspired by the* **New York Times** *counterpart. Having started at the bottom, and left at the top, how did those years in ascendance impact your personal growth?*

My years at the *Daily News* were wonderful preparation for thinking in rapid-fire fashion and for solving problems one on top of another. I became accustomed to creating a cover in a few hours, reworking a story three or four times to satisfy editors, and making art out of completely non-visual stories. At newspapers, you get used to designing pages out of nothing. And I had had the wonderful opportunity

"And I can't say enough about the importance of strong editorial direction, of having the good fortune to work with an editor who has a precise vision for the publication and respect for design."

to work with one of the great magazine editors of all time, Clay Felker, who spent one short year as features editor of the *Daily News.*

My transition to the *Times* was not so easy. *The New York Times Magazine* took itself much more seriously than *The Daily News Magazine.* The stakes were higher. And its storied design history (including art directors Ruth Ansel, Roger Black and Diana LaGuardia) was an intimidating act to follow. The magazine's then-editor was a famously difficult man who had made it close to impossible to do good work. But in that short first year he was fired, and then Diana LaGuardia, the art director who had hired me, left and everything changed. Looking back, I don't think I yet had the design chops to ascend to the art director's position, but I

[1] "Remains of the Day" cover for The New York Times Magazine *(September 23, 2001). [2] "The Rooting Teuton,"* The New York Times Style Magazine; *photography by Jean-Baptiste Mondino (February 20, 2005). [3] "White Mischief,"* The New York Times Style Magazine; *photography by Raymond Meier (August 28, 2005).*

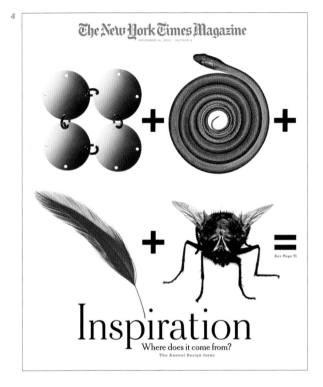

was prepared to try because of my rough and tumble training at the *Daily News*. I learned on the job.

You are constantly working on a series of magazines for The New York Times: The New York Times Magazine, T (style), Play (sports) and Key (real estate). Each magazine requires a brave and strong team, as well as the ability to search for talent and to collaborate with many parties across mediums. How do you achieve this? Do you have any recommendations for the young and restless publishers-to-be?

I've been doing these magazines for over twenty years. I've worked with at least six different editors (that's unusual because during an editorial changeover, the art director is the first to go), several major redesigns, and the launch of the completely new *T: The New York Times*

Style Magazine. I've had many truly talented designers on my staff because I know I am only as good as the designers I work with, so I see the hiring component as the most important part of my job. I'm very good at choosing those people. And I also think I'm good at working with them. I have strong, clear ideas about what the *Times's* magazines should look and feel like, and I communicate those ideas fairly clearly. But no one can do it alone. It's important to empower people, and let them take things to a new place.

And I can't say enough about the importance of strong editorial direction, of having the good fortune to work with an editor who has a precise vision for the publication and respect for design. Gerry Marzorati, the editor of *The Sunday Magazine*, and Stefano Tonchi, the editor

of *T*, have been remarkable partners, and I give each of them huge credit for our ability to create memorable work.

You were recently interviewed by Debbie Millman for her radio show Design Matters, in which you talked about your experience with publishing after 9/11. Your cover—photographed by Fred Conrad—became an overnight icon and inspiration, so much so that a year later two beams of light were installed as a memorial where the building footprints used to stand. Events and situations like this one need to be treated carefully, especially when you have the kind of distribution The New York Times has attained. How do you balance the emotional and the journalistic aspects of a story through design?

I don't think you balance the emotional and journalistic aspects of a story so

[4, 5] "Inspiration: Where Does It Come From?" cover and article for The New York Times Magazine *(November 30, 2003).*

much as you respond appropriately to different situations. You know your audience, you know your mission, and you rely on the journalists you work with to keep you on the right path. In this case we were called upon to rise far beyond the normal solutions—to dig a lot deeper. And we called on other artists and collaborators for their input: Julian LaVerdiere and Paul Myoda, whose concept became the Towers of Light; Fred Conrad, whose original photograph provided the groundwork for the digital rendering; and my then-editor Adam Moss, who asked the question, "What would the memorial look like?" before anyone else dared to ask it. It gives me goose bumps every year to see those beams of light rise above lower Manhattan.

You are a self-professed magazine junkie and newspaper devourer. Working as a visual journalist, you are always in search of information that will keep you growing and make you better. Are there any particular favorites?

I do love to read the newspaper—on paper, not online. It is my habit and my pleasure in the morning. But design is about everything else. It's all about the stories you tell, and the research you do and, in the news business, it is about editing the world for the reader.

I love to visit newsstands, and pour through what's happening in small presses and foreign publications. It is a very fertile moment in the culture right now.

There is much talk about the convergence of high and low—in fashion and fine art, and in design and architecture. And just about everyone is making movies. I think we in the magazine business are in a particularly good place to weigh in on those issues.

Publishing the kind of content that you do, you are constantly learning about multiple subjects and find yourself exposed to new things. So, we have to ask, is there anything out there you wish to do beyond editorial design?

Every once in a great while I think I might like to go back to painting.

It seems so simple now.

---

[6] The New York Times Style Magazine *covers (Spring 2005, Fall 2006, Fall 2006, Fall 2005).* [7] The New York Times Style Magazine *cover (Fall 2004).*

"Collaboration with great people, for great ideas is the only work I'm interested in participating in. I've worked very hard at creating a situation in my practice that allows me to carefully choose my professional relationships. Having that choice is the sweetest reward."

Rebeca
Méndez

Detail of "Homeland #1", a series consisting of six 20' x 8' murals. Permanent installation at the University of Cincinnati Recreation Center, C-Store (2006).

JENNIFER
MORLA

NATIONALITY
American

YEAR BORN
1955

CURRENTLY RESIDING IN
San Francisco, California, United States

YEARS IN THE BUSINESS
31

CURRENT POSITION/FIRM
President and creative director, Morla Design
Vice president and creative director, Design Within Reach
Adjunct professor, California College of the Arts

PREVIOUS EMPLOYMENT
PBS
Levi's

DESIGN EDUCATION
BFA, graphic design, Massachusetts College of Art (1978)

It's hard to define a West Coast aesthetic or sensibility, but in the work of Jennifer Morla one can find many of its most pleasing attributes. It's vibrant, colorful and intense in execution, and it's energetic, exploratory and enterprising in attitude. Morla moved from New York to San Francisco in 1977, working at PBS and Levi's before opening her own studio in 1984 at the age of 28. It was a ripe time and place for designers willing to take the design profession into new territory, one that Morla was instrumental in defining. Most recently she became creative director of Design Within Reach and was responsible for all its brand manifestations (catalogue, stores, new product launches) while still running Morla Design.

"A great designer is a good listener. It is what I try to teach and instill in my office and with students. Design must always be appropriate. It will allow you to inject individuality into every project, resulting in a fresh solution to every problem."

Before establishing your own firm you worked as an in-house designer for Levi's and PBS. And twenty years later you have taken on another in-house role as creative director for Design Within Reach. What is it about this type of environment that you enjoy?

I truly do not feel that there is much difference between being creative director for my in-house team versus being creative director for my studio. Bottom line: Every CEO is a client. But our responsibility is delivering meaningful design to our audience, not the client.

You started Morla Design in 1984 in San Francisco, where the new technology was being embraced by the likes of April Greiman and Emigre. How influential was this period of change in our profession?

It was radical, especially in California and specifically in the San Francisco area where Apple formed the nucleus of digital design. That said, I did not feel that the aesthetic of design was contingent on the aesthetic of software. It was a new medium, with graphic elements (the pixel) that allowed for new forms of experimentation within a new language. My office was all on Macs by 1989, which allowed me to experiment—most especially with book design—in a way that the laborious confines of traditional cut and paste would have never allowed me to do.

What have been some of the biggest challenges in maintaining a successful and relevant practice since 1984?

A great designer is a good listener. It is what I try to teach and instill in my office and with students. Design must always be appropriate. It will allow you to inject individuality into every project, resulting in a fresh solution to every problem.

[1] Gift poster for Levi's brand, for Levi Strauss & Co.; design with Angela Williams; illustration by Jennifer Morla; photography by Jock McDonald (1998). [2] Brochure for Levi's Red Version Jeans, for The Curious Company; design with Hizam Haron; photography by Lionel Deluy; copywriting by The Curious Company (2002). [3] Exhibition announcement poster for the California College of Arts & Crafts; design with John Underwood and Sara Scheider (1999).

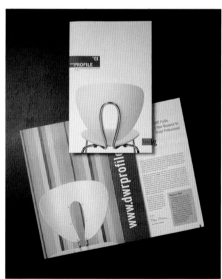

[4] DWR Profile for Design Within Reach; design with Hizam Haron and Brian Singer; photography by Russell Abraham, Bill Acheson, Tony Cunha, Stefano Massei and Julius Shulman; copywriting by Rob Forbes, Cathy Lang Ho, Dung Ngo and Rick Joy (2003). [5] Poster for the Mexican Museum 20th anniversary for Bacchus Press; design with Craig Bailey (1995).

Aside from your current position at Design Within Reach, you are keeping Morla Design active. What do you hope to achieve through that venue?

When I was offered the position of creative director at Design With Reach, I refocused Morla Design to respond to the needs of educational and art institution clients. Current clients include Stanford University's postgraduate literature department. We create their annual poster series and define the graphic language of this influential department.

Design Within Reach (DWR) offered me the opportunity to create a world-class environment that fosters design in every venue: product, print, retail and web. Although I had done extensive work in each one of those areas, it was increasingly rare to work with a client where I could be responsible for the creative side in totality. The manifestation of that total vision could only be accomplished in-house. I have an extremely talented team that continues to evolve DWR into one of the few public companies that are truly design driven.

Over the course of your career you have been heavily involved with AIGA: as a member on the national board and as president of the San Francisco chapter. What keeps you involved in this organization?

We are the AIGA. It is the collective voice of the design community. And it is this community that I have learned from, and have supported, since 1980. As president of AIGA San Francisco in the early 1990s, I had the opportunity to invite and enjoy the international company of Andre Putman, Jean Paul Goode, Javier Mariscal, and Eiko Ishioka. But of even greater enrichment was my exposure to the dedication of the local San Francisco design community. We enjoyed and rejoiced in showcasing San Francisco and international talent.

As a member of the AIGA National Board, I embraced the opportunity to further expose our profession to the public at large. We are ubiquitous but often invisible. AIGA is the platform for critical discourse, professional dialogue, student support and, quite simply, it serves as the cornerstone for the design community. AIGA and I believe in the power of our creativity.

[6] Olympic bid poster for "San Franciso: 2012" for BASOC; design with Hizam Haron; photography by Jock McDonald and Photodisc (2002). [7, 8] Poster for AIGA Landor Associates lecture series in San Francisco; design with Brian Singer; copywriting by Landor Associates (2003).

JENNIFER
STERLING

With an infinite sense of attention to detail and a methodical commitment to intricate typography, Jennifer Sterling has designed a multitude of projects that have long fascinated the design profession. During the digitally-obsessed years of the dot-com era in the late 1990s, Sterling's tactile designs—usually aided by letterpress, intriguing binding methods or sophisticated paper choices—proved to be an invaluable reminder of the power of tangible design. After five years as art director with Tolleson Design in San Francisco, Sterling established her own firm in 1996, creating annual reports, identities, posters and packaging. She currently teaches at Academy of Art University in San Francisco.

NATIONALITY
American

YEAR BORN
1964

CURRENTLY RESIDING IN
San Francisco, California, United States

YEARS IN BUSINESS
12

CURRENT POSITION/FIRM
Founder, Jennifer Sterling Design
Teacher, Academy of Art University

PREVIOUS EMPLOYMENT
Art director for Tolleson Design

DESIGN EDUCATION
Art Institute of South Florida

How did your interest in typography and design develop?

I grew up in a house of avid readers. We had an extensive library that included a range of subjects... science, history, literature, poetry, religion and art. Some of which dated back centuries. Most of my childhood I had a book in my hands. I wasn't aware of it making an impression on me as a design element; however, looking back I can see a distinct divide in the design of books as marketing directors changed the course of book design after the 1960s. Grids and details and nuance were much more elegantly approached prior to this time. Some of my favorite books were actually older mathematical and science textbooks. Perhaps it was generational but it appeared as if someone thoughtful designed these books and enjoyed their life.

There is one typeface that played a recurring role in your work, Garamond. What is it about this serif that made you use it over and over?

When work is published it is often asked of the designer to list the fonts used. I may have just used the old style numbers of Garamond (a particular favorite) so it appears as if I use it to exclusion. Although I use it quite a bit, I actually use hundreds of fonts. I don't have a favorite font. I think all fonts have a voice and sometimes that voice has a range. I believe typography has the same responsibility as photography or illustration to convey the concept. With that said, I do like the voice of Garamond for its range. It can feel both academic and poetic, which lends itself to many clients. When I use it I usually will create a new typeface that I use only in numerical form or as a detail.

I'll frequently change its voice by pairing it with a more utilitarian sans serif. I also like the low x-height. I can use a tightly leaded page and it still feels open.

A lot of your work is extremely tactile, using letterpress and die-cutting regularly on rich papers and even metal. Why do you pursue this quality in your work, given that it is already rich in its design?

I think it goes back to the environment in which I was raised. The richness and variety of books... the lack of utter sameness is what appeals to me. I feel materials should support the concept. I don't necessarily think "paper" when I think "brochure." One client approached me for a press kit design and was perhaps expecting or envisioned some manner of a 9" × 12" paper folder. However, his company was entirely based online. His product

1
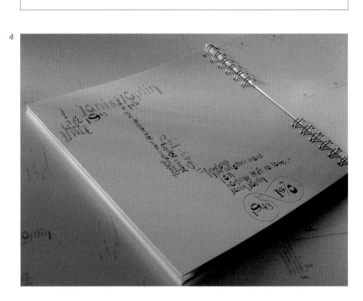

2

3

4

[1] Poster for Southern California Scool of Architecture (2000). [2] Packaging for David Maisel (2004). [3] CD packaging for Bhoss (1999). [4] Paper promotion for Fox River (2001).

5

was a paperless world of streaming video, with live performances and interviews. To design a paper form of this world was at odds with his product. I ended up creating a rubber bag only large enough to hold multiple DVDs. All future items created were synthetic based in form.

People don't need to purchase books anymore... the information is free. So with the exception of novels, textbooks, manuals, bestsellers, etc., which need to be designed in a straightforward manner, books are being purchased for completely different reasons. A certain loveliness factor. I think this divide will continue to grow. I have purchased books in languages I don't speak just for the loveliness of the book itself. Yet there are many that still strike me as aspirational landfill.

How important has teaching been for you?

I have taught on and off at both CCA and AAU since 1996 as an adjunct professor in thesis and advanced typography in graphic design. I didn't have a realization of the importance of design until many years into the profession. I think it was due in part to my early environment. While it allowed great exposure to design, it was more of a byproduct to the information. It's not to say art as a profession was discouraged—it just wasn't encouraged. My father was a managing partner for Deloitte and Touche in Manhattan, yet he built a darkroom in our house as he enjoyed photography. My sister received a scholarship for creative writing, yet ended up becoming a physician and doing her residency at Yale New Haven.

The message being, art is something at which to be accomplished yet not to undertake as a profession. Teaching has forced me to articulate and therefore come to appreciate a profession that for many years I dismissed as "my sister saves lives—I save four-point type."

Good design has a very important role to play in messaging. You can change people's behavior in environmental, political and cultural ways that affect generations to come. I stress that aspect of the profession while teaching and enjoy the light that flickers over a student's face when finally realizing the import and responsibility of their profession.

[5] *Book design of* 365: AIGA Year in Design 21, *by AIGA (2001).*

JESSICA
HELFAND

NATIONALITY	American
YEAR BORN	1960
CURRENTLY RESIDING IN	Connecticut, United States
YEARS IN THE BUSINESS	14
CURRENT POSITION/FIRM	Partner, Winterhouse Studio/Institute/Editions
PREVIOUS EMPLOYMENT	Principal, Jessica Helfand Studio, Ltd. (1993–96) Design director, *Philadelphia Inquirer* magazine (1990–93)
DESIGN EDUCATION	BA, graphic design and architectural theory, Yale University (1982) MFA, graphic design, Yale University (1989)

If there is any remote way to tie design with the Pixar film **The Incredibles**, *gardening, or Ken (of Barbie fame), Jessica Helfand will find it. As a writer for Design Observer, Helfand has developed a sensibility that is equal parts inquisitive, entertaining and critical. She is equally adept at writing seminal books on Paul Rand, volvelles (wheel charts), technology, and scrapbooking—not to mention her work in the early 1980s as a writer for daytime soap operas. Helfand began her design career as an editorial designer, first for Roger Black and then for the* **Philadelphia Inquirer** *Magazine. She later worked as an independent designer from 1993–97, then she formed Winterhouse Studio, a design and publishing firm, with her husband and partner, William Drenttel.*

As we were coming up with our list of "includees" for this book, we started by placing names under different categories. We kept moving your name between "designer" and "writer" until we settled on just putting it down twice. How important is it for you to design and write? How do the two inform each other in your case?

I am overjoyed to be considered an "includee" in both lists because I feel unbalanced when I let one of these categories go. I think visually, but I draw constantly, and to me, talking and drawing are two halves of a whole; I can't do one without the other. I sometimes tell my students that I write to figure out what I can't figure out in the studio, and vice versa. About five years ago, I was making such a mess in the studio that I was banished to a little annex space in our house: that's where I do more experimental things, all of them with my hands. There's no talking there (my children know this) and no computer in sight. So that's become the third piece of the triangle: writing/designing/making things.

With Design Observer you have developed a platform where you have the liberty to write about any topic that strikes your fancy. And, whether it's The Incredibles or scrapbooks, you happily do. Before blogging, you were a traditional writer with deadlines and editors. How has your writing evolved in the last four years?

It's alternately liberating and terrifying to have no real editor, although Bill and Michael Bierut and I use each other for this (and we all edit our contributors). The liberating part is casting a wider lens—writing about the intersection between design and a larger civilization—and seeing where it takes us. Our readers are all over the world, and I've become more attentive to thinking about design with an eye to more international thinking. Obviously, this invites political thinking, which is not always welcome among our readers. Still, we set out to keep the quality of writing high, which invites pretty well-crafted comments mostly—and that has been extremely gratifying.

I'm also interested in how graphic design—which is by definition a mass-produced medium—relates to first-person writing. If it's personal, is its public role devalued? Design Observer has more male writers (and more male commenters) than women, which occasionally irks me also. I question my participation, which in turn makes me write more first-person narratives, which sometimes gets me

1

2

3

4
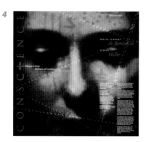

in trouble. (Children, PG-rated movies, gardening, food—you get the picture.) When I wrote about scrapbooks, I hit a nerve. I was critical of the millions of women who are devoted to this phenomenon, and they thought I was attacking them. One of the reasons I am writing a book on the subject now is to find out why people (read: women) adhere so passionately to craft. Where's the line between public and personal, professional and amateur, self and family, universal and unique? And incidentally, it's only recently that scrapbooking has become such a gendered activity; Thomas Jefferson and Mark Twain were both avid scrapbookers.

Another facet of your career is teaching. You have been part of the Yale University School of Art's MFA graphic design program since 1996. Yale is a school teeming with talent at both faculty and student level. What role has this environment played in your career?

My role at Yale has been as a senior critic, working with the second year thesis students on the development of a body of work. So, in a sense, my role there is curatorial, which has turned out to be wonderful because it simultaneously addresses both ideas and form, writing and making. These years have also corresponded to my children's growth—so I've evolved as an educator in tandem with growing as a parent. I'd like to think I've gotten better at both (wishful thinking, probably), but I do know that I've gotten tougher. I love my children (as well as many of my students), but I am extremely aware that neither set of relationships hinges on popularity. In retrospect, I think that as growing up as the youngest child in my family, the idea of being in charge was very much a learned behavior for me.

Teaching informs the way I work because it makes me think—about how to cultivate someone else's work without telegraphing my own ideas; about how to encourage without predicting the outcome; and perhaps most of all, about using criticism as a tool for shaping someone's thinking, not skewering their ego. I've seen many critics do the latter, which is, to my mind, nothing short of malpractice. Still, such torture endures in many programs around the world.

It's obvious that your life is devoted to design, and as if all this weren't enough, you are married to Bill Drenttel, a designer and writer, equally obsessed (in a good way!) with the profession. You share a home, a

[1] *Editorial spreads for* Philadelphia Inquirer Magazine *(1990-93).* **[2]** *Collages/spreads from an experimental book on visualizing biography (1990).*
[3] *"In My Beginning Is My End," artists book on T.S. Eliot (part of same ongoing project on visualizing biography) (1989).* **[4]** *Poster for AIGA Philadelphia lecture series, "2 × 2: Dialogues on Design" (1992).*

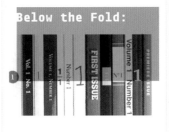

studio, an imprint and a blog. How do you traverse between home life and design life? Or is it all one big, happy blur?

We share it all—home and studio, children and dogs, books, a blog, even a boat. (A very little, used motorboat that we keep on a nearby lake: our children named it Winterboat.) And we disagree—a LOT—on certain things. He's focused like a laser beam, and I am the consummate, multi-tasking plate-spinner. (He was also captain of his debating team in high school. Enough said!) But recently we were interviewed together on tape, and I was startled to see how much I pushed back. And I suddenly realized, the tension may be deeply felt, passionately expressed and excruciating to bear—but it's always respectful. We do love each other dearly, after all.

I would also say that our talents are for the most part complementary: we don't do the same thing. Bill's a great writer but can't spell to save his life. (He's really dyslexic.) I draw, but I am hugely challenged three-dimensionally—Bill's really good at that. He's also an incredible book designer because he's been collecting books since he was sixteen years old and has probably spent more time looking at books than anyone I have ever met. When our children were tiny, he'd read to them before they went to bed, and I'd overhear him. "Alice in Wonderland, Title Page. Alice in Wonderland, Half-Title." Both our children knew what endpapers were before they were toilet trained.

The short answer is that there is a lot of divide-and-conquer between us. This is one of the reasons we always lecture together. It obliges us to refresh our sense of the work we're doing, which is hugely therapeutic. (And we get to take a trip together without the children—perhaps equally therapeutic.)

But I do need my own outlets. Teaching has become that, but it's also why I have a painting studio now. As hard as it is to imagine our children grown and out of the house, this is the part of my life I imagine expanding one day. And this slow, even dormant piece of my life probably has more to do with graphic design than almost anything else—more than teaching, blogging, writing, editing, curating, parenting, and a million other activities that consume my energy. Being alone in a studio with no computers: that's the future.

[5] *Typography and package design, Hautboy Hill Farm Milk (2004).* **[6]** *Typography and package design, Winterhouse Maple Syrup (2006).* **[7]** *Covers for* Below the Fold, *issues (01) our collection of volume one number one journals, and (02) danger.* **[8]** *Essay commissioned for the 2nd edition of* The End of Print *by Lewis Blackwell and David Carson.* **[9]** *Interface and web design for* Millennium *and* Newsweek *(1999-2000).*

"I teach because I love the discourse. I love the dialogue that happens during the process. I also feel a responsibility to my profession to teach students that what we do is important, thoughtful and a true, meaningful craft."

Carin
Goldberg

"It's of concern to me that many younger designers are bypassing phone conversations and client meetings, opting for e-mails and PDF presentations instead. It takes only a few attempts at this method to realize these 'convenient' ways of doing business don't lead to the best results."

Petrula
Vrontikis

Detail of: *Book* Inspiration=Ideas: A Creativity Sourcebook for Graphic Designers, *Rockport Publishers (2002).*

LAURIE
DEMARTINO

During the mid- to late 1990s, Minneapolis became one of the most remarkable design hubs to surface during the hectic dot-com years. The city captured the attention of the design profession. At its epicenter was Laurie DeMartino—after transplanting her design firm, then named Studio d Design, from Philadelphia in 1991—with her astutely detailed aesthetic that blended infinitely massaged typography with richly textured patterns into intricate layouts that never sacrificed hierarchy or communication over style. Her promotional work for French Paper, specifically Twelve Identities in 1999, was cause of obsession for many designers.

NATIONALITY
Italian and German

YEAR BORN
1964

CURRENTLY RESIDING IN
Minneapolis, Minnesota, United States

YEARS IN THE BUSINESS
21

CURRENT POSITION/FIRM
Principal, Laurie DeMartino Design Co.

PREVIOUS EMPLOYMENT
After college I worked for a firm that specialized in packaging design for national cosmetic brands in New York (1986-90). After several years I moved to Philadelphia and formed Studio d Design (1990-95), which led to Laurie DeMartino Design (1995-present), currently in Minneapolis.

DESIGN EDUCATION
BFA, communication design, Kutztown University (1986)

1

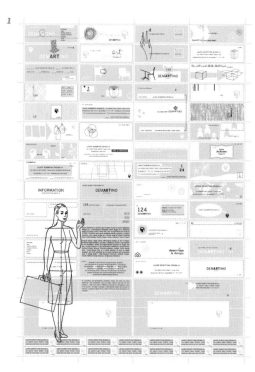

2

[1] Label poster for Laurie DeMartino Design (2004). **[2]** "Doo The Dishes" dinner plates for Pop Ink (2006).

"How do I divide my time? Since I have a small design studio, my time is spent writing proposals, sketching, designing, illustrating, presenting, and obsessing about it all. In the hours at home, there is a continuous dialogue about design with my husband, and precious time spent raising our six-year-old daughter, Grace."

[3] "Hurricane Katrina Poster" for The Hurricane Poster Project (2005). [4] Beverage cups for Target stores; illustration by Paulina Reyes (1999).
[5, 6, 7] Minneapolis College of Art and Design Admissions Catalogue (2002).

LAURIE
HAYCOCK MAKELA

NATIONALITY

American

YEAR BORN

1956

CURRENTLY RESIDING IN

Stockholm, Sweden

YEARS IN THE BUSINESS

100

CURRENT POSITION/FIRM

o-b-o-k

PREVIOUS EMPLOYMENT

Director of graphic design department,
Art Center College of Design (2001-02)
Co-director of graphic design, designer in residence,
Cranbrook Academy of Art (1997-01)
Walker Art Center (1990-97)

DESIGN EDUCATION

MFA, Cranbrook Academy of Art (1992)
MFA, Rhode Island School of Design (incomplete, 1982)
BA, University of California, Berkeley (1981)

"Challenging the status quo" is a cliché to avoid, yet the work, passion and influence of Laurie Haycock Makela has unmistakably embodied what the phrase genuinely entails. In her tenure as design director of the Walker Art Center, Haycock Makela created the antithesis to an identity—inconsistent, wildly varying, interpretative—that became a cohesive whole only after years of use. As co-director of the 2-D design department at Cranbrook, along with P. Scott Makela (may he rest in peace), she ignited its evolution as an unabashedly and unapologetically expressive environment unlike anything before it. Her embrace of technology and emotion produced a body of work that may have proven to be uncomfortable for some—and that's perhaps the biggest compliment to her approach.

Perhaps one of your most influential and memorable contributions to the profession was your time as co-chair of the 2-D design department at Cranbrook Academy of Art in Michigan from 1997 to 2001 with your late husband P. Scott Makela. The reputation of the program along with the work produced and the energy of the students was widely discussed, for better or for worse. What are some of your memories from this period?

Cranbrook was a supremely intimate experience of suspended time, endless space and joyful collaboration. I do not know of any other place in the world that requires that students, faculty and visitors live and work twenty-four hours a day together, with the exception of overseas group travel. As a petri dish of design experiments, Scott and I encouraged everything but traditional problem solving. Students made music, videos, performances, fonts—beautiful and difficult works. As for memories, students like Mikon, Jeff, Brigid, Paul, Brian and many, many others hold a place in my heart, contributing to our practice and the lives of every Cranbrook student. My memories, of course, are veiled by Scott's death, but perhaps that was an education in itself. Scott was a transcendent figure—passionate, productive, generous and immensely creative. He liked to shock, and in his sudden death, no one will ever forget the experience of real, unsimulated shock. Okay, here's a memory. The head of metals, the lovely Gary Griffin, regularly mountain biked with Scott. A few days after Scott died, Gary asked me if he could melt down Scott's wedding ring to its original form. Under normal circumstances, you might think this inappropriate, but Gary said, "You guys played with media fire—let's

"Cranbrook was a supremely intimate experience of suspended time, endless space and joyful collaboration. I do not know of any other place in the world that requires that students, faculty and visitors live and work twenty-four hours a day together."

EXPERIENCE DESIGN GROUP   PERSUASIVE EXPERIENCE   HUMANITARIAN EXPERIENCE   ENVIRONMENTAL EXPERIENCE

[1] *Identity for Experience Design Group, Konstfack, Stockholm (2008).* **[2]** Whereishere by Lewis Blackwell, P. Scott Makela and Laurie Haycock Makela *(1998).* **[3, 5]** MONKJUNK, *a meditation on drugs, greed, spirituality, surrender, and a labor of sibling love; in collaboration with her brother (2008).* **[4, 7]** *Poster for "Walker Design Now" (1996).* **[6, 8]** *Collaborative posters with students from the Communication Design department at HfG, Karlsruhe.*

do the real thing." I will never forget Gary's humanity in the aftermath of Scott's death. We burned the ring down to its essence.

Was there any pressure or particular challenge in taking over the program from Katherine and Michael McCoy, who had previously presided as co-chairs for almost twenty-five years?

Kathy and Mike supported our appointment. As elegant thinkers, they understood better than most that change begets change.

During this time—and as is customary of Cranbrook's chairs to act as artists in residence—you ran the design studio Words

> **"Every project, every curator, every artist, every designer had the opportunity to create a voice, a signature, a message; in this way, we established our unmistakable identity."**

+ Pictures for Business + Culture, doing work for clients like Nike and MTV. How were you able to practice and teach at the same time? And how did the two influence each other?

Kathy and Mike promoted theory and practice. We promoted practice and theory. We kicked off our tenure with the motto, "The Audience Is Real," and I was fond of saying, "Experience as Theory."

In 1998 you published Whereishere, a book that baffled, intrigued, and provoked the

design profession. How important was this book for you?

The book was imperfect. I wish we had focused our interest in sexuality in a more direct way.

Before Cranbrook you were the director of the design department at the Walker Art Center in Minneapolis, where you transformed its visual style from what Peter Hall described as an "unwavering adherence to the clinical International Style"* into a remarkably flexible and unconventional approach that would set up the Walker, to this day, as one of the most innovative museums in terms of its design approach. How did this work evolve during your tenure?

The work evolved because of director Kathy Halbriech's vision and support, and the extraordinary talents of interns like Mark Nelson, Santiago Piedrafita, Deb Littlejohn, and designer Matt Eller. The participation of Matthew Carter cannot be underestimated. My goal was to provide an intoxicating environment for design experimentation. No dogma, no design manual. Every project, every curator, every artist, every designer had the opportunity to create a voice, a signature, a message; in this way, we established our unmistakable identity.

In 2002 you moved to Stockholm to establish a new design firm, o-b-o-k (ord, bilder, objekt and kunskap [words pictures objects and knowledge], with Ronald Jones, an artist and critic. What was the impetus for this move?

Change.

Okay, there's more. As an ex-patriot, I have learned to see all cultures, class, political systems, religions, wars, diseases, histories and humanity as an interrelated whole. Personal reinvention is risk, and risk involves failure. At the end of my days in the U.S., I began to see "graphic" design as irrelevant. I no longer cared about new typefaces, youth culture and the 10 percent who have access to technology. As a social welfare state, Sweden rejected postmodernism, and the aggressive hubris of Americans. I have learned the grace of failure and humility in Sweden, to which I am grateful.

As this is a book about women in design, my next comments will be undoubtedly unpopular, but nonetheless they are my truths. I have been deeply influenced by three wildly flawed men: my brother, a Zen monk, taught me the power of unattachment; my first husband, P. Scott Makela, taught me the power of passion; and my second husband, Ronald Jones, taught me the power of knowledge. I teach my son and daughter the power of detachment, passion and knowledge, and they now hold all the secrets of the world.

---

* *"Truly, Madly, Deeply: Laurie Haycock and Scott Makela" by Peter Hall, from* 365: AIGA Year in Design

LOUISE
SANDHAUS

NATIONALITY
American

YEAR BORN
1955

CURRENTLY RESIDING IN
Los Angeles, California, United States

CURRENT POSITION/FIRM
Full-time faculty, California Institute of the Arts
Principal, Louise Sandhaus Design

PREVIOUS EMPLOYMENT
Tons!

DESIGN EDUCATION
Graduate Laureate, Jan van Eyck Akademie (1996)
MFA (1994), BFA (1993), graphic design,
California Institute of the Arts
AS, advertising design, Art Institute
of Fort Lauderdale (1976)

With a career straddling education and practice, Louise Sandhaus is equally comfortable designing identities, web sites, posters, books and museum exhibits, or organizing exhibits and conference programming about design and education. And she has been a part of the California Institute of the Arts as faculty and director—co-director from 1998 to 2004 and on her own until 2006—of the graphic design program. Before becoming a staple of the California design scene, Sandhaus's work and education stretched back to Boston in the early 1980s. Her lectures and writing display a topical variety—including remarkably fresh approaches on new media and technology—delivered through precise language that never fails to inform, educate and entertain.

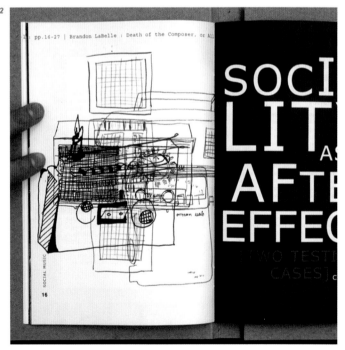

[1, 2] Documentation of Social Music broadcast, Kunstradio, Vienna for Errant Bodies Press; illustrations by Gillian Coe, Ed Fella, Tahli Fisher, Adam Linden, Jennifer McKnight, Emily Morishita, Jordan Rosenfeld, Brian Roettinger, Carol Soh, Jon Sueda and Brad Tucker (2002).

3

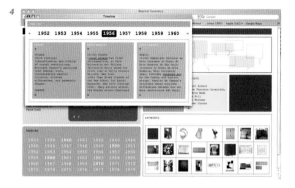

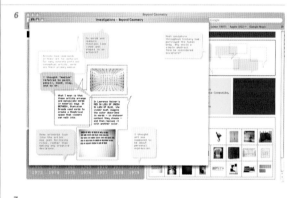

7

[3] Banner for the Urban Forest Project by AIGA NY, Worldstudio, and Times Square Alliance (2006). [4, 5, 6] "Beyond Geometry" web site for Los Angeles County Museum of Art; in collaboration with Tim Durfee and Joel Fox (2004). [7] Logo for Pitch; in collaboration with Derrick Schultz (2007).

LUBA
LUKOVA

With no more than one or two colors and a minimal use of form and line, Luba Lukova can convey a message, feeling or story with pinpoint accuracy and emotion. After graduating from Bulgaria's National Academy of Fine Arts—a six-year program—in the late 1980s, Lukova was appointed by the then-Communist government to work at the theater of a small town as its graphic designer—the very first poster she did there is now in the permanent collection of MoMA—and after three years, in 1991, she moved to New York. Since then, Lukova's work has appeared in the form of posters and editorial illustrations and, as a whole, has lent itself to gripping solo exhibitions.

In 1991 you took your first trip to the U.S. and stumbled upon your own work while book browsing in New York—in Graphis Poster Annual, to be specific. With ten slides and a copy of the above-mentioned book you went on an interview with The New York Times. Did you realize that moment would be a catalyst to a new life? Did you expect that New York would be your home for such a long time?

I realized clearly back then that my decision to stay in New York would change my life. I've lived in New York for sixteen years now, and that realization proved to be true. All of the important moments in my professional life have happened here, and my career wouldn't be the same if I hadn't come to the U.S. I loved the city from the first sight. Once I read about a famous opera singer who, after visiting New York, got so energized that he said there were vitamins in the air. I felt exactly the same way, and I hope I won't lose that enthusiasm.

Your approach can be described as simple, moving, often guttural, always honest and, most of all, engaging. How did this work philosophy come to be? How do you go about finding these qualities within your projects?

Probably the greatest influence in shaping my beliefs came from my work at the theater. After I graduated I found a job as a graphic designer in a theater company in Bulgaria. When I did my first theater posters I realized that all the plays I had to read were basically about the same thing: human relationships. And yet, the audience is never bored watching these fables over and over again because people need to see themselves in art. So, it was very natural to me to use the human figure as my visual alphabet. The work at the theater is like a laboratory of humanity, and to do a theater poster is to find that distilled substance that will carry the essence of the text. Theater is always alive; real people play in front of real people. I guess that obsession I have with accessibility and engaging the viewer comes again from the theater: You need the audience's reaction and understanding to be able to continue with your work.

To answer the second part of your question: How do I find these qualities within my projects? Well, usually projects with such qualities find me. New clients often approach me by saying they want something moving and passionate. In that sense, I don't make much difference between personal and commissioned work. I put my own feelings into the client's project.

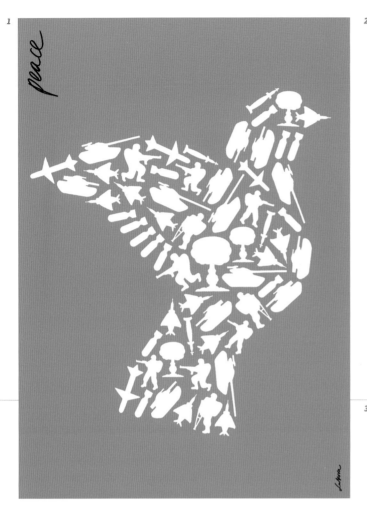

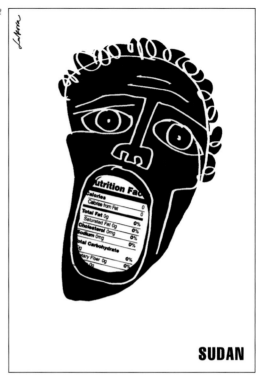

[1] *Peace poster for War Resisters League (1999).* **[2]** *Sudan poster for International Anti-Poverty Law Center (1998).* **[3]** *Logo for Say It Loud! (2003).*
[4] *Love poster for Scheufelen (1999).*

You've taught at The School of Visual Arts for many years now, and you frequently participate in educational programs across the nation. You have noted a major difference between your education in Bulgaria and the curriculums across the U.S. in the lack of a basic artistic skill base. How important do you consider drawing to be for a designer? Would you propose any changes be made in our design education?

Drawing is extremely important. I think the skills of our hands enrich our thinking capabilities. You don't have to be Leonardo or Michelangelo, but when you draw you observe and make visual associations, which in turn help you to be a better thinker. Unfortunately, the contemporary designers can't draw, and the educational system is to blame. Change is definitely needed in that direction.

Your work is prone to imitation and even plagiarism. How do you cope with this issue?

First, we need to distinguish between influence and plagiarism. It is flattering to be influential to someone. And there is nothing wrong to be influenced by work you like. An infringement is a different story, and when that happens we have to protect our intellectual property. As of now, I've noticed that people who appropriate from others instead of digging into their own souls usually don't go very far.

Your work spans many kinds of clients and an even broader range of subjects—an enriching manifestation of being a designer. Is there a topic or a client out there in the big wide world that you would like to take on as a challenge? A new medium you would like to tackle?

Oh, there are so many things that I'd like to try. Still, I guess I will always be interested in exploring humanity and drawing. I am thinking now about a hybrid project between theater and my images. That has been in my head for a couple of years, and I hope to realize it soon.

[5] Poster for the Immigrant Theater Festival (1994). [6] Poster of The Taming of the Shrew *for La MaMa e.t.c., Columbia University (1998).*

MARGO
CHASE

NATIONALITY
American

YEAR BORN
1958

CURRENTLY RESIDING IN
Los Angeles, California, United States

YEARS IN THE BUSINESS
21

CURRENT POSITION/FIRM
Owner and executive creative director,
Chase Design Group

DESIGN EDUCATION
BS, biology, minor in design
Two years master's work in medical illustration

Through an organically textured, layered and detailed design sensibility, Margo Chase has produced work for an extraordinary range of clients—from Madonna and Cher, to the popular TV series Buffy the Vampire Slayer and the feature film Bram Stoker's Dracula, to the USA Network and Perdu, a lingerie store in Saudi Arabia. Through the years and the differing industries, Chase has managed to infuse her design with an inimitable approach that always feels crafted by the human hand—no surprise, given her interest in biology and medical illustration—and unique to each project.

There is a very controlled, organic quality to your work, and you were originally a biology major. Coincidence?

Probably not. I've always been fascinated by organic form. I loved biology for many reasons, but the beauty of natural forms, both living and non-living, intrigued me from the start. The influence of these forms on my work was unconscious, however. I never intentionally tried to make things feel organic; they just came out that way.

You have maintained a unique, hard-to-describe aesthetic that is a medley, and this is meant as a compliment, of Goth and modernism. How do you feel your work has evolved over the course of twenty years?

I'm really not sure how I feel about the Goth label. I've heard it a lot, so it must be true. I started doing design in the mid-1980s when there were strong gothic trends in fashion and interior design. I know my early work was influenced by everything going on around me, where I traveled, what I read, what the fashions were. I think it's impossible and maybe even counterproductive to try to work in a vacuum, so I paid attention to everything. One of the things I love most about design is the excuse it gives me to become a sponge. I love books and I have a huge collection that fills one entire wall of my studio. I collect books on everything from typography to textiles. Looking back, I can see the influence on my work of my progression from one interest to another.

The look of the work I do now is much different from what I was doing when I started. My first clients were all in the music business, so the work could be edgy and experimental. My design was self-referential and there was lots of room for personal expression. I made lots of design decisions based on gut and intuition rather than research.

Today my clients are much larger and more corporate, so the work isn't about me anymore. I spend time listening to consumers and trying to figure out what they'll like. I use my skills, taste and expertise to make and direct design that will connect with people I often have little in common with. Today I'm getting a chance to deliver on my belief that good design can change minds and behavior.

We have to ask... How cool is it to have designed the identity for one of the most successful and pop-defining TV series, Buffy the Vampire Slayer?

CHINESE LAUNDRY

The *Buffy* project came as a result of the logo we did for *Bram Stoker's Dracula*. For a few years we got every vampire project there was. Style can be a trap though. When I got tired of designing for vampires, it took years and lots of fast-talking to convince more conservative clients that I had breadth. They were afraid they were going to get "Buffy the Cosmetics Line," or "Dracula the Financial Services Company" if they hired me.

You've had good success designing for the entertainment industry—like logos for WB's Angel's, Madonna, Cher and even Dennis Rodman/Nike. In contrast to other industries you work with, how do these projects stand out?

Working with celebrities has its good and bad aspects. It's wonderful to work with talented artists who have great vision. Designers who work with celebrities like Madonna get lots of exposure and even some celebrity by association. And, of course, it's fun to do cool work. The downside is that design for entertainment isn't usually valued in the same way that design for other products is. Design doesn't sell music; music sells music. Design for the music business is often seen as a decorative commodity, so the budgets are often quite small and the deadlines are extremely short.

You have designed more than a dozen typefaces, and you develop custom and proprietary typefaces for your clients. How did you develop an interest in typeface design?

My interest in type and lettering was influenced by two people: my mother and Pierre Rademaker, one of my first design instructors. Among her many talents, my mother is a calligrapher. I grew up watching her make beautiful forms by hand with strange pens and brushes.

When I was in college studying biology, I took a few design classes as electives. One of my instructors was Pierre, who was obsessed with type and lettering. His lectures made me see type in a completely new way. I had always taken type for granted, but Pierre saw type as something malleable that could be formed and changed. My interest started there and has never left.

You founded Chase Design Group in 1986, when design was divided by those who embraced the Mac and those who didn't. What role did this environment, and shift, play in the beginning of your career?

[1] *Identity, packaging and car for Chinese Laundry (2007).* **[2]** *Environmental design for Belkin Electronics (2007).*

I wasn't sure about the computer at first. I was doing lots of lettering by hand. It was quite intricate and ornate. The first things designed on the Mac were very primitive and digital. Rudy VanderLans's *Emigre* magazine was filled with bitmap typefaces that looked extremely geometric and stiff. I didn't want my work to look like that.

I waited until 1990 to get my first computer. By then Adobe Illustrator and Photoshop had evolved enough that I could do the kind of work I wanted. Illustrator was an incredible gift. I had been inking everything by hand on drafting film using French curves. It was slow and labor intensive. Corrections were a nightmare. The Mac changed everything for me. Even though I still did all the early sketches by hand, Illustrator freed me from the labor of the final inking and allowed me to change and edit things as much as I wanted. The computer as a design tool was a fabulous revelation then—and it still is.

In the first years after the Mac was introduced, I watched several designers' careers stall when they couldn't or didn't want to learn to use the computer. Today it would be hard to find a designer who can't use a Mac. But I think it's important to be able to use traditional methods when appropriate. Too many designers today haven't learned to use their hands to create images in traditional ways.

How do you keep your practice challenging and moving forward?

Keeping things challenging seems to come naturally when you run your own business. It's never easy, but it's never boring! There are constant challenges, from finding talented designers and smart strategists, to managing existing clients, finding new ones, and figuring out how to pay for everything.

These days, when I'm not working, I'm flying. I got my pilot's license three years ago, and I've been flying competitive aerobatics for the last year. There's nothing more inspiring than being up in the sky, looking upside down at the world. Flying aerobatic sequences requires control and precision. It's a bit like designing in the sky with an airplane. After a weekend spent flying, I go back to work on Monday with a whole new attitude!

[3] Witch's Brew *book collection for Chronicle Books (2001).* **[4]** *Identity for* Buffy the Vampire Slayer *(1997).* **[5]** *Identity for* Charmed *(1998).* **[6]** *Identity for* Bram Stoker's Dracula *(1992).* **[7]** *Identity for Marais (2002).* **[8]** *Identity for Madonna,* Like a Prayer *(1989).* **[9]** *Identity for Bonnie Raitt (1991).*

MÓNICA
PEÓN

NATIONALITY
Mexican

YEAR BORN
1969

CURRENTLY RESIDING IN
Mexico City, Mexico

YEARS IN THE BUSINESS
16

CURRENT POSITION/FIRM
Co-founder, Igloo Design

PREVIOUS EMPLOYMENT
Designer at Studio Dumbar, Netherlands (1998-99)

DESIGN EDUCATION
MFA, Cranbrook Academy of Art (1998)
BA, communication design,
UAM-AZC, Mexico City (1992)

Hailing from Mexico City, with a Master's degree from Cranbrook—during Laurie Haycock Makela's time—and a year's worth at the venerable Studio Dumbar in the Netherlands, it comes as no shock that the work of Mónica Peón is eccentric, layering many influences and inspirations through an eclectic design aesthetic. Peón works across many mediums, including illustration, editorial design and motion graphics. During the late 1990s, she was involved with the influential Mexican design magazine Matiz as a designer as well as a contributor, sharing her experiences abroad, illuminating an otherwise bleak design discourse in the Mexican design community.

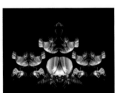

[1] The death of personality, "Tu No Existes" street poster campaign (2003-05). [2] Heavyweight travel illustration cover for BIG magazine issue #3 (2006). [3] Animation for the design conference "Design, be glocal" (2001).

4

5

6

7

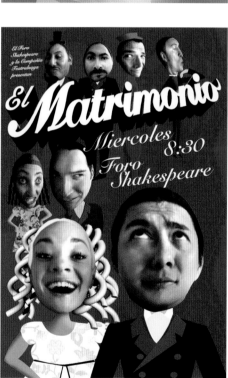

Time as lived by Mónica Peón:

Hot potato time: adrenaline rush for solving problems and working really fast to meet unreal deadlines.

Daydreaming/inspiration time: alone time while driving, taking my dog for a walk, talking with friends, parties, reading, movies, TV, travel, web surfing.

Yoga time: for health, centering and unwinding; for my teacher-training, and thus to help others help themselves.

Night dreaming: as inspirational as daydreaming, if not more.

Family time: the quality is what counts.

[4] *Promotional poster and branding for Academia de Artes Visuales (AAVI) (2005).* **[5]** *Channel branding for Cine Latino (2005).* **[6]** *Print ad for Absolut Ruby Red, in collaboration with Griselda Ojeda (2007).* **[7]** *Theater poster for El Matrimonio (Marriage) by Nicolai Gogol (2004).*

NATIONALITY
American

YEAR BORN
1965

CURRENTLY RESIDING IN
Venice, California, United States

YEARS IN THE BUSINESS
14

CURRENT POSITION/FIRM
Partner, AdamsMorioka, Inc.

DESIGN EDUCATION
BFA, California Institute of the Arts (1988)

NOREEN
MORIOKA

The art of conversation is generally not a designer's strong point (true, most make do) but for Noreen Morioka, it seems it's not just an art but also a way of life. And business. It is a trait that has helped establish AdamsMorioka—founded in 1994 with partner Sean Adams—as a firm with an incisive portfolio that combines graphic buoyancy with an assertive sense of purpose honed by her business acumen. And humor. Morioka is a permanent fixture in the design community through her involvement with AIGA and her work for industry-shaping organizations like Adobe and Mohawk. And her laughter and vitality not only precede her, but they are also contagious.

Along with business partner Sean Adams, you've run AdamsMorioka since 1994. How has your practice evolved over the years?

When we first started, we both had our own projects and dealt with each of them separately. Eventually, we concluded that Sean was much more talented with executing ideas, and I was more comfortable with working and communicating with our clients.

Although we've changed responsibilities, clients and even co-workers, one thing that remains is our friendship. We've known each other since CalArts, and to this day, Sean is one of my closest friends.

Before establishing your own firm, you worked with April Greiman for two years, after working in Tokyo for two years at Landor Associates Tokyo. How have these two early experiences shaped your career?

Actually, there are three great experiences that were the foundation to my values and ethics in our profession. My first job was for John Bricker at Gensler Associates in San Francisco. John taught me the importance of compassion and kindness for designers in our profession. He was a tough boss and demanded the work be well crafted and executed, but if the work was strong he would be the first to celebrate and promote the individuals behind the work. He taught me that ego was destructive unless you used it to champion others.

From there, Lou Danziger recommended that I go to Japan, and after 105 interviews I finally landed a design job with Landor Tokyo. The creative director at that time was Fumi Sasada, who warned me that he was hiring me to be an inspiration to the team; that my western way of thinking and designing would never be accepted, and that I would help his all-Japanese team become a bit more international. For two years, we worked on over twelve corporate identities, and for two years my ideas never got out of the first round of sketches. In fact, after six identity projects, it became comical to the team. On one project, we were asked to design concepts in a Japanese color palette. On the day of the crit, Fumi looked at my exploration and said, "Morioka, I asked for a Japanese color palette, not a Chinese one."

There's a famous saying in Japan that if a nail is sticking up, eventually it will get hit down. I never gave up hope that one day my designs would get to the final round. Even though I did not succeed in doing so, I left Landor humbled and respected by Fumi and his team.

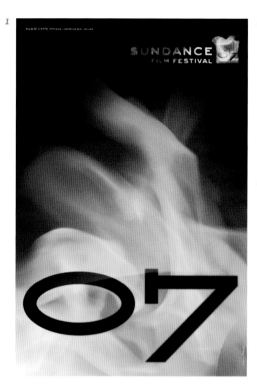

Obviously, working for a superstar like April Greiman was a wonderful opportunity. She hired me during college as one of her interns, then after returning from Japan, I was hired again as designer. April and her work always received great praise and criticism simultaneously. I remember she designed a call for an entries announcement for the annual AIGA design competition. It was a huge poster with digitized brains, complex typography and several layers of images. I thought it was amazing, but along with wonderful cards praising the poster, there were also cruel and mean notes criticizing everything from the size of the poster, to the amount of folds it had. I couldn't believe how petty and disrespectful our profession can be, but I learned that being the true critic of your work is more important than what others think.

[1, 2] Identity and materials for The Sundance Film Festival 2007 for the Sundance Institute; in collaboration with Jan Fleming and the Sundance Creative Team (2007). [3] Sundance Resort web site; in collaboration with Jan Fleming (2007). [4, 5] Identity and materials for The Sundance Film Festival 2006 for the Sundance Institute; in collaboration with Jan Fleming and the Sundance Creative Team (2006). [6] Identity and building facade for REDCAT Theater—Roy and Edna Disney CalArts Theater (2004).

Help someone see the world
in a new way. Volunteer.

Los Angeles Public Library Adult Literacy Program 213 228 7037

We preemptively stated that we understand the seriousness of your work, but we have to admit that, overall, it feels "happy." We mean this as a compliment too. How would you describe your aesthetic tendencies? What is it influenced or inspired by?

Perhaps I might use the word *optimistic* instead? Quite frankly, it is pretty easy to be critical and negative, and I think that our profession is trained from the early design classes to think this way in order to do better. I recently met a high level Buddhist priest who said that it was obvious that I suffered many hardships to see the humor and joy in situations. Maybe that's it?

More seriously, at the core of our process is the modernistic principle that problems have solutions. This base understanding is why we continually are drawn to an optimistic message. As you know, modernism evolved during World War II, and the mentality of rationing, working hard and thinking positively to end the war created messages that evoked emotional resonance.

You are very involved in the business side of AdamsMorioka, securing new clients and maintaining existing ones. What is your approach to selling design?

You don't sell design. Like the medical profession, clients—like patients—come to you when they have problem. Think about your favorite doctor—how they treat you, care for you and advise you—

and then think of how you work with your clients.

Whether it's your involvement with AIGA or designing the coveted paper promotions, you are continually involved and present with the design community. Why is this important to you?

There is no better advocate for the design profession then another designer. The only way people will understand the value of design is for us to celebrate everyone's successes and provide a community of support.

You are funny. Do you have a good joke that works well on paper?

No, I think it may fall flat.

[7, 8] Trade show LED "Lightwall" Adobe Systems Inc. (2004). [9] Poster for the Adult Literacy Program at Los Angeles Public Library (2007). [10] Disney Club House identity system (2001).

"My big interest now is how design relates to everyday situations, from making your bed to raising your kids. Design is a form of thought and action, as well as an approach to creativity. Design is a tool that can be used by anyone on earth. Design isn't just about making stuff; it's about making stuff happen."

Ellen
Lupton

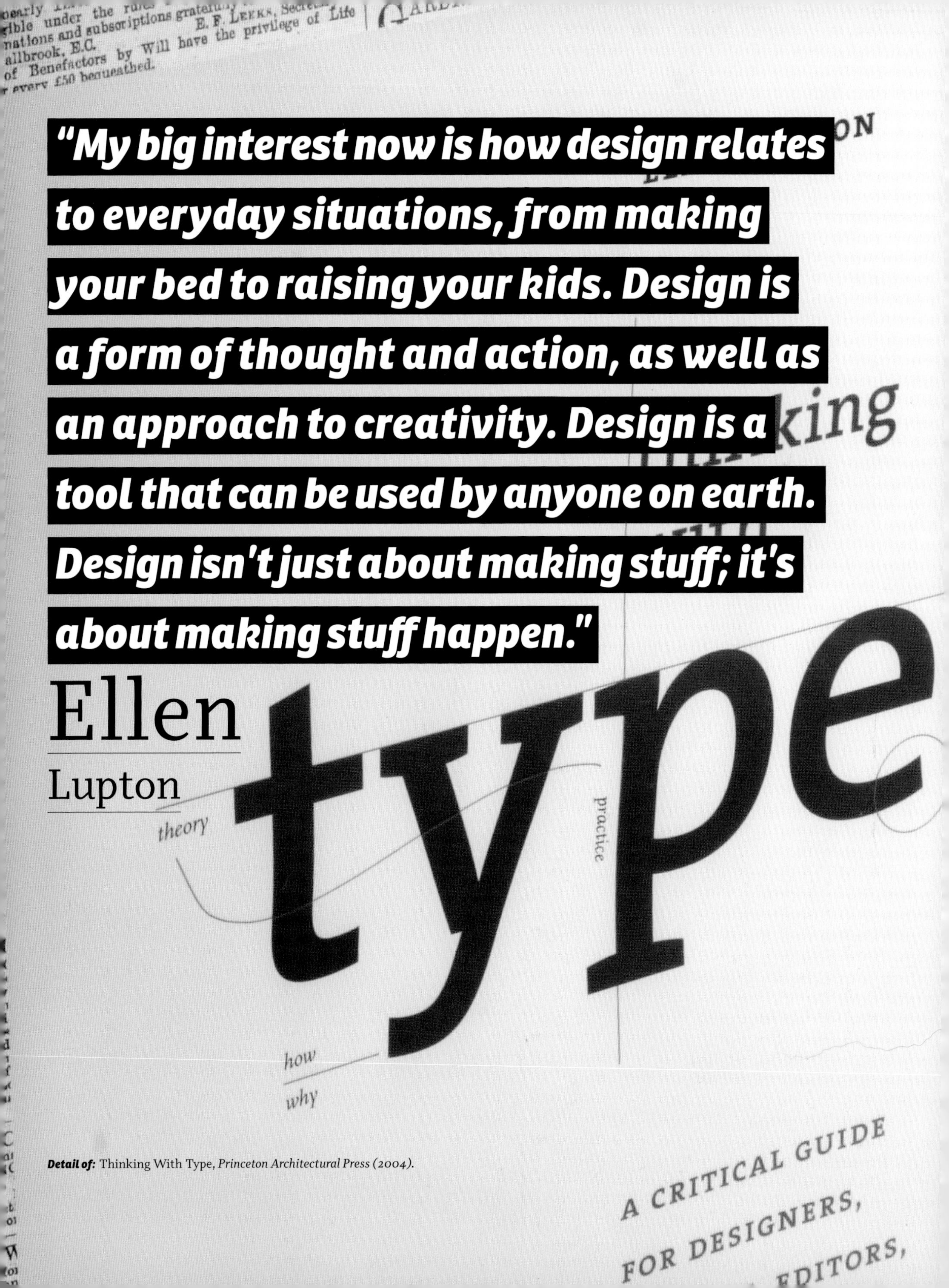

theory

type

practice

how

why

Detail of: Thinking With Type, *Princeton Architectural Press (2004).*

A CRITICAL GUIDE
FOR DESIGNERS,
EDITORS,

"From day one I instinctively believed design was about making life better and more meaningful. The process of creating something of beauty, value and usefulness thrills me today as much as it did thirty years ago."

Ann
Willoughby

Detail of: *Identity for Kevin Carroll Katalyst (2004).*

Photo by Andrea Ciotti

PAOLA
ANTONELLI

From Aerogel in **Mutant Materials in Contemporary Design,** *to the frisbee in* **Humble Masterpieces,** *to a manhole in* **SAFE: Design Takes On Risk,** *to a vase made by bees in* **Design and the Elastic Mind,** *Paola Antonelli celebrates objects, materials, spaces and ideas that would otherwise pass unacknowledged. As senior curator of the Department of Architecture and Design in New York's Museum of Modern Art (MoMA)—which she joined in 1994—Antonelli has mounted exhibitions that establish design as an intrinsic, momentous and delightful ingredient of culture and everyday life, exploring its commonplace applications as well as its experimental possibilities, and exposing it to a broad audience... including those that only wanted to see Claude Monet's "Water Lilies."*

NATIONALITY
Italian

YEAR BORN
1963

CURRENTLY RESIDING IN
New York, New York, United States

YEARS IN THE BUSINESS
All my life

CURRENT POSITION/FIRM
Senior curator, Department of Architecture and Design, The Museum of Modern Art (MoMA)

PREVIOUS EMPLOYMENT
Visiting professor, Harvard University Graduate School of Design, (2002-present)
Editor, *Abitare* (1992-94)
Lecturer, University of California, Los Angeles (1990-93)
Contributing editor, *Domus* (1987-91)

DESIGN EDUCATION
MA, architecture, Polytechnic Institute of Milan (1990)
Economic and social disciplines,
Bocconi University, Milan (1988-89)

1

2

[1] SAFE: Design Takes On Risk *exhibition, The Museum of Modern Art (2005).* *[2]* Humble Masterpieces *exhibition, The Museum of Modern Art (2004).*

You have been at MoMA since 1994 and, in this time, brought an exalted sense of relevance to everyday and commercially-available design that deserves to be shown on par with contemporary art. How have MoMA and its audience embraced this notion? Has interest in this aspect increased?

People are very, very interested in design, most of them just do not realize it until they stumble upon it. Design exhibitions are always packed and the discussion is lively. I still have not managed to convince major publications to hire design critics, though. My puzzle is not the audience, but rather the editors that still live in denial of the importance of design.

You must see hundreds of objects, spaces and ideas routinely. What does it take for something to catch your attention?

As an answer, I'd like to use here a wall text for the show that is currently on in our 3rd floor galleries in our *Just In* show, about recent acquisitions. It took Christian Larsen, curatorial assistant, Research and Collections, Department of Architecture and Design, and me several days to get it right and I could never put it better:

There are no hard and fast rules, but there are several criteria that come into play in the discussion:

Form and Meaning. Certainly an important criterion in an art museum, and yet an elusive and subjective one, beauty is today tied to meaning. Objects have to communicate values that go well beyond their formal—and functional—presence, starting from the designer's idea and intention. The best objects embody these concepts in a transparent way.

Function and Meaning. Just like form, function has also changed dramatically in the last few decades. Some objects are designed to provide certain emotions, feelings, and inspiration, and these aspects are also considered part of their functional makeup.

Innovation. Good designers take scientific and technological revolutions and transform them into objects that anybody can use. Curators are constantly looking for objects that solve new problems or address old ones in a new way, as well as for objects that introduce new and promising forms, materials, or structures.

Cultural Impact. MoMA has always privileged objects that, whether mass-marketed or developed experimentally in a designer's workshop, have the power to influence and touch the greatest number of people. Their impact can be either direct, effective the minute they get purchased and brought into people's lives, or building up in time through the inspiration they give to other designers.

Process. Curators—and people—do not take objects at face value, anymore. The way they are designed and built; the economy of means evident in their production, distribution, and use; the way they address complexity by celebrating simplicity; respect and honesty in use of materials. Consideration of the entire life cycle of the product.

Necessity. Here comes the ultimate litmus test: if this object had never been designed and manufactured, would the world miss out, even just a bit? As disarming as this question might seem, it really works. Try it at home.

Phrases like "Antonelli has the power to make or break designs and designers alike"[1], or being included in Time's 2007 list of "25 Creative Icons"[2], or named one of Art Review's "Power 100" is probably flattering, but does it also bear certain pressures or obligations? As a very public champion of design, how do you maintain this aspect of your life?

It is flattering, definitely, and having the power to make designers—I honestly do not consider breaking them a good use of the little time I have on earth—is one of the most wonderful parts of my job. Of course, there are pressures and obligations, but they are nothing compared to the advantages. It is not that different from being a politician, although I think that curators take their obligations as public figures far more seriously than politicians.

Since this is a book about graphic design, we would like to particularly ask your opinion about what you think makes visual communication relevant in the big world of Design (with a capital D) and if, in the distant future, an exhibition on, say, "The Power of the Beautifully Designed Annual Report" could happen?

Visual communication is extremely important today, although I am not sure that the annual report is the application that I would focus a show on. I am enthralled by the synthesis of great amounts of data, for instance in the work of Lisa Strausfeld, Ben Fry, Martin Wattenberg, or Laura Kurgan, and great part of my current show, *Design and the Elastic Mind*, is devoted to them. Graphic design is today more important than ever and its definition needs to be reassessed—and is being reassessed in a lively debate.

[1] *"Paola the Populist" by Linda Tischler for* Fast Company, *October 2007, issue 119.*
[2] *"Visionaries: Looking at the future through the eyes of 25 creative icons,"* Time, *August 19, 2007.*

PETRULA
VRONTIKIS

NATIONALITY
Greek American (2nd generation)

YEAR BORN
1961

CURRENTLY RESIDING IN
Los Angeles, California, United States

YEARS IN THE BUSINESS
18

CURRENT POSITION/FIRM
Creative director, Vrontikis Design Office
Senior faculty, Art Center College of Design

DESIGN EDUCATION
BFA, California State University (1984)
Major in graphic design, University of Denver (1979–80)

As a teacher since 1989 at Art Center College of Design in Pasadena, Petrula Vrontikis does not limit her educational attitude to young students only. Through her practice, workshops and numerous articles, or her book Inspiration=Ideas: A Creativity Sourcebook for Graphic Designers, *she empowers both clients and designers. Since she established her design firm in the same year, it's no surprise that both disciplines would overlap. Vrontikis's involvement with the design community is reflected in her roles co-organizing the Schools of Thought education conferences, programming the student conferences at two AIGA National conferences, and co-chairing the wildly popular* The Design Conference That Just Happens to Be in Park City *with Rick Tharp (may he rest in peace).*

You are a designer. You are also a teacher. A writer. A lecturer. And overall, you are a professional advisor to eager minds. How did you end up in this multi-faceted position?

I'd love to say that it was serendipity, or that I came to this point in my career by saving April Greiman's dog from a fire and earning her lifelong devotion and patronage, but sadly, no.

It sounds simple, but one thing led to another. I got to know colleagues in AIGA and through attending various conferences. I spent time with them talking about design and teaching. Some were editors who asked me to write (or contribute to) articles and books. Some headed up graphic design departments at colleges and asked me to present to their students. Some invitations came from leaders of AIGA chapters and Art Directors Clubs, asking me to speak to their groups.

These experiences were, and continue to be, great practice for me to formalize and refine my views on how we learn, create and practice our craft.

Do you find it hard to go back and forth, or does it come so naturally you wouldn't have it any other way?

The year I started my business, I started teaching. I've always done it this way and would feel isolated without both. I feel more authentic about my role as a graphic design teacher when I'm practicing graphic design every day.

Wearing all these hats has forced me to become highly efficient with my time because there's not much of it. Being busy

> **"I feel more authentic about my role as a graphic design teacher when I'm practicing graphic design every day."**

makes me feel purposeful. I appreciate opportunities to practice and refine what I can do. It's also a great way to keep learning and growing as a person.

Your studio mantra, "Listen, think, design—in that order," is something that you take very seriously and objectively. While it seems obvious at first glance, it is not easy to actually live it day-to-day. Can you elaborate on this process?

If design fails or falls short, it's usually because this process has been taken out

of order. Over the years I've observed students, staff and myself diving into design without digesting what the client said, or without thinking it through. We struggle with what we think is a time management problem when it's really a process problem.

You are constantly giving workshops to students and professionals alike, where "real life" plays a key role. You advise attendees to talk to their clients and really get to know them, to get the job done in time and to be professional at all times. You also encourage them to talk budgets, expectations and design value. What comes out of these frank conversations?

What comes out of this hardnosed practice of professionalism is a client's appreciation of what designers do, and designers realize how much faith clients put in our work. If clients and designers are able to clarify their expectations and discuss their concerns early, projects progress more smoothly. The key is to have these frank discussions at the beginning.

Unfortunately, many designers have these discussions after a problem is encountered, putting them at a terrible disadvantage that tends to lead to mistrust. Ultimately, the client decides to take their business elsewhere.

The process sounds agonizingly pedantic and—frankly—unsexy, but it is critical for a designer to head off potential disaster from the outset. It not only makes good business sense, but it also allows the designer to create a finished product that exceeds the expectations of the client, which is good, since the client is the one with the checkbook.

Do you believe people go home with renewed convictions and methods?

I certainly hope so. It's hard to break old habits. These habits often come from the attitudes designers observed in school. Many graphic design teachers were frustrated with—or not all that interested in—the design business. An "us and them" relationship is cultivated early on.

Sometimes the people who hear me speak about business practice say that I help them see these principles in a new way—they become not so complicated and worrisome. That's my message. It's about clear communication, and it must be practiced over and over in order for us to have confidence in how much difference it makes in our effectiveness as creative professionals.

[1] In-store poster for an exhibition of designs by Marimekko at the Fashion Institute of Design and Merchandising, and merchandising sale of Marimekko-inspired bed linens and bath items at Crate and Barrel (2004). [2] Book Inspiration=Ideas: A Creativity Sourcebook for Graphic Designers, *Rockport; design with Ania Borysiewicz and Rebecca Au Williams (2002). [3] Wine label for Think Pink, for Red Car Wine Company (2005). [4] Marketing launch materials for E! Entertainment Television (1990).*

5

6

It's of concern to me that many younger designers are bypassing phone conversations and client meetings, opting for e-mails and PDF presentations instead. It takes only a few attempts at this method to realize these "convenient" ways of doing business don't lead to the best results.

Hopefully I can impress upon designers that even if you are a good writer (and few graphic designers are), e-mail communication is often not read as it's intended. Sending PDFs off to a client severely weakens the position of the designer as a key advisor and collaborator.

My message to an audience is that clients want to work with confident and creative designers who listen to them and understand good business. It's the key to a thriving career, as opposed to de-

signers just getting by and complaining endlessly about why they aren't able to do their best.

You opened your firm in 1989—almost two decades ago. You have had the opportunity to work with small and large clients on a wide range of projects that have obtained many awards and have been published widely. Is there any work that is still on your dream list?

I'd like to run away with the yoga circus and design for scuba diving resorts in exotic places. (A girl can dream.)

Okay, seriously: I'm beginning to realize one of the items on the dream list. It's a recent business venture called "ib4e: Ideas Before Experiences" (ib4epartners. com). I've partnered with an architect and a market research expert to consult

The purposeful time allocation of Petrula Vrontikis:

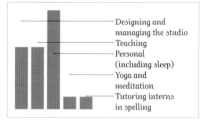

Designing and managing the studio
Teaching
Personal (including sleep)
Yoga and meditation
Tutoring interns in spelling

on projects in the initial development phase. We help clients craft and visualize experiences. Our expertise is the development of ideas, often using brainstorming techniques that help us and our clients discover unexplored solutions. It's really enjoyable to collaborate with other disciplines in this innovative context.

[5] Wine label for The Table for Red Car Wine Company; illustration by Leigh Wells (2001). [6] Subway poster for the Tokyo opening of Monsoon restaurant for Kozo Hasegawa, Global-Dining, Inc.; design by Ania Borysiewicz (1999).

REBECA
MÉNDEZ

NATIONALITY	Mexican and United States citizen
YEAR BORN	1962
CURRENTLY RESIDING IN	Los Angeles, California, United States
YEARS IN THE BUSINESS	20
CURRENT POSITION/FIRM	Principal, Rebeca Méndez Design Professor, University of California, Los Angeles, design | Média arts
PREVIOUS EMPLOYMENT	Creative director, Ogilvy & Mather, Brand Integration Group (1998-2003) Art director, Wieden+Kennedy (1997-98)
DESIGN EDUCATION	MFA, media design program, Art Center College of Design (1996) BFA, communication design, Art Center College of Design (1984)

Fully embracing and blending being a designer and an artist, Rebeca Méndez has allowed herself to produce client-driven work—from posters, to collateral, to environmental graphics. She also explores her personal interests through photography and video—with group and solo exhibitions to her credit. Over the course of her career, Méndez has been able to pursue both passions, taking her to seemingly opposite positions that only she could bridge, like moving from creative director at Ogilvy & Mather's Brand Integration Group in Los Angeles to an art residency at The Institute of Gunnar Gunnarsson in Iceland.

Few people know that you were an amateur gymnast in Mexico—with the goal of going to the Moscow Olympics in 1980 when, unfortunately, Mexico decided not to participate for political reasons. Heartbroken, you found yourself moving to the U.S. and attending Art Center College of Design. What led you to choose design? And why Art Center?

I qualified for the junior Olympic team in Mexico City at age ten and continued training an average of eight hours a day to become the national champion at age seventeen, with the goal of going to Moscow in 1980 for the Olympics. Mexico followed the United States boycott of the Moscow Olympics in 1980 and did not participate. So my fifteen years of intense focus and training suddenly seemed to have no purpose, and I felt very lost. This feeling was compounded by my family's decision to move to the United States that same year. I was very happy in Mexico City.

How I chose design is a long yet logical story. Both my parents studied chemical engineering, which instilled in me a scientific mind. At the same time, my father's passions are Mexico's history, art and archeology, so I grew up traveling throughout Mexico and learning its rich culture. My father belonged to La Mesa Redonda de Palenque, which is a gathering of researchers on Mayan studies. At a very early age, all the kids helped my father trace Mayan glyphs, so my love for typography and iconography began there. My mother's influence was equally strong, as she loves beauty and patterns in nature, and she expressed her creativity every day with us. Yet, my primary choice of study was in physics and mathematics, as I wanted to be an astronaut. But, I was talked out of these areas of study by friends and family. My cousin Laura Ruelas was studying industrial design at the Universidad Metropolitana de Xochimilco and introduced me to both industrial and graphic design. The fields were so new that nobody could talk me out of them, and simply, that's why I ended up in design. I didn't know much about the discipline of design, just that it seemed like a creative, contemporary field with a balance of both the irrational and rational mind. Once I was in the U.S., I was advised by a professor at San Diego State University to go to Art Center, CalArts or SVA. I drove to Art Center and was very impressed by the work in the gallery, and I applied. I'm sure that if I'd driven to CalArts first, I would have applied to CalArts. Both are

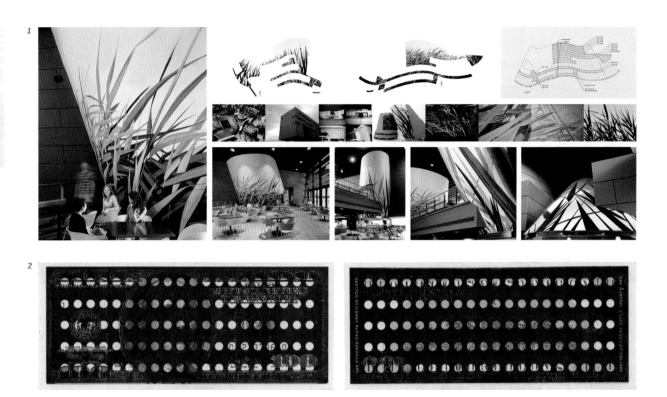

amazing schools. I started at Art Center in the fall of 1981.

As a working designer you have yet to work in your home country, Mexico. Is this something you might actively pursue?

I have never worked as a designer outside of the United States, but as an academic, I've lectured and given workshops in various countries, including Mexico, Chile, Taiwan, the Netherlands and the UK. Currently I'm collaborating with architect Enrique Norten in a few projects, and there are several possibilities that might bring me to work in Mexico. I'm really looking forward to bringing all that I've learned back to Mexico.

And speaking of this worldly gap, how do you nurture the bridge between your nationality and your design work?

Design is intrinsic to Mexican culture, as one can see by the sophistication and complexity in all Mesoamerican cultures, specifically the Olmecs (1200 B.C.), known as the progenitor civilization of later Mesoamerican civilizations. The Olmecs are credited with the invention of the calendar and the concept of zero. So we not only have highly evolved design manifestations, but we also have refined design thinking; there is nothing to bridge but much to remember. My design work is the expression of my multiculturalism/multiethnicity. I'm an amalgam of various cultures and peoples, which may manifest as a capacity to allow chaos and multiplicity to coexist with order and minimalism.

Beyond your work as a designer, you are an avid traveler in search of nature images that

express the everyday vastness, stillness and emptiness of our world. This has lead to interesting projects such as the upcoming art residency at the Gunnar Gunnarsson Klaustrið in Iceland. What attracted you to this research? How do your photography and design work coexist?

I knew at a very early stage in my design career that I wanted to balance my life as a designer and my life as an artist. My MFA's emphasis was in video art, and it's taken me over ten years since my graduate degree to create the conditions to also practice as an artist. So, the residency in Iceland is a way to isolate and protect time dedicated solely to my art practice. What I love about Iceland is that it is a geologically young land, thus it is extremely active, with volcanoes constantly erupting, causing dust clouds and haze, exploding geysers, boiling sulfur mud pools, iceberg

---

[1] "Grass #1" and "Grass #2," permanent art installation at the Marché, at the University of Cincinnati Recreation Center; architecture by Thom Mayne and his firm Morphosis (2006). **[2]** "Crude American Dollars, $100," a self-generated project created in response to the invasion of Iraq (2006). The following text goes alongside the work: "06.06.2006 / PETROLEUM: Nymex Crude Future ($71.65/bbl) / Reported Killed by the Military Intervention in Iraq: 42,646 Civilians and 2,476 U.S. Military. / Missing or Captured: 17,869. / Wounded in Action: 17,869. / Journalists Killed: 97."

lagoons and subterranean boiling rivers. There is an unusual, performatory aspect to Iceland's natural forces due to its difference in intensities (mass and speed). My research focuses on capturing this force of sensation. Thus, Patagonia, the Sahara Desert and the Mexican jungle have also been locations for my photography and film shoots. Iceland's history (it is the oldest existing democracy) and people also fascinate me, and I'm deeply inspired by their music—Johann Jóhannsson, Hilmar Örn Hilmarsson, Sigur Rós, Amina, Múm and, above all, Björk.

"How do I divide my time? Very fluidly between my studio, my art practice, my teaching and my personal life. Sometimes I feel that Time divides me, not the other way around."

As far as how my artwork and design coexist, sometimes they do and sometimes they don't. I can perform "cleanly" as both a designer and an artist, but the areas I enjoy treading on most are more messy, as they are at the threshold of boundaries; they are at the interior of the exterior where categories, rules and positions leak, where the edges blur, in the in-between, the ambiguous, the composite. So far as a designer I have created identities, systems, order; and as an artist I research where identity, system, and order clouds. It seems that as an artist I'm trying to obliterate all I learned as a designer. Lately, my collaborations have been with great people who also see dis-ciplinary boundaries as unnecessary, so what I create in the end can be art and can be design, all according to what language you use to codify it and what; circles you frequent. My dear friend and cultural historian Sande Cohen says that language is fascist... I fully agree.

As the lead of Brand Lab at UCLA, you have focused your research on the strategy, organization, culture and public identity of complex organizations. This is not the only way in which you are deeply invested in design education—a great passion of yours. What do you see in your future, as you relate to the next generation of students?

I'm much more interested in instilling in our students how to regain their independent minds. I make an effort in teaching them how to ask questions themselves, rather than solving problems. By learning how to ask questions, a person creates opportunities and has the capacity of invention. As a problem solver, you are simply a servant to industry, which has been the demise of much of education in general and the design discipline in particular. Design has been undergoing CPR for many generations; it is by understanding that it's not about the world of design (how much money I get) but about the design of the world (sustainable evolution) that design will mature and have the confidence and vitality to act in its full capacity.

This is what I tell my students: Remember that at the core of the art and design discipline is analysis, and foster a critical mind. Also, practice three things simultaneously: (1) Experiment: Create work for yourself, independent of clients, responding to your own questions and curiosity; (2) Collaborate: Create work and/or a collective with your peers and friends, especially those who are not in your discipline—writers, architects, artists, musicians, scientists; (3) Do your professional work with integrity—by neither blindly serving the industry nor abandoning your personal convictions and values. Soon you'll see that your experimental work will become your professional work, and you will craft your own practice independent from the dominant culture.

Along your trajectory, you have had the opportunity to collaborate with architects, video artists, film directors and artists in many mediums. What would you say are the rewards and challenges of such collaborations? From what you have learned in the past, what do you foresee in your collaborative future?

My collaborations have not been just with people in other disciplines—they have been with amazing individuals, like video artist Bill Viola, architects Frank Gehry, Thom Mayne, Enrique Norten and Greg Lynn, and film director Mike Figgis. Not only does my mind open by stepping into another discipline and it's methodologies, but I am also able to work hand in hand, day in and day out with these great minds. Sometimes the learning curve is huge, and I need to be on my toes, but other times I realize how the creative process is vastly similar and thus we simply "play" like Frank Gehry told me.

Collaboration with great people, for great ideas is the only work I'm interested in participating in. I've worked very hard at creating a situation in my practice that allows me to carefully choose my professional relationships. Having that choice is the sweetest reward.

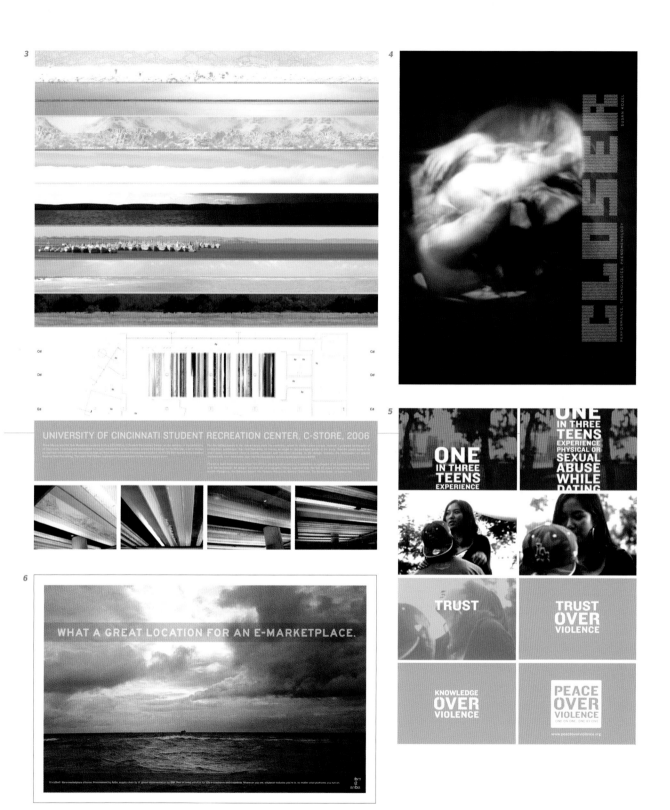

[3] *"Homeland #1," a series consisting of six 20' × 8' murals; permanent art installation at the University of Cincinnati Recreation Center, C-Store (2006).*
[4] *Book design for* Closer: Performance, Technologies, Phenomenology *by Susan Kozel, MIT Press (2008).* **[5]** *360° brand identity and public service announcement for Peace Over Violence; director of photography Michael D. Powers (2006).* **[6]** *E-marketplace national print and outdoor advertising campaign for IBM; in collaboration with Chris Wall; photography by Pete Seaward (2000).*

"**I love books, and I love storytelling. I love understanding the text and trying to imagine the way a text could be represented. I'm not academic and cringe at the thought of a serious discussion about the books I've read, but I enjoy taking that leap of faith that is necessary to change words into something visual.**"

Barbara
deWilde

Detail of: "May" Martha Stewart Living opening page.

ROBYNNE
RAYE

NATIONALITY	
American	
YEAR BORN	
1964	
CURRENTLY RESIDING IN	
Seattle, Washington, United States	
YEARS IN THE BUSINESS	
20+	
CURRENT POSITION/FIRM	
Co-founder, Modern Dog Design Co. Teacher, Cornish College of the Arts	
PREVIOUS EMPLOYMENT	
Burger slinger, Jack in the Box Disc jockey (1983-86) and publicity director (1985-87), KUGS, WWU College radio station	
DESIGN EDUCATION	
BA, Western Washington University (1987)	

Lacking any solid job offers—or any job offers for that matter—after arriving in Seattle, Robynne Raye founded Modern Dog with her college friend Michael Strassburger in 1987. For the past two decades Raye has been energetically pumping out work that spans posters, packaging, identity and other impossible-to-categorize work with a consistent sense of exploration, playfulness and doggedness that has defined her work and established her (and Modern Dog, of course) as one of Seattle's most distinctive studios and representatives. Generous with her time and energy, Raye lectures around the country and has been teaching at Cornish College of the Arts since 2000.

This may be hard to believe for some, but you founded Modern Dog more than twenty years ago and have been producing work across three different decades—sorry, are we making you feel like a dinosaur?—yet your work seems to have an eternal freshness. How have you managed to keep things evolving and interesting in your work?

The most significant contributing factor is that I still create work I enjoy doing on a daily basis. I think a lot of designers get into a creative corner and feel like they can't get out. I've never felt trapped. At the end of the day I go home and look forward to coming back because, quite honestly, I laugh a lot and I really enjoy the company of my co-workers.

Speaking of decades, you have probably seen the profession change by leaps and bounds both technologically and in spirit. How have you adjusted to the continuous shifts?

No unusual or fascinating story here. I work on a MacBook Pro, but I still have a circa 1987 waxer and X-Acto knife nearby as I still like getting my hands involved whenever possible. I also love Sumi ink because there's no black that's blacker.

In the design world, Seattle is known as a tremendous hotbed for poster design, and rightly so. Did you ever consider a less saturated market? Did the city itself become a source that informed your work and sensibility?

I can't imagine not living in Seattle because so much of my life is invested here. I don't know if my design sensibilities can be entirely credited to one place, but living here definitely plays a role.

In the 1980s, Seattle was a working class city where it was possible to live on $600 a month. We started Modern Dog in 1987, paying $60 a month for our studio space. The only equipment we needed was a table, T-square and a phone line (insert birds chirping, "Cheap, Cheap, Cheap").

But it's not so much Seattle at large but the people Mike and I knew. We were immersed in music culture because all of our friends were in bands. It's hard to ignore what's around you. I spent my early adulthood laughing out loud while reading Lynda Barry comics and Matt Groening's pre-*Simpsons Life in Hell* cartoon strip in *The Rocket*, a free biweekly music rag. (My best friend even met her future husband through a "Guitarist Wanted" ad in *The Rocket*.) Being around musicians was, and still is, inspiring. As

1

2

3

4

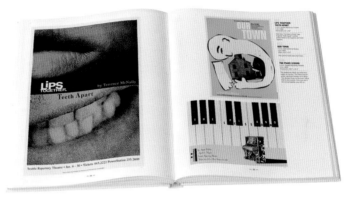

> **"I work on a MacBook Pro but I still have a circa 1987 waxer and X-Acto knife nearby as I still like getting my hands involved whenever possible. I also love Sumi ink because there's no blacker black that's blacker."**

I've always gravitated toward do-it-your-selfers, which partly explains how Mike and I could go straight from college into starting a design company, there was no one telling us otherwise. Having a young company in the late 1980s and early 1990s really benefited us. We initially got a lot of poster work just because we decided that doing theater posters wasn't that far off from the music posters we were already doing for our friends' bands. We were able to experiment, take risks visually and have fun. It's an approach we still enjoy doing today.

You are best known for your poster work, but we bet you have other talents. Identity design? Advertising? Maybe an annual report here and there?

I've never designed an annual report, but it's on my list of things to do before I die. I would agree that I'm primarily known as a poster designer because that's what shows up in the design books and gets collected by museums. This past year I've worked on a variety of projects that included posters but also book design, identity work for an online media company, and new product development and packaging for a green dog products company.

You also lecture, teach and impart workshops. How important is it for you to share what you've learned?

Simply put, I enjoy sharing the wisdom I've gained over the years. Most students don't understand that a career as a designer is a risky one. If you want it, you have to go and make it happen. Students believe if they are talented, someone will come knocking, and it just doesn't happen that way. I know that teaching someone to be creative is next to impossible, but one of my strengths as an instructor is that I'm pretty good at pulling it out of anyone who is willing to try. My classroom environment encourages students to take risks without fear of failure.

[1] *Identity for Brown Paper Tickets (2002).* **[2, 4]** *Book* Modern Dog, 20 Years of Poster Art, *co-authored with Mike Strassburger, Chronicle Books (2008).*
[3] *Poster for the Icograda Seattle Design Week conference (2006).*

If I feel someone isn't giving it 100 percent, I'm not afraid to tell them. (And I don't walk on eggshells while doing so.) I feel that an uncompromisingly honest environment is most conducive to learning.

It's also common to find you stirring the pot with posters that are considered controversial by some. Between us (and the thousands of people who will read this book), why do it? Wouldn't it be easier to do posters with flowers and call it a day?

You know, it's not like I come to work and think, *Gee, I'm going to create a controversial poster today*. But it's true that I really

The Hurricane Poster Project received hundreds of posters from the U.S. and abroad. All proceeds from the sale of limited editions were donated to the American Red Cross.

enjoy living in the United States and taking full advantage of the First Amendment when I feel I have something to say. The most controversial poster I ever did was created in 2005 in response to Hurricane Katrina, and to this day I'm still getting hate mail over it. There's even a rumor that a designer is using it as an example of "bad graphic design" in design conferences. Ironically, I was recently asked by the Musée des Arts Décoratifs (which displays their collections at the Louvre) to send them a print for their permanent archives. Just goes to show you, what's one man's Britney Spears is another man's Mötley Crüe.

By now, a book on Modern Dog should be on bookshelves as well. Is this an important achievement/milestone for you and your

partner, Michael Strassburger? Can we expect Volume 2 in 2028?

Well, I almost forgot that we did it, but thanks for reminding me. (Okay, just joking.) Mike and I are really excited about it. The book spans a twenty-year timeline and provides insight into how Modern Dog approaches poster projects. Even for me, when I look at it, I'm amazed that a body of work that diverse came from one company. I don't know of any other design book like it. We were lucky to get a great editor at Chronicle, Alan Rapp, and a lot of helpful and smart people advised us.

Will I still have expectations in 2028? I'm enjoying being here right now. I really don't find myself thinking too much about the future.

[5] *Poster for* Art Walk *2007 by the Greenwood Arts Council (2007).* **[6]** Liz Phair *poster for the Crocodile Cafe (2005).* **[7]** *Dog biscuit packaging for Olive (2007).* **[8]** wtf? *sour lemon tarts packaging featuring President Bush (2006).* **[9]** *Poster for the annual Sasquatch Music Festival sponsored by House of Blues (2006).*

SHARON
WERNER

Through a richly layered aesthetic that weaves a combination of hand-crafted nostalgia with culture-savvy modernity through typography, illustrations, decorative motives, and evocative imagery, Sharon Werner has been producing work for a variety of notable clients like Target, VH1 and Moët Hennessey. Upon graduating from college in 1985, Werner worked for Duffy & Partners, and in 1991 established her design firm, Werner Design Werks, giving Minneapolis (and now St. Paul) one of its most iconic practitioners that would come to define the burgeoning design scene of the Twin Cities. While the output of WDW is akin to that of larger design firms, Werner has consistently operated a very small studio of only two people—and that includes her.

NATIONALITY
American

YEAR BORN
1961

CURRENTLY RESIDING IN
Minneapolis, Minnesota, United States

YEARS IN THE BUSINESS
16

CURRENT POSITION/FIRM
Principal, Werner Design Werks, Inc.

PREVIOUS EMPLOYMENT
Duffy & Partners (1985-91)

DESIGN EDUCATION
Minnesota State University (1985)

Prior to starting your own shop, you worked at Duffy & Partners. How did this experience inform how you handle your own business? What were the key lessons you learned, or things you wanted to avoid?

I learned an incredible amount about design and the business of design from both Joe Duffy and Charles Anderson (who was there for the first three or so years of my time there). But the most impactful lesson I took away from there is the importance of doing smart work, no matter who the client is and how much money they do or don't have. This work, in turn, will breed more great projects and hopefully more smart work, and so on. Has it worked for us? Well, basically I think so—some days or weeks more than others.

At the time I was working at Duffy, we were partially owned initially by Fallon

Advertising and then the Michael Peters Group. Through that I realized that partnerships are difficult to manage in a design firm and that I would be wise to avoid that situation.

Having started with no clients and no prospects, your current client list is remarkable—Target, VH1, Amazon.com, MTV Latino, Chronicle Books, just to name a few—giving the impression of a large design firm, yet you have remained small. How have you been able to maintain this modus operandi?

We've been very fortunate to have been given the opportunity to work with great clients even though we are just a two-person studio. It is a deliberate decision to remain small because it allows us to be selective in the projects we take on. There have been times when it was tempting to staff up to take on more projects (read

between the lines, more money!), but I didn't want to create this large machine that I would have to fuel all the time.

I think that during our workday we are considerably more productive than firms with far more people. We don't need staff meetings to find out the job status or multiple, drawn-out conversations to make sure everyone in the office is on the same page. We just look around our monitors and say, "Oh, that's cool," and move forward.

We also present ourselves from a professional standpoint much as a larger firm does; we submit very detailed proposals, contracts and timelines. There is a sense of comfort for clients, when all expectations and deliverables are outlined and agreed upon. It also helps us—if a client

changes the deliverables we have something to refer back to.

One project many designers talk about is Mrs. Meyer's cleaning products. Can you talk about how this particular experience, and your involvement from the very beginning, evolved into such an iconic project?

Mrs. Meyer's is one of our favorite clients and, luckily, one of our favorite products too. That's a bonus!

The Mrs. Meyer's story from the Werner Design Werks perspective:

Monica Nassif, the founder of Mrs. Meyer's, asked us if we would be interested in working on a new aromatherapeutic brand of cleaning products. They already had an existing high-end line of aromatherapeutic products called Caldrea,

and Monica posed the project as follows: "Someone is going to rip off this idea at a lower price point, so I'd rather do it myself!" Brilliant strategy!

From the beginning, Monica was going to approach this brand unlike most large, mass market cleaning brands; her goal was to merchandise all categories of the cleaning aisle together, i.e., laundry detergent would be shelved next to the dish soap. This is referred to as brand blocking, and it hadn't yet been done in this category.

So with that we worked with them to give the brand a name. We landed on Mrs. Meyer's, Monica's mother's name. Monica grew up on a farm in Iowa; there were nine children, cats, dogs and other stray pets. Who wouldn't believe that

Mrs. Meyer would know how to keep a clean home?

We suddenly had a great brand story that was true, and both Sarah and I could completely relate, too. You see, Mrs. Meyer was also very much like our own Midwestern mothers—thrifty, hard-working and no-nonsense.

Thelma Meyer and her husband, Vern, tour the country in the Clean Home Tour concession trailer, talking about everything from getting stains out to raising kids. Thelma has appeared on local as well as national TV as the real face of Mrs. Meyer's.

Because we are channeling our own mothers, Sarah and I are able to write most of the copy and, of course, become two of the gatekeepers of the brand. The

---

[1] *Grand Connect Writing Kit for Pam Lohmann; design and illustration with Sarah Nelson (2004).* **[2]** *Identity and packaging of Mrs. Meyer's Clean Day, for Clean & Company LLC; design with Sarah Nelson (2001).* **[3]** *Talent Portfolio Books for Caryn Model and Talent Management; design with Sarah Nelson; illustration by Sarah Nelson (2007).* **[4]** *Clean Home Tour Trailer of Mrs. Meyer's Clean Day, for Clean & Company LLC; design with Sarah Nelson and Paul Sieka (2006).*

5

6

7

8

9

10

question that is frequently asked of everyone is, "Would Thelma say that, or would she grow that in her Iowa garden?" When in doubt, we call Thelma or Viola or Helen (our moms)!

Back to your original question: I think the reason Mrs. Meyer's is an iconic brand is only partly due to the package design. Mrs. Meyer's Clean Day has what every brand hopes for: a real story that almost everyone can identify with, a great product that lives up to the story, and last, but we hope not least, a nice package that communicates the story well.

You have been in the Twin Cities area for over two decades, including its heyday in the mid-1990s. How has the design scene evolved? And what role does it play in your practice?

I debated over this question for a long time and came to the conclusion that it depends on which heyday you're referring to—the designers' financial heyday of the late 1980s when Duffy was doing posters with fifteen spot colors, or the design heyday of the mid-1990s when clients closed their wallets a little and designers had to work really hard to get something produced.

I personally love the mid-1990s when clients were smarter with how they spent their budgets; it really appealed to my Midwestern values. I loved scrounging for things that would give big impact for little money. And clients were completely accepting that there may be a bit of a grittiness to the design, because that's what they could afford, and it was real. Ah, life was good!

Now, you have big brands with endless budgets trying to mimic that grittiness, so they look like small brands; and you have small start-up brands trying to communicate luxury, so they look like big brands without the budgets to carry it through. It's all upside down.

So what's a designer to do? Tell the story of the brand in the best way possible and let fads and trends go—unless that, of course, is the story!

[5] 10 Cane packaging for Moët Hennessey; design with Sarah Nelson; illustration by Elvis Swift; photograph by Lars Topelmann (2006). **[6, 7]** Hillbilly Hollywood by Debby Bull, Rizzoli, New York; design with Sarah Nelson; image collection by Debby Bull (2000). **[8, 9]** Inspiration, a Natural Neighborhood advertising for CPDC; design with Sarah Nelson; illustration by Sharon Werner; writing by Lisa Pemrick (2006). **[10]** Elvis Swift, illustration promo for Joanie Bernstein; design with Sarah Nelson; illustrattion by Elvis Swift (2007).

SUSAN
KARE

NATIONALITY
American

CURRENTLY RESIDING IN
San Francisco, California, United States

YEARS IN THE BUSINESS
21

CURRENT POSITION/FIRM
Partner, Susan Kare LLP
Creative director, Chumby Industries, Inc.
Co-founder, Glam.com

PREVIOUS EMPLOYMENT
Apple Computer, Inc. (1982–86)
NeXT, Inc. (1986–88)
General Magic, Inc. (2004-present)

DESIGN EDUCATION
BA, summa cum laude, art major,
Mount Holyoke College (1975)
MA, Ph.D., fine arts, New York University (1978)

In 1984, before anyone had done anything remotely similar, Apple introduced a graphical user interface with its groundbreaking Mac OS. Equally formidable was Susan Kare's unprecedented work in developing the icons that would come to signify this revolutionary operating system—the Happy Mac, the trash can, and even the terrifying bomb, among the most memorable. After Apple, Kare was creative director of Steve Jobs's NeXT computer company, and later she designed Microsoft's Windows 3.0 operating system. Kare started her own firm in 1989 and has since established herself as an expert in the field of user interface design, invariably infusing her work with playfulness, simplicity and accessibility.

It has been more than twenty years since you famously designed the iconography of the original Macintosh operating system, and since then you have continued to innovate and thrive in the field of interface design. How formative was that experience?

I continue to be grateful for that opportunity. It was a chance to work on a project that was of great interest and a good match for my skills, to work with many dedicated and talented engineers, and to work in an environment where great emphasis was placed on striving for excellence and creativity at every instance.

Since there are only a handful of major operating systems, you have had to take your specialty to other mediums, like handheld devices and online applications. How have you, as both designer and busi-

ness owner, been able to transition across technologies?

To some degree, design work is design work. I enjoy working in many mediums, including traditional graphic design and bit-map graphic design. Although I particularly enjoy the challenge of developing images for devices with limited screen real estate, there are many other interesting design problems on the web and on new devices. My firm also does corporate identity work and some product design. (There is a line of Susan Kare products such as magnets, cards and notebooks, developed for and sold by the Museum of Modern Art in New York.)

You have been working across three decades that have seen major improvements in the breadth of technology, but your work has consistently revolved around pixels—some-

times more of them, usually less. How do you keep your work evolving within this constraint?

Well, my work is often focused on designing symbols, or graphics for user interfaces. The problems to solve involve metaphor, imagery and communication. The actual specifications of how many or few pixels are secondary to figuring out design solutions. That being said, I love the challenge of expressing an idea in a limited grid of pixels, and there are still plenty of requests for 15 × 15 pixel images. At the same time, creating infinitely resizable images in Adobe Illustrator is something I enjoy tremendously and is a medium I often employ in my projects.

In an era when more is more and the option of fully-colored and highly-detailed interfaces is possible, how do you achieve the

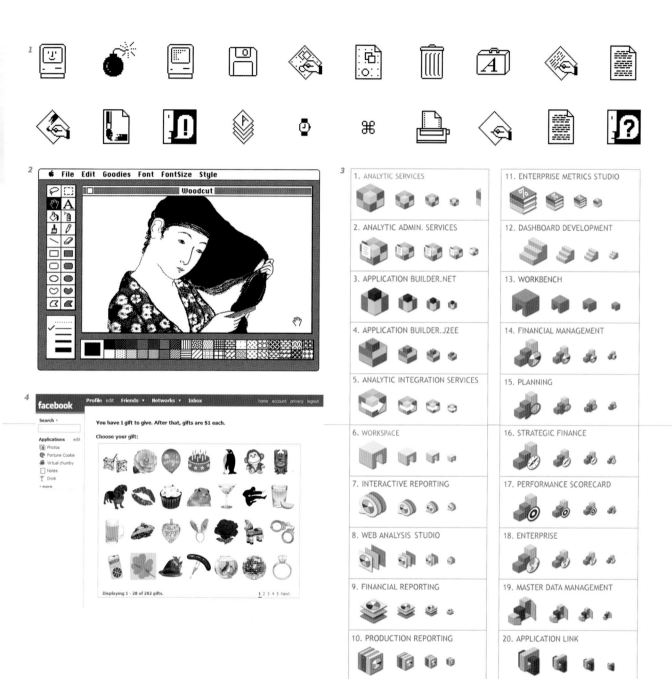

[1] Icons for Macintosh operating system for Apple Computer (1984). [2] Macintosh MacPaint window for Apple Computer (1983). [3] Product icons for Hyperion (2005). [4] Icon gifts for Facebook (2007).

5  6

7

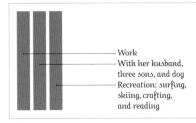

— Work
— With her husband, three sons, and dog
— Recreation: surfing, skiing, crafting, and reading

clarity, simplicity and directness necessary for the best user experience?

Well, I believe the interface should not compete with the data, so I tend to favor a minimal approach. Just because you can use a million colors doesn't mean you necessarily should.

How do you see your practice, as well as the role of the interface designer, evolving in the next five or ten years?

Right now my design practice is in overdrive and I'm busier than ever (and getting less sleep than ever), but I am working on the most creative projects ever—UI graphics, packaging and charms for Chumby Industries, a Facebook gift shop, illustrating a business book, and a new logo for San Francisco Water and Power. It's a time when we're able to expand the nature of the design projects we take on. I definitely see technology and fashion merging, and I hope to participate.

[5] *Weather icons for WeatherBug (2004).* **[6, 7]** *Logo and web site for Chumby Industries, Inc. (2007).*

8

PLANT WATER WEED

PLANT WATER WEED

FEED HARVEST SHOP

PLANT WATER WEED FEED PICK SHOP HOME

PLANT WATER WEED FEED HARVEST SHOP HOME   HOME HOME HOME HOME

APHID   WHITEFLY   CATERPILLAR

HOT + DRY   HOT + HUMID   MILD + BREEZY   MILD   CLOUDY + BREEZY   CLOUDY   SHOWERS   RAIN   HEAVY RAIN

Tomato Tomato Marigold SUNflower CORN PUMPKIN PEPPER POLE beans TULIP Daffodil Iris

Watermelon Watermelon ZUCCHINI HOT PEPPER CARROT STRAWBERRY Onion Zinnia Foxglove VENUS flytrap CACTUS

ROSE ROSE ROSE PEPPER Zinnia DAISY TULIP Pumpkin Orchid Orchid cosmos

WIND CHIME

GNOMES

HUMMINGBIRD FEEDER

[8] *Phone game graphics for Digital Chocolate (2004).*

GROUNDBREAKERS

Promotional journals for Start Here, by Little Fury (2006).

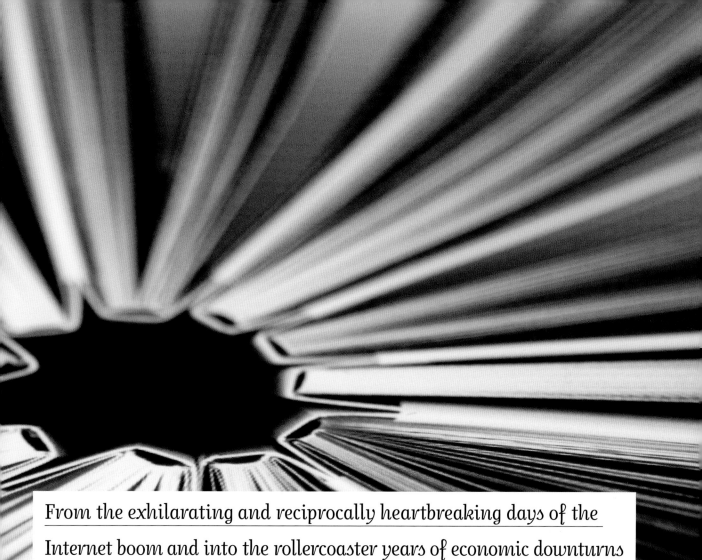

From the exhilarating and reciprocally heartbreaking days of the Internet boom and into the rollercoaster years of economic downturns and upswings that have sinuously defined the twenty-first century, graphic designers have responded to each unannounced curve by adapting to new delivery mediums, embracing uncommon business models, engaging in entrepreneurial ventures and, most ardently, expanding the definition of what a designer is. These designers are extending the breadth, increasing the influence and raising the expectations of our profession—collaboratively cementing the efforts and influences of their predecessors.

ALICE
RAWSTHORN

NATIONALITY
British

YEAR BORN
1958

CURRENTLY RESIDING IN
London, United Kingdom

YEARS IN THE BUSINESS
20+

CURRENT POSITION/FIRM
Design critic, *International Herald Tribune*

PREVIOUS EMPLOYMENT
Architecture and design critic,
Financial Times (1999-2001)
Director, The Design Museum, London (2001-06)

DESIGN EDUCATION
MA, art and architectural history,
University of Cambridge (1980)

Wielding an incomparably eloquent and accessible writing style, Alice Rawsthorn has given design a lucid voice in the mainstream through her weekly design column for the International Herald Tribune. With 240,000 copies in circulation and 4.6 million unique visitors a month through its web site, she does not shy away from featuring graphic designers like Stefan Sagmeister, Graphic Thought Facility or Irma Boom, or writing about design-centric topics like flexible identities. In her previous role as director of the Design Museum in London, Rawsthorn's emphasis on design brought the legendary work of Saul Bass, Peter Saville and Robert Brownjohn to its halls—much to designers' frenzied interest and gratitude.

Many Design (capital D on purpose) writers tend to narrow their definition of Design to fashion, architecture or product design. You have grandly embraced visual communication as part of the design discourse. Why is this important, and of interest, to you?

I can't imagine writing about design without exploring visual communication. We're bombarded by so many visual images in our daily lives that it is arguably the most ubiquitous area of design; it is also the area that people outside the design community think they know least about but are most intrigued by once they look into it. Personally, I'm fascinated by visual communication, as it encapsulates so many of the qualities I love most about design—it's dynamic, richly fetishistic, and constantly changing.

Although I write for civilians—general readers, rather than designers—in my *International Herald Tribune* columns, I really enjoy the insider discourse around graphic design on blogs like Design Observer and in magazines such as *Dot Dot Dot*. I look forward to the emergence of a similar debate in multimedia design.

As director of the Design Museum in London you organized exhibitions on some of graphic design's most notable figures like Saul Bass, Peter Saville and Robert Brownjohn. How do you feel these shows compare in popularity and appreciation by the public in contrast to other design subjects like, say, furniture?

The graphic design exhibitions we staged at the Design Museum were extremely successful, both in terms of visitor numbers, which were higher than for most of

our furniture design shows, and the critical response. The educational projects, talks and debates that accompanied those exhibitions were very popular, too. Whenever a great graphic designer like Matthew Carter or the late Alan Fletcher came to speak, their talks sold out swiftly. People even flew in from other countries to hear them. Although the craziest incident was for the opening party of *The Peter Saville Show*, when an invitation was auctioned on eBay and sold for over $1,000.

These graphics exhibitions proved popular partly because graphic design is such an important part of the industry that they attracted a large professional audience, as well as thousands of graphic design students. As graphic design was then a relatively unusual theme for museums, we were careful to choose subjects

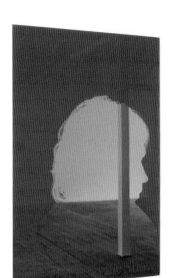

that crossed over into other areas of contemporary culture, thereby broadening the audience. For obvious reasons, the Saul Bass and Robert Brownjohn retrospectives had huge appeal for movie buffs, which we enhanced in the media coverage and in collaboration with the National Film Theatre. Similarly *The Peter Saville Show* attracted music fans. New Order, one of the bands Peter worked with, even recorded a special soundtrack for the exhibition. And Alan Fletcher's talk was part of a collaboration with Tate on pop culture in 1960s Britain.

The success of such crossover projects enabled us to stage more esoteric graphics shows, knowing that the audience would be smaller. A good example was *You Are Here*, a fantastic exhibition on the history of information design, from

"How do I divide my time? As enjoyably and efficiently as possible."

eighteenth-century orreries, to Google. Everyone who came to see it loved the show, but it didn't attract as many visitors as graphics blockbusters like Saul Bass and Peter Saville. That said, it's one of the exhibitions I'm proudest of having put on at the Design Museum.

Currently, you write the weekly design column for the* International Herald Tribune (IHT) *where the range of subjects you cover is downright extraordinary. How do you keep matters fresh and topical?

One of the joys of writing about design is that it is such an eclectic discipline,

encompassing so many different areas of our lives. This eclecticism makes it very challenging to write about, and also very invigorating. In my *IHT* columns, I've had to come to grips with everything from why $8 plastic monoblocs are the world's most popular chairs, to why roundabouts are the most efficient forms of traffic management, to the mysteries of user interface software and the physics of the football. I am very lucky in that the senior editors at *IHT* have been staunchly supportive from the start and understood that there is much, much more to design than expensive, uncomfortable chairs being auctioned at Sotheby's.

I try to keep the columns fresh and topical by reading as much—and as widely—as possible in a constant search for new ideas and interesting themes. Often the

[1] *Exhibition graphics for the* Alan Fletcher *retrospective at the Design Museum by Graphic Thought Facility (2006).* **[2]** *Exhibition poster for* The Peter Saville Show *at the Design Museum by Graphic Thought Facility (2004).*

3

4

5

best ideas come from the least likely sources, or a chance conversation with someone who's an expert in a field I know nothing about but turns out to be in flux because of a design innovation. It probably helps that I'm naturally curious—I've always loved discovering and learning about new ideas, and observing changes—and I really enjoy the subject. Design is such a dynamic and engaging discipline that I can't imagine having as much fun writing about anything else.

You've written two immersive monographs; one on Yves Saint Laurent and another for Marc Newson. Of course, this is a much different process and experience than writing a weekly column. What were some of the most rewarding aspects of these endeavors? The hardest?

The books were very different. I agreed to write the introductory essay to Marc's monograph as a favor to a friend. It's a relatively short essay, which was fun to write and taught me a lot about product design and Marc's evolution as a designer. We later collaborated again on various Design Museum projects, including a retrospective of Marc's work.

The Yves Saint Laurent book was completely different as it was a full-fledged biography and the single most challenging project of my career. It was fantastically rewarding, and a great opportunity to explore areas I'd written about as a *Financial Times (FT)* journalist—fashion, design, post-war French history and contemporary French politics

(I was a foreign correspondent for the *FT* in Paris)—as well as art and gay culture.

Making the transition from short, snappy journalism to writing a narrative of far greater length with credible characters and dramatic pace was very difficult, more so than I'd anticipated. I couldn't have done it without the help of my U.S. editor, Nan A. Talese at Doubleday, who was brilliant at identifying my weaknesses and giving me the confidence to address them.

Could we egg you on for an equally in-depth look at a graphic designer? Pretty please?

It sounds very tempting.

---

[3] *Design Museum identity by Graphic Thought Facility (2003).* **[4]** Designer of the Year *exhibition graphics at the Design Museum by Graphic Thought Facility (2003).* **[5]** Designer of the Year *exhibition graphics at the Design Museum by Graphic Thought Facility (2006).*

NATIONALITY	
British	
YEAR BORN	
1973	
CURRENTLY RESIDING IN	
Brooklyn, New York, United States	
YEARS IN THE BUSINESS	
11	
CURRENT POSITION/FIRM	
Chair, MFA in design criticism, School of Visual Arts	
PREVIOUS EMPLOYMENT	
Program director, American Institute of Graphic Arts (1998–2002)	
DESIGN EDUCATION	
MA, history of design, Royal College of Art/Victoria & Albert Museum (1996)	

ALICE
TWEMLOW

Photo by Yoko Inoue

Establishing high standards for design criticism and writing—whether through teaching or leading by example—has not been a priority among designers, mostly because there are few design writers who are not practicing designers that would rather spend time designing. Luckily there is Alice Twemlow, a gifted writer with an education in English literature, a Master's degree in history of design, and an in-progress Ph.D. in design criticism—as a result, Twemlow's essays are persistently well informed and exhaustively researched while being illuminating and challenging. In her role as chair of the new MFA in design criticism at SVA, Twemlow is poised to elevate the standards and practice of design criticism and writing. Finally.

You have an MA in history of design, are currently working on your Ph.D. on design criticism, write extensively about design, curate design conferences and shows, and teach at more than one design school. There is only one way to put it: Why design?

Why, thank you. Well, my interest in design started off as something personal and close to home, and now it's amplified because I'm also intrigued by its role in every aspect of the public realm. I grew up in a household that was filled with design: My mother used to be an interior designer and my dad an illustrator and a lecturer in graphic design, plus they are both sharp-eyed antique dealers. So a combination of nature and nurture meant that I had little choice but to see the world through a design lens. The part I had control of, however, was how to engage with design. I didn't want to

go to art school and train as a designer; I loved writing too much. So I went off to university to study English literature and, when I discovered there was an academic discipline called history of design, I leapt upon it, returning to design not as a practitioner but as an investigator. I quickly found that I love to research and to write about design in its many forms and contexts. I guess that's why I'm now starting four years of graduate research.

Your writing always feels accessible even when you are dealing with complex strains of criticism or exposing unknown historical facts and figures in loving detail. How do you approach writing?

Warily. I said before that I love writing, but I should clarify that the love I feel is very intense and short-lived and that the usual sensation is more of a muddy

mixture of fear, hate, resentment and frustration. I find writing hard, and I am very slow. But when a paragraph or even a phrase turns out as well as I'd imagined it, I get such a giddy rush that I lose all memory of the pain. Until I take on another assignment. The fact that my writing feels accessible is due to editing. I'm an average editor, but my husband, David Womack, is brilliant, and if he has time he'll always help. Although I'm starting to learn his advice, which boils down to this: Get rid of all the qualifiers (the *possibly*s, *perhaps*s and *almost*s) and always cut the first paragraph!

You have been writing about design for a decade now; how has the acceptance of design writing changed within the profession in this time? Do you feel your audience has grown or matured?

I love this question because I'm really interested in the relationship between a writer/critic and their readership—it's going to be a thread that runs through my Ph.D. dissertation—and whenever I interview a critic, or research their work, I'm always looking for an indication of dialogue between author and reader, or at least a response on the part of the reader. Did a piece stimulate a reader to have her own critical opinions? And how do we know? One of the basic measures of reader response is the letters page in a publication, a format now superseded by the online comments section—a letters page with ADD. But are there other measures of a piece of criticism's ability to resonate and to provoke action? Well, that's a question for me to address in my research, but back to your question. Acceptance of design writing within the profession has clearly increased in the last

decade. The fact that we can launch an MFA in design criticism is testament to that. But I'm interested in the response to design writing from people beyond the profession, and that has not changed enough for my liking in the last decade. We still have a long way to go, I think, before there are design sections in national newspapers, and the general public sees that design's implications extend beyond sections like *Style & Fashion* and *Home & Garden* in *The New York Times*. This situation is just as much the fault of the writers and editors as it is of the public; if we wrote more compellingly about design's role in healthcare, warfare, and housing and our editors actually made room for such articles, then perhaps the public would respond. Within the design profession, even if the audience for design writing has grown (mainly because so many designers now are also writers),

that doesn't mean that it has also matured. Thanks to the comments sections of blogs and web sites we have a much clearer view of our audience now than we did when I started to write. I think this is great in principle, but I'm not encouraged by the kinds of comments that tend to get posted; as a whole they don't suggest that the design readership has matured particularly. One of my favorite examples of this lack of maturity—lack of a lot of things—was a comment posted in response to a review of Jonathan Barnbrook's monograph. The poster prefaced his comment by explaining that he hadn't actually read the book, nor had he even seen it.

As director or co-director of conferences, how do you approach these tasks?

I think the conference is both a weird and a wonderful medium that remains

[1, 2, 3] Poster, advertisement and logo variations for the School of Visual Arts MFA in Design Critisism; design by Walker Art Center (2007).

under-exploited in terms of its potential for exploring and exchanging ideas. I've produced and directed several design conferences, both at AIGA while I was their program director, and beyond, and I've consulted on many more. I approach the direction of a conference as a curator does an exhibition or an editor a themed issue of a magazine, except, because I'm dealing with something live, I also have to be a bit of a rock concert producer, too. I'm a big proponent of themes for conferences—as an attendee of those without them, I always feel at sea. But the program doesn't have to be as cohesive as you suggest in your question. It's important to leave some of the threads hanging. It's also a good idea to throw into the mix some disruptive or simply non-sequitur elements. If it's all too tightly resolved, the audience will feel like there's no room

for them to make their own associative connections. Picking a theme is always tough. It has to fascinate you personally, but then it also has to be something that's in the air and of interest at the moment people are coming to the conference, which can be up to two years after you have to choose it.

We were not there, but legend has it that Voice, the 2002 AIGA National Conference in Washington, DC that was postponed due to September 11, was perhaps one of the best. Ever. You directed that conference. Can you tell us a little about this one in particular?

Yes, it was a corker. It evolved from the final presentation of the previous conference, which was a souped-up, glitzy extravaganza that crystallized the excesses of its moment and its venue—millennial dot-com fever and Las Vegas,

respectively. In the wrapping-up of that 1999 conference, Michael Bierut drew the attention of the 3,000-strong audience to ideas and sentiments that were beginning to stir in the corridors of the conference, and of graphic design itself, but that had not been given a place on the main stage—namely, the 1999 resurrection and rewording of Ken Garland's 1964 "First Things First" manifesto. I had heard the same rumblings and predicted a pendulum shift away from the show-biz aspects of design and towards an engagement with social and political issues. That's how *Voice* evolved. The real trick with that conference was to make sure the content was powerful and inspiring but neither preachy nor what Bierut referred to as "broccoli"—stuff that was good for you, but dull. So while some of the presenters were intense—

[4] Poster for AIGA's Voice Conference; design by Cahan and Associates (2001). [5] Logo for the second iteration of AIGA's Voice Conference; design by AdamsMorioka (2001). [6] "The Decriminalization of Ornament," opening spread in EYE Magazine; design by Esterson Associates (April 2004).

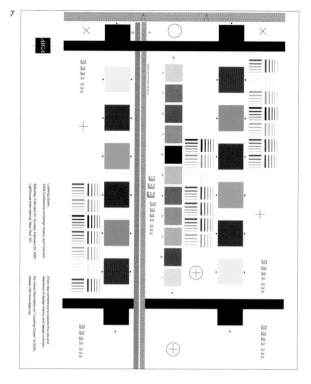

artists Sue Coe, James Nachtwey and Alfredo Jaar, for example—I left room for humor with Matt Groening, Dave Eggers and Joe Garden of *The Onion.*

The hardest part for me, of course, was dealing with my own shock in response to 9/11 while trying, for AIGA's sake, to resuscitate a conference. There were many elements of the first version that didn't make it through to the rescheduled one, speakers such as the activist collective RTMark, hip hop producer Dan the Automator, author Naomi Klein, radio documentarian David Isay, designer Bruce Mau, Zimbabwean designer and educator Saki Mafundikwa, and industrial designer Bill Stumpf. Ah well. In the end, all I did was to assemble a really good conference. What made the event poignant and memorable was its timing—

it materialized, in its slightly injured but more resilient form, in March 2002, six months after 9/11 and at exactly the moment when everyone was ready for the kind of catharsis that it could provide.

In the fall of 2008, the very first crop of students began their courses at D-Crit, the new MFA in design criticism at the School of Visual Arts, which you are chairing and have co-founded with Steven Heller. This must be terribly exciting. What are you most looking forward to? And what do you want to achieve personally, as well as professionally, with this program?

Yup, this is exciting alright. I'm looking forward to what the students themselves bring to D-Crit. So far it's all been about my and Steven Heller's vision for the program—and our imaginations can only stretch so far. What I'm hoping for is a

diverse group of students with different ideas about what design criticism might be. My objective for the program, beyond delivering a stellar educational experience for fledgling critics, is to improve the level of public design discourse. As for personal goals, conceiving, formulating and then chairing a brand new MFA is a pretty engaging challenge. I hope my efforts ensure that the program lives up to its promise. I had just decided I'd like to transition from being a freelance writer and lecturer to a situation where I'd be working more fully in education, when I was offered this amazing opportunity at SVA. I think I'll make a good chair; I've always loved teaching and I'd eventually like a position where I can teach, research, write books and have a salary. Doesn't that sound good?!

[7] Poster for AIGA's Looking Closer *conference; design by Paul Elliman (2001).* *[8] Poster for AIGA NY's evening with Wim Crouwel and Massimo Vignelli; design by AIGA/NY board (2007).*

" *I am much more interested in writing about design for non-specialist audiences. I want to tell broader cultural stories through the lens of design, and my ambition is to draw people's attention to the role of design for the first time.*"

Emily
King

Detail of: *Table of contents of* Robert Brownjohn, Sex and Typography, *Princeton Architectural Press (2005).*

ALLYSON
LACK

Bouncing between three U.S. states in her design upbringing, Allyson Lack received a bachelor's in marketing from the University of Maryland, followed by a crash course in graphic design from Portfolio Center in Atlanta, landing a job at Houston-based Rigsby Hull Design—where she met her future partners—followed by a senior design position back in Maryland at Rutka Weadock in Baltimore, and, finally, going back to Houston to establish the Texas office as a partner of Principle, where she focuses on print and packaging work for clients as varied as Nordstrom, The Walters Art Museum, and more.

NATIONALITY

American

YEAR BORN

1976

CURRENTLY RESIDING IN

Houston, Texas, United States

YEARS IN THE BUSINESS

8

CURRENT POSITION/FIRM

Partner, Principle

PREVIOUS EMPLOYMENT

Rigsby Hull Design (2000-01)
Rutka Weadock Design (2001-04)

DESIGN EDUCATION

BS, science and marketing,
University of Maryland (1998)
Graduate studies, graphic design,
Portfolio Center (2000)

[1] *Collateral materials for The Walters Art Museum (2005-07).*

A day in the life of Allyson Lack:

- Phone calls
- Business development
- E-mailing
- Managing projects
- Brainstorming
- Designing
- Miscellaneous

- Driving
- Eating/cooking
- Exercising
- Dog walking
- Playing
- Dreaming

2

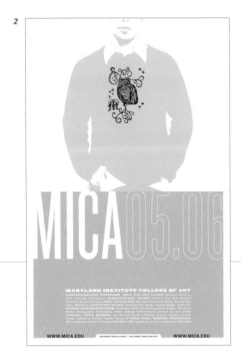

3

4

5

6

[2] *Admission recruiting poster for the Maryland Institute College of Art (MICA) (2005).* [3] *Identity, invitation and collateral for the 2007 Honor Award gala National Building Museum's annual fund-raiser (2007).* [4] *2007 Holiday gift card campaign for Nordstrom (2006).* [5, 6] *Packaging for Paddywax Journey of the Bee candles (2006).*

JENNIFER
SUKIS

After almost seven years of lending her talents to design firms—for nearly three years at Rigsby Hull Design, where she met her future partners, and for nearly four years at Aue Design Studio—Jennifer Sukis established the Ohio office of Principle in 2004. With a knack for the unconventional, Sukis is prone to design novelties like a self-warming holiday card, an inflatable invitation or an illuminated manuscript that is, literally, illuminated… much like her personality and approach to design.

NATIONALITY
American

YEAR BORN
1976

CURRENTLY RESIDING IN
Cleveland, Ohio, United States

YEARS IN THE BUSINESS
9

CURRENT POSITION/FIRM
Partner, Principle

PREVIOUS EMPLOYMENT
Rigsby Hull Design (1998-2000)
Aue Design Studio (2000-04)

DESIGN EDUCATION
BFA, visual communication design,
Kent State University (2000)

1

2

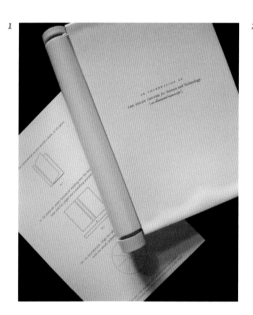

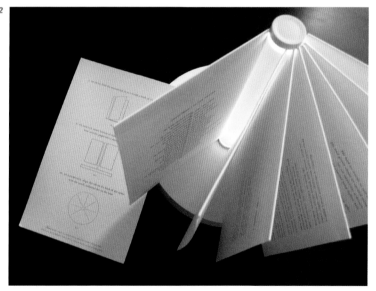

[1, 2] John Carroll University Illuminated Manuscript (2005).

"*How do I divide my time?
Coffee is first, followed by e-mail, and writing my daily
to-do list. Usually I work until two or three with little
breaks in between to let my pooch out. If we're busy you
will find me at my desk late into the night, but I try to
spend my evenings cooking, hiking, playing around online,
watching movies, reading or listening to podcasts.*"

[3, 6] *Welcome Kit for Progressive Auto Insurance customers (2004).* **[4]** *Identity redesign for Ultradent Products, Inc. (2006).* **[5]** *Packaging for Paddywax Destinations Collection (2006).* **[7]** *Web site for Progressive TripSense (2006).*

PAMELA
ZUCCKER

Somewhere between Detroit, Atlanta, Houston and Quebec lies the secret to the design versatility of Pamela Zuccher. After attending The Portfolio Center in Atlanta, Zuccher spent four years at Rigsby Hull Design—where she met her future partners—later running her own firm, Pomme Studio, in Québec. With her accumulated experience in branding, advertising and packaging for small and large clients, she founded the Québec office of Principle in 2004.

NATIONALITY

American

YEAR BORN

1974

CURRENTLY RESIDING IN

Québec, Canada and Detroit, Michigan, United States

YEARS IN THE BUSINESS

10

CURRENT POSITION/FIRM

Partner, Principle

PREVIOUS EMPLOYMENT

Rigsby Hull Design (1998-2002)
Pomme Studio

DESIGN EDUCATION

BFA, University of Michigan (1996)
Graduate studies, graphic design, Portfolio Center (1998)

1

[1] Packaging for Paddywax Classic Collection (2005).

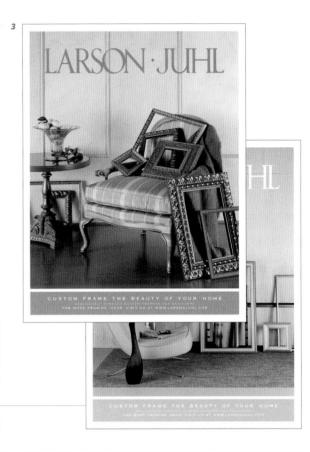

[2, 3] Campaign for Larson-Juhl Consumer (2005–07). *[4, 5]* Packaging for NapaStyle specialty foods (2006–07).

AMY
FRANCESCHINI

NATIONALITY

American

YEAR BORN

1970

CURRENTLY RESIDING IN

San Francisco, California, United States

YEARS IN THE BUSINESS

18

CURRENT POSITION/FIRM

Founder, Futurefarmers
Co-founder, Free Soil
Professor of art, visual arts, University of San Francisco

Before sustainability, accountability and responsibility towards the world became global talking points and matters of pride for those who embraced them, Amy Franceschini has steadily, earnestly, and actively produced a range of work filtered through these concepts—and then some—for more than a decade. In 1995 Franceschini founded Futurefarmers, a group best described in their own words: "Relevant to the time and space surrounding us." Futurefarmers produces client-driven work, self-initiated endeavors, and public projects, ranging in the extremes from editorial illustrations to experimental undertakings like powering a Nintendo Game Boy with voltage from lemon trees. Franceschini teaches media theory and practice courses at Stanford University and the San Francisco Art Institute.

We have to admit that we are a little baffled in trying to summarize what you do. So, for the record and to get us rolling, could you give us your elevator pitch?

I make things. I work with people who have common questions and concerns about the complex world that we are part of. I do not bind myself to one medium, as ideas and context drive the medium that best illustrates the question at hand.

I am an artist and educator. I founded Futurefarmers in 1995 as a means to bring together multidisciplinary practitioners to create new work. I co-founded Free Soil in 2005. This is a group of researchers, gardeners, artists and writers who share their research in an online blog [www.free-soil.org].

You are equally adept in a variety of online and offline mediums. To what do you attribute this ability to jump from one project to another?

I guess it is a matter of curiosity and trust that I can learn how to do whatever I need to learn in order to make what is in my head. As I mentioned before, medium is really a byproduct of an idea. The root of my interests is questions. I have many questions, and I often meet people who have similar questions. I find it important to put a form around these questions.

I work with many other practitioners, researchers and artists. This allows for a broader range of questions and outcomes.

There is a peculiar (and very satisfying) aesthetic to your design work—the minty, pinkish color palettes, the tiny worlds within larger canvases, the pixels... How did this develop?

The color palette was influenced by my mother's trips to India. She always returned with lovely photos of the amazing colored architecture, especially from her guru's ashram, Sai Baba. His ashram is incredibly baroque and insanely colorful.

In terms of worlds within worlds, this is just a natural inclination to mimic the "natural" world that surrounds us. There are so many worlds going on at once; while I type, the hummingbird outside is visiting our garden, the neighbors are enjoying her, I am trying to ignore the bouncing Eudora symbol in my toolbar, the plane overhead is casting a shadow on the car outside—who is in that plane, where are they going?...

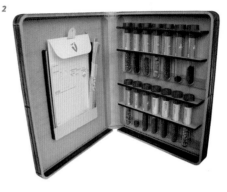

I feel that it is important to find connections between all of these things that surround us and incorporate them into a visual system.

You started Futurefarmers in 1995, right as the Gold Rush of the Internet started. What was your experience during this time as a small enterprise?

I really feel like I was just in the right place at the right time. It was a very strange time for me, to be twenty-five years old and being approached by huge companies. Money was flying around like mad, and small studios were becoming huge companies overnight. We had to make a very conscious decision around 1998 to stay small. Luckily, my partners and I were all in agreement that we wanted to do "good" work. We felt that if we grew larger we would become managers and our creative time would be lost. In our hearts, I was an artist, Josh On was an activist, and we did design to allow us to focus on our true loves as much as possible. So we have stayed small since then and only do work that makes sense either financially or conceptually.

Of course, it was very hard to turn down offers to be bought out and million dollar jobs, but we did.

Once the wave was over in the late 1990s and into the twenty-first century, did your career or outlook on what you wanted to do change?

I don't think I ever aimed to be a designer or run a design studio, so the whole ride was really day-to-day. I never felt entirely satisfied by design, so I decided to go to grad school in 2002 to focus more on my art interest. While in grad school I had time to reflect on the work Future-

[1, 2, 3] *Victory Garden posters, seed library, seed packaging and bikebarrow for SF MoMA (2006-07).*

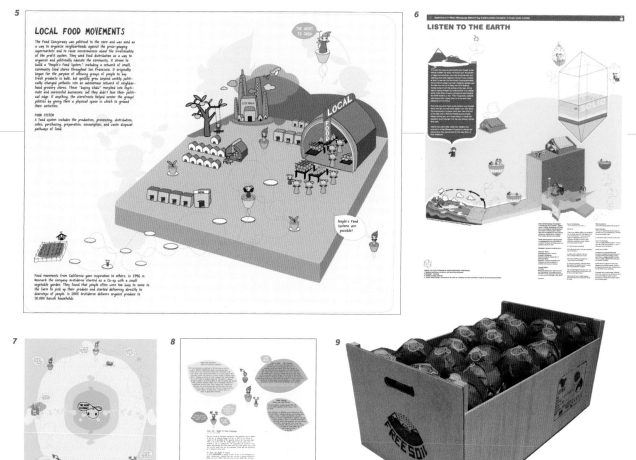

[4] *Futurefarmers book cover for IDN (2002).* [5, 7, 8, 9] *F.R.U.I.T. poster, wrapper and box for Smart Museum of Art—University of Chicago (2004).*
[6] *Impossible Projects poster for Rooseum Museum of Art, Malmo, Sweden (2005).*

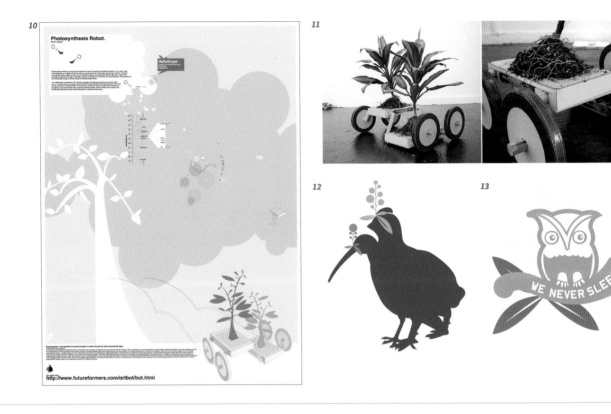

farmers had done. Through two years of reflection and graduate work at Stanford I realized that I really enjoy the merging of disciplines and that Futurefarmers had to become that bridge.

You've been a proponent of sustainability and community for some time, and it's only been a few years since those notions have entered the mainstream consciousness. How has this larger concern and acceptance affected Futurefarmers? Do you find your work to have a larger public now?

It is interesting how many illustration jobs we have gotten recently that are accompanying "green" or "global warming" stories. When it comes down to it, the jobs we are doing seem only to be part of a green trend. I speak with some of the

editors to ask them to develop the stories a bit more critically, but not many of them seem interested in critical content. I can only hope that our illustrations lead people to dig deeper into these issues that are only scraping the surface of larger, more complex situations.

It must be fascinating to be one of your students. Since your career has been anything but conventional, what is your approach to teaching?

I love teaching, but it is the biggest challenge. I feel that I am most effective as a teacher in a non-institutional setting or short-term workshop scenario—a situation where students are there because they want to be.

Since I am now a professor at a university, I try to bring a democratic approach to my classes, such that each student can also be the teacher. This is not an easy task, but I truly believe that the traditional way of teaching is problematic and that our educational system needs to be overturned. Seats in rows and rooms without windows are like vampires. It is time to take teaching out into the world and look at things together.

Collective experience is the most powerful learning tool, thus I try as much as possible to get my students out into the world and collaborating with each other and real-life practitioners.

[10, 11] Photosynthesis Robot poster and Photosynthesis Robot for Foxy Gallery (2006). [12, 13] Logos for Futurefarmers (2006).

BRYN
MOOTH

Photo by Hal Barkan

There is an optimistic range of attitudes that HOW magazine—and its wildly popular conferences—have achieved: friendly, accessible, entertaining, informative and empowering. Pretty much the same can be said of HOW's editor of nine years, and staff member for thirteen, Bryn Mooth. Along with her team's, Mooth's editing sensibilities extend beyond the bimonthly magazine as HOW has evolved into an all-encompassing experience that bridges its information-rich publication, with its invariably packed business and creativity conferences, and its inspirational annuals that celebrate everything from self-promotion to in-house design. Mooth's presence ricochets between her editorial letters both offline and online and as crowd-energizer at the conferences—never missing an opportunity to smile.

NATIONALITY

American

YEAR BORN

1967

CURRENTLY RESIDING IN

Cincinnati, Ohio, United States

YEARS IN THE BUSINESS

17

CURRENT POSITION/FIRM

Editor, *HOW* magazine

YEARS AT HOW

13 years on staff, plus 4 additional years as contributing editor and writer

PREVIOUS EMPLOYMENT

Created, edited and published a custom lifestyle magazine for a segment of American Express cardholders

[1] HOW *magazine covers; photo by Hal Barkan.* **[2]** HOW *magazine cover, "Creativity issue"; art direction by Tricia Bateman (June 2007).* **[3]** *"Cardboard Couture" by Amy Leibrock,* HOW *magazine; art direction by Tricia Bateman (2007).*

4

5

"How do I divide my time?"

HOW magazine:
- *Developing editorial plans*
- *Assigning and editing articles, working with outside writers*
- *Writing*
- *Production editing*
- *Managing staff*

HOW events:
- *Developing programming*
- *Inviting and working with speakers*
- *Marketing support*
- *Hosting events*
- *Developing new events*

Digital/online HOW projects:
- *Managing HOWdesign.com*
- *Writing bimonthly newsletter*
- *Contributing to HOW blog*
- *Developing/managing digital products like compilations and online webcasts*
- *Marketing support*

6

7

[4] HOW magazine covers; photo by Hal Barkan. [5] "Developing a Formula" by Romy Ashby, HOW magazine; art direction by Tricia Bateman (2005). [6] "The Birth of Odile" by Tamye Riggs, HOW magazine; art direction by Tricia Bateman (2007). [Authors' note: Odile is one of the typefaces being used in this book.] [7] HOW magazine cover, "Typography Issue"; art direction by Bridgid McCarren (2008).

CATELIJNE
VAN MIDDELKOOP

NATIONALITY
Dutch

YEAR BORN
1975

CURRENTLY RESIDING IN
Rotterdam, The Netherlands

YEARS IN THE BUSINESS
7

CURRENT POSITION/FIRM
Partner, Strange Attractors Design
Professor, graphic design, The Royal Academy of Art
in The Hague
Guest teacher, Design Academy Eindhoven

DESIGN EDUCATION
Royal Academy of Art, The Hague,
Department of Graphic & Typographic Design (2000)
MFA, Cranbrook Academy of Art (2002)

Ornate, complex, and anomalous are characteristics that could render graphic design unapproachable, but in the dexterous hands (and mind) of Catelijne van Middelkoop these are adjectives that only begin to compliment the visual language that she has developed over the years as one of the founding partners of Strange Attractors, the Hague- and New York-based firm she co-founded with partner Ryan Pescatore Frisk in 2001. Together they work on a bewildering range of projects from motion graphics, to interactive, print, environmental and identity design. A third generation Dutch designer, van Middelkoop is currently on the National Board of Directors of the Association of Dutch Designers/BNO.

[1] Little Yellow Writing Hood *animation for FSI FontShop International; in collaboration with Ryan Pescatore Frisk (2005).* **[2]** *"The Visual Rhetoric of the Supreme Being," published by ONOMATOPEE, written by Max Bruinsma (2007).*

3

4

5

6

7

[3] The New Typographers, *Sage Publications; in collaboration with with Ryan Pescatore Frisk (2005). [4]* Cranbrook Catalogue, *Cranbrook Academy of Art (2002). [5, 6]* Big Type Says More *installation for Museum Boijmans van Beuningen; in collaboration with with Ryan Pescatore Frisk (2006). [7] "TokyoChat" video for Tokyo.Now, commissioned by W+K Tokyo Lab (2006).*

DEBBIE
MILLMAN

Since brands are an inherent part of her life, it's safe to compare Debbie Millman to the venerable Swiss Army knife: ingenious, versatile, dependable, and, just ever so slightly, dangerous! While her professional career spans more than two decades, it's only recently that her years of simmering experience, knowledge and passion for design have funneled through a variety of means. Millman lectures across the country; hosts an addictive Internet radio show, Design Matters; teaches at SVA; writes on her personal blog as well as on Speak Up; and recently published an exposé (of sorts) of designers' innermost thoughts, How to Think Like a Great Graphic Designer. The only thing missing from her arsenal would be mirror writing... Oh, yes, she does that, too.

NATIONALITY
American

YEAR BORN
1961

CURRENTLY RESIDING IN
New York, New York, United States

YEARS IN THE BUSINESS
25

CURRENT POSITION/FIRM
President of design, Sterling Brands

PREVIOUS EMPLOYMENT
Senior vice president, Interbrand (1993-95)
Director of marketing,
Frankfurt Balkind Partners (1992-93)
Designer and editor, Rave Communications (1985-88)

DESIGN EDUCATION
BA, University at Albany,
State University of New York (1983)
Certificate, Harvard University (2003)

Most people know you from your radio show, Design Matters, your commitment and contributions to AIGA and, of course, your writing on the beloved Speak Up— sorry for the bias, readers. But that only covers the past few years. What have you been up to all this time?

Working! For me, there is little difference between working and non-working. I love everything that I do (well, almost everything), so what I do does not really feel like work, so to speak. It is all part of the life I have always dreamed of living.

Why the sudden, almost Napoleonic, public burst that has made you one of the most recognizable figures in our industry?

Eddie Cantor, a star of stage, screen, radio and TV from 1904 to 1960, famously said, "It took me twenty years to become

an overnight success." For me, it was twenty-one.

Much of the design work you and Sterling Brands do is for large (well, very large) retail clients that must move millions of shelf units to stay competitive. How do you respond to this kind of responsibility? And how does design make a difference?

I have a lot of opinions about what we do. I think that packaging and brand design are not just about design anymore. There is no more "mass market" in which to target a product. There is no one demographic picture of the planet. I recently saw cultural anthropologist Grant McCracken speak, and he discussed how, while lifestyle typologies expanded to first three, then six, then nine and then twelve typologies, there is now too much variation, and we have

reached categorical exhaustion. As a result, I have come to believe that the term *brand design* ultimately undermines the job we do as brand consultants, marketers, designers and strategists. Brand design is not only about design. It is the perfect, meticulously crafted balance of cultural anthropology, behavioral psychology, commerce and creativity. It is about cultural anthropology because what we do in our culture—whether it is an obsession with celebrity or politics or weather—has a major impact on the brands around us. It is about psychology because if we don't fundamentally understand the brain circuitry of our audience and really know what they are thinking—and why they are thinking it!—we will not be able to solicit their imagination. It is about commerce because understanding the marketplace

1

2

3

4

and the messaging impacts and influences perception. It is about creativity because if we don't create a compelling package, then consumers won't notice it and buy it. So, short answer, I take this responsibility very, very seriously.

So when you are not strategizing about the next item currently sitting in our fridges, you devote a lot of your time—six months a year—to Design Matters, your live Internet radio show, now in its fifth season. Besides skipping sleep altogether, how do you go about putting together each show?

The first thing necessary for a great show is a great guest. I have an endless list of artists, designers and thinkers that I admire, and I start several months before each season by personally e-mailing or calling folks and inviting them on the show. This is actually extremely diffi-

> **"As far as my love for this business—'Who casts not up his eye to the sun when it rises?' All I know is that design is in my DNA."**

cult, as I have to book twenty-five guests before I even go on the air, and I am often scheduling guests between three months to nearly a year in advance. After my guest list is secured, Jen Simon (my chief researcher) amasses as much material as she can on my guests: books, articles, reviews and so forth. Jen is an amazing librarian, and she culls material that I use to develop the questions I pose to my guests (which I develop in the week before the show). I also begin the show each week with a monologue wherein I try to weave together several threads: cultural commentary, a personal anecdote and something that is either inspired by my

guest, or something I think they would appreciate. Altogether, the preparation for each show is about ten to fifteen hours per week. Or it could be more if my guest is also a writer, and I need to read or re-read everything they have published! But I love every second of it!

On top of being exhausting, it must be exhilarating to interview all these amazing people. What have you discovered, in general, about dealing with the industry's leading practitioners?

Other than Massimo Vignelli and Milton Glaser (who are both in their 70s), everyone is insecure. Everyone wonders

[1] Identity and packaging of Celestial Seasonings Tea for Hain Celestial (2007). **[2]** Identity for Burger King (2002). **[3]** Identity and packaging of Gevalia Tea for Kraft Foods North America (2003). **[4]** Identity of Hellmann's Mayonnaise for Unilever Foods (2005).

if they're good enough or smart enough or brave enough. Everyone.

You also write. A lot. You have been contributing to Speak Up since 2003, you write a column for Print magazine and, as of this writing, you have published two books. What is it about writing on design that keeps you going at it?

Not knowing the answers to the questions I still have.

As though all of this wasn't enough, you also find the time to teach at the School of Visual Arts, where your class is probably the only one of its kind: teaching designers how to talk about design. What prompted you to take this on?

I think when we give something of ourselves, what we get in return is immeasurable. We might be giving back because someone gave to us, or we are giving back because we know we should. Either way, when we do this, something remarkable happens: We get a uniquely human, mutually-shared experience. And in that experience, continuity develops. You give something away, you get something in return, and the cycle is perpetuated. I had a lot of great teachers along the way. They profoundly impacted who I am. I realized that what I was taught about design and business I didn't learn in school, and I wanted to help prepare a new generation of designers with what has taken me my whole career to learn. Plus, I never stop learning from my students. They keep me on my toes!

And just to clarify... You are not a graphic designer, per se. So why so much love and passion for this profession?

Actually, I studied design, and the first ten years of my career were as a practicing designer. But in order to work at Frankfurt Balkind (in 1993), Aubrey Balkind would only hire me as a salesperson. I would've worked there as the janitor, if that is what it would've taken to get a job there. That started me down a different path that I've journeyed ever since. I found that I had a natural inclination for business development, which grew into running accounts, which grew into running a business.

As far as my love for this business—"Who casts not up his eye to the sun when it rises?" All I know is that design is in my DNA.

[5] Identity and packaging of Tropicana Pure Premium Orange Juice for PepsiCo North America (2006). [6] Identity of Optimum for Cablevision (2004).
[7] Identity, bottle design and packaging of Four Roses Bourbon for Seagram (1999). [8] Identity and packaging of Hershey's Bar for Hershey's Chocolate (2002).

"*I find writing hard, and I am very slow. But when a paragraph or even a phrase turns out as well as I'd imagined it, I get such a giddy rush that I lose all memory of the pain.*"

Alice
Twemlow

DEBORAH
ADLER

NATIONALITY	American
YEAR BORN	1975
CURRENTLY RESIDING IN	New York, New York, United States
YEARS IN THE BUSINESS	5
CURRENT POSITION/FIRM	Senior designer, Milton Glaser, Inc
DESIGN EDUCATION	MFA, design, School of Visual Arts (2002)

It is not your typical graduate thesis project that lands on the shelves of nearly 1,500 Target stores nationwide, but the revolutionary proposal by Deborah Adler in her 2002 thesis at SVA's designer as author MFA program achieved the unthinkable. Adler's effort of heroic proportions—updating a design problem that had been unaddressed for the past half century—allowed her to establish a partnership with Target and a collaboration with Milton Glaser that has been widely celebrated and acknowledged in the mainstream media. A happy side effect of this was that Adler landed a coveted position working for Glaser, working on identity systems, magazines, book jackets, product packaging, and restaurant interiors—not a bad return on her education investment.

1

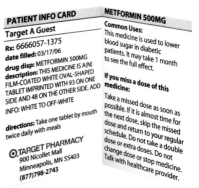

[1] *Packaging of ClearRx prescription system for Target Corporation (2005).*

2

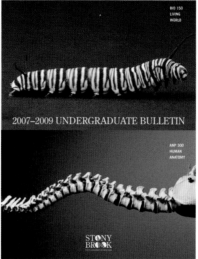

3

4

KIND

5

Jonathan Teller
Managing Partner

The Kind Group
27 W 24th St Suite 10-C
New York, NY 10010
Tel: 212 645 0800 x11
Fax: 212 645 0755
Mobile: 212 203 6184
jonathan@thekindgroup.com

6

KIND

7

"I used to work on projects endlessly. At 4:50 p.m., on April 28, 2007, it all changed—my daughter, Sophia, was born and my new role as mother overruled all others. Now I've found ways to return to my design career, working with Milton and in other ventures on my own. So these days I'm dividing my time between the endless mysteries of motherhood and the wondrous satisfactions of design."

[2] Bulletin covers for Stony Brook University* (2005-06). [3, 6] Jasmine Food Court at Stony Brook University* (2006). [4, 5] Logo and business card for The Kind Group (2007). [7] Packaging system of Advanced Wound Care for Medline Industries, Inc.* (2007).

*Art direction by Milton Glaser.

KING

NATIONALITY	British
YEAR BORN	1967
CURRENTLY RESIDING IN	London, United Kingdom

YEARS IN THE BUSINESS

I am not sure when business started, or if it ever has. I graduated with a BA in 1989, an MA in 1993 and a Ph.D. in 2000, but I always worked alongside and in between, teaching first and later writing.

CURRENT POSITION/FIRM

No firm, no position, just me.

DESIGN EDUCATION

MA, history of design, RCA/V&A (1993)
Ph.D., with a thesis concentrating on the design of type, Kingston University, London (2000)

Working independently, yet in collaboration with other designers and authors, Emily King has contributed a range of unique books to the design canon. With Restart: New Systems in Graphic Design, A Century of Movie Posters: From Silent to Art House, and C/ID: Visual Identity and Branding for the Arts, King brings together a sophisticated selection of work aided by her commanding writing. In the astounding Robert Brownjohn: Sex and Typography, she weaves together the life and work of this influential designer. With an endless thirst for exploring design topics and a desire to bring them to the attention of those outside the profession, it's reassuring to know that our collective stories and work are in capable hands.

In your Master's thesis Taking Credit: Film title sequences, 1955–1965, you thank notable designers such as Saul Bass and Alan Fletcher for helping with your research. Looking back, how have these interactions impacted your career? Any suggestions on how to approach big name designers, a usually intimidating task for students?

If you are contacting a big name designer, or anyone you admire, you must be aware that they have been approached many times before. It is only good manners to read and research to the fullest extent, to the point that you are sure that any question you plan to ask has not been answered elsewhere. Eventually this will work out much better for you too, as you will come away with original, relevant and more interesting information. I did not follow my own advice when I contacted Saul Bass. He had the good grace

to meet me in his studio, but all I did was pitch him a bunch of questions he had been asked many times before. He gave me fabulous answers, but over the course of my research I discovered that they were word-for-word anecdotes, which is no more than I deserved. Similarly, I didn't do adequate research before my first encounter with Alan, but we had a combative and eventually fun encounter that was the basis for lots of future work.

When you are telling a story, or setting down a historical track, it is fantastic to meet the protagonists. A face-to-face encounter helps you understand and sense things that are inaccessible otherwise. Sitting across from Bass, looking at him over the sea of small African and Asian sculptures that covered his desk, overhearing a conversation with his wife

about that night's dinner, gave me a sense of his story, in spite of my bad manners in not having done my research properly. Similarly, drinking whisky with Alan in the Pentagram studio in Needham Road, with its nineteenth-century Lyons Teashop sign pinned to the raw brick wall, gave me a feel (almost a smell) for the evolution of design in Britain in the 1960s and 1970s.

If you have something important and original to ask, you should never feel intimidated. If you just want to see someone to tick them off your list, then you should not have the presumption to take up their time.

And a particular bugbear: the very generalized questionnaire that would take an age to answer properly, yet is in no way aimed specifically at its subject

1

2

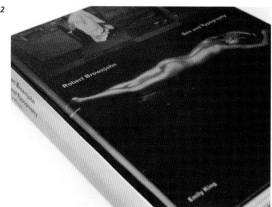

(the opposite of this very well-researched, thoughtful set of questions). It is the height of bad manners to send these things out indiscriminately, and I cannot imagine why students do it!

Have you noticed any changes, for good or bad, in the the increase of design criticism and the understanding of graphic design by the general public?

If there has been any great change, I am not sure I have noticed it.

There is more graphic design criticism around, mostly online, but then there is more of every kind of writing. Proportionately, there may well be less attention paid to graphics. I don't think there is any greater understanding of graphic design by the general public. Sure, people practice it more on an amateur level and know the names of the fonts they use, but if anything that has become a barrier to the general understanding of how it can be a serious profession. I realize that this sounds snobbish, and I want to temper it by saying that I am not against the wide practice of graphic design at all—I love the way my daughter makes a title page for every one of her school projects and is encouraged to think visually—but I do think there is a gulf between that

and my historical focus (although, obviously, I would acknowledge that there are threads that connect the two). In terms of understanding how design describes and creates the world beyond being merely a service industry and recognizing that some design is truly great and that design is very difficult to do well, I am not sure things have changed at all in the period I have been writing in. If anything, I think the divorce between graphics and music has lessened public appreciation and understanding of design. I don't think anyone is following and analyzing design in the way that they did when, say, Peter Saville designed the record covers for Joy Division and New Order.

Most people still refuse to believe that I am not a design practitioner, or at least a frustrated design practitioner. Art historians are the worst in this respect: In general they seem unable to grasp that my relationship to design is the same as theirs to art. They seem unable to acknowledge that design could be worthy of study. Generally, I try and explain my position by saying that I am not a designer manqué, but a historian manqué. This people seem to understand, but it is depressing that I can only clarify what I do in negative terms.

And, to keep up the negative tone, I think a lot of designers still don't acknowledge that a valid history can emerge outside of practice. Very recently a prominent British graphic designer told me that he didn't believe that non-designers could have any insight into graphic design history. Bless him, I think he thought I was a designer myself.

In 2005 you published a biography, Robert Brownjohn: Sex and Typography, on the very talented yet troubled designer. Why were you attracted to this particular profile?

I was immediately drawn to the subject by my interest in film title sequences, which is the subject of my MA thesis. The opportunity to write about Robert Brownjohn emerged when his daughter Eliza moved to London with an amazing archive. For me the most exciting part of the project, apart from Brownjohn's brilliant work and posthumous charisma, was the way in which the story threaded through the history of twentieth-century design. With the link back via Moholy-Nagy to the Bauhaus, through mid-century American modernism, New York in the jazz era, and into 1960s London pop, the story of Brownjohn's life and work prompted me to rethink the connections between various highpoints of graphic design history and,

[1] Restart: New Systems in Graphic Design, *by Christian Küsters and Emily King, Universe (2001).* **[2]** Robert Brownjohn: Sex and Typography, *by Emily King, Princeton Architectural Press (2005).*

3

4

indeed, the broader cultural history of the twentieth century.

Another key project was curating the retrospective of Alan Fletcher, one of the most celebrated and well-known designers, for the London Design Museum in the fall of 2006. Fletcher passed away shortly before the show opened. Can you talk about this whole experience?

Curating the retrospective of Alan Fletcher's work was an enormous honor. Alan embodied what it is to be a graphic designer in Britain; in fact, he pretty much invented the British manifestation of the profession. His work formed the basis of much of the design thinking of the last fifty years and remains extremely relevant today. To be the first historian to trawl through his archive in its entirety and tell his story was a fantastic privilege.

We were very lucky that Alan was involved in much of the planning of the show, but losing him that September was very painful. Obviously, I felt under a huge amount of pressure to do him justice. During this period I was very glad to have the support of Graphic Thought Fa-

cility, who were designing the show. Alan picked people carefully and while we went through a period of feeling anxious about creating a successful exhibition, we did know that he had positively chosen our input.

On the opening night I was very relieved to be told by Alan's family, colleagues and friends that I had created a picture of the designer that they had known.

You were recently the editor at Frieze—a magazine focused on contemporary art and culture—and curating exhibitions, but you are also writing for other publications such as 032C and Print. Is it challenging to go back and forth between being the editor and being edited? How do these varied activities shape your work?

I have just resigned as design editor of *Frieze*, handing the position on to Gina Bell, a very talented design writer who is currently based in New York. I enjoyed doing it a great deal but felt that after several years it was time to move on, and I also thought the magazine might benefit from relocating its design focus to the States for a time.

Among the things I most enjoyed about writing for *Frieze* was the slight shift in perspective involved in writing about design for an art audience. I am an avid follower of contemporary art, and writing for art readers—particularly the artists themselves—was an exciting challenge. It is interesting to look at one of your passions in the light of another.

In general I am much more interested in writing about design for non-specialist audiences. I want to tell broader cultural stories through the lens of design, and my ambition is to draw people's attention to the role of design for the first time. I have done some writing in mainstream newspapers and would love to do more, but (and this harks back to the issue about the interest of the general public) most dailies employ only architecture critics, choosing to cover the rest of design purely in terms of lifestyle, as things to buy.

I know part of the responsibility for this situation lies with me. I should hound those papers until they publish me. But while I am finding lots of other rewarding venues for my work, it is hard to get on the case.

[3] Movie Poster, *by Emily King, Mitchell Beazley (2003).* **[4]** Designed by Peter Saville, *edited by Emily King, Princeton Architectural Press (2003).*

"As for my office, it is anywhere I happen to be with my laptop and cell phone."

Jhoana
Mora

Detail of: Identity for Esquina Norte; organized and art directed by Jhoana Mora (2007).

NATIONALITY	
American	

YEAR BORN	
1969	

CURRENTLY RESIDING IN	
Peoria, Illinois, United States	

YEARS IN THE BUSINESS	
13	

CURRENT POSITION/FIRM	
Acquisitions editor, Rockport Publishers	

YEARS AT STEP	
12 (in two parts)	

DESIGN EDUCATION

My education was in journalism. Anything I learned about design was learned on the job, which turned out to be a great education!

EMILY
POTTS

As far as many young designers are concerned, the comprehensive and versatile STEP magazine found in today's newsstands has existed in its current format for ages. It certainly looks and feels that way, thanks in part to the watchful and guiding eye of Emily Potts, the magazine's editor for twelve years, who oversaw the overwhelming transformation from Step-by-Step Graphics—a magazine with a loyal readership that reveled in the practical advice and insight it offered—into STEP Inside Design in 2002, with a luscious new design and completely fresh editorial approach. In 2006 Potts left STEP to join Rockport as acquisitions editor, where she has procured authoring contributions from many of the industry relationships she has fostered throughout her career.

[1] STEP *magazine cover, "Women of Design" issue (November/December 2005).* **[2]** *"The Establishment" by Emily Potts,* STEP *magazine (November/ December 2005).* **[3]** *"Memorable Moments" by Aaris Sherin,* STEP *magazine (November/December 2005).*

"I love being a mom, and I love my work. It's quite a balancing act, but I wouldn't have it any other way. I hope that I'm setting a good example for my girls by demonstrating that women can be successful and fulfilled both professionally and personally. Of course, success is a relative term, and for me it's achieving this professional/personal balance."

[4] STEP magazine cover, "Premier Issue" issue (July/August 2002). [5] "Fresh Talent" by Michelle Taute, STEP magazine (March/April 2004). [6] "Designer Fetishes" by Romy Ashby, STEP magazine (November/December 2002). [7] "Ox" by Allan Haley, STEP magazine (July/August 2002). [8] STEP magazine ongoing feature "Q&A" [Where designers interview designers]. [9] STEP magazine page detail. [10] "5w's" by Emily Potts [Where the who, what, where, when and why of a topic is explored by a writer], STEP magazine (July/August 2002). [11] STEP magazine cover, "Design Annual 100" (March/April 2004).

ESTHER
MUN

NATIONALITY	Korean
YEAR BORN	1978
CURRENTLY RESIDING IN	New York, New York, United States
YEARS IN THE BUSINESS	7
CURRENT POSITION/FIRM	Partner, Little Fury
PREVIOUS EMPLOYMENT	Duffy & Partners (2003–05) Pentagram Design (2002–03)
DESIGN EDUCATION	BA, School of Visual Arts (2001)

Within a span of seven years Esther Mun has worked at two of the most recognized design firms, Pentagram and Duffy & Partners, where she has honed her packaging and identity sensibilities that allowed her to jumpstart her own design firm, Little Fury, as co-founder with Tina Chang—with whom she shares in common an education at the School of Visual Arts and moving to the U.S. from Korea at an early age. Mun and Chang are also co-founders of Start Here, a clever line of notebooks that can be linked together—perhaps a noble metaphor for these two young designers.

[1, 2] Identity and packaging of Help Remedy Products for Help Remedies, Inc.; structure design by ChappsMalina, Inc. (2007). [3] Rembrandt rebranding and packaging for Mother New York and Johnson & Johnson (2007).

TINA
CHANG

From Pentagram, to MTV, to the Public Theater and Martha Stewart Living Omnimedia, Tina Chang has amassed an enviable amount of experience producing work at these varied career stops. Along with her partner, Esther Mun, Chang is co-founder of Little Fury and Start Here—together they produce packaging and branding for a range of clients. Chang has taught at the School of Visual Arts (her alma mater) and served on the board of the AIGA New York chapter.

NATIONALITY
Korean

YEAR BORN
1976

CURRENTLY RESIDING IN
New York, New York, United States

YEARS IN THE BUSINESS
9

CURRENT POSITION/FIRM
Partner, Little Fury

PREVIOUS EMPLOYMENT
Martha Stewart Living Omnimedia (2005-06)
MTV (2003)
Pentagram Design (1999-2003)

DESIGN EDUCATION
BA, School of Visual Arts (1999)

1

2

3

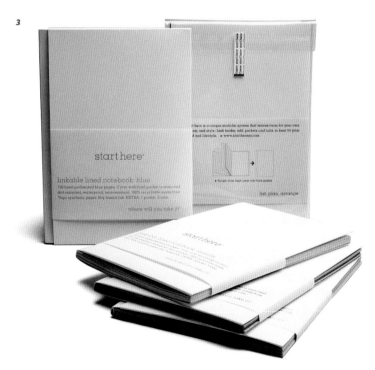

[1, 2] Rembrandt rebranding and packaging for Mother New York and Johnson & Johnson (2007). [3] Start Here product line by Little Fury (ongoing).

NATIONALITY	French
YEAR BORN	1977
CURRENTLY RESIDING IN	Paris, France
YEARS IN THE BUSINESS	7
CURRENT POSITION/FIRM	Independent graphic designer
PREVIOUS EMPLOYMENT	Atelier de Création Graphique (2001–04) Qui Resiste (2000–01)
DESIGN EDUCATION	Ecole Nationale Supérieure des Arts Décoratifs, Paris (2000)

FANETTE
MELLIER

Through an exquisite color sensibility and a penchant for pleasing geometric figures, the work of Fanette Mellier feels remarkably unique and unconventional. After graduating from the prominent École Nationale Supérieure des Arts Décoratifs, Mellier spent seven months with type designer Pierre di Sciullo and then three years with legendary French designer Pierre Bernard. Since 2004, Mellier has worked as an independent designer producing work for cultural institutions through poster, book and identity design. Mellier also designs typefaces—some incredibly unconventional and intriguing—that are usually found throughout her projects, further authenticating her individual approach to design.

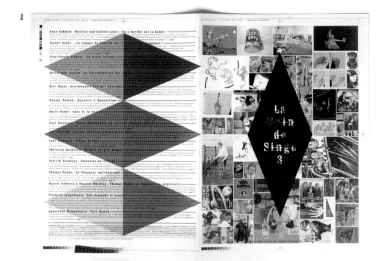

[1] Design of La Main de Singe, a literature newspaper (2005). [2] Street posters of a poem by Laure Limongi, as placed during the "Graphisme dans la rue" festival (2007). [3] Cover design for R. by Céline Minard, where the ink was changed on press to produce alternate colors (2003).

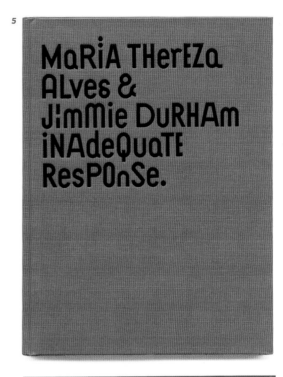

[4] Design of the cultural booklet Sortir à Gentilly *(2006–07). [5] Art catalogue for* Maria Thereza Alves and Jimmie Durham Inadequate Response *(2007). [6] Poster for* Biennale de la jeune creation, *Houilles (2006). [7] Book cover for* Dans la zone d'activité *by Eric Chevillard (2007).*

GEORGIANNA
STOUT

NATIONALITY	American
YEAR BORN	1967
CURRENTLY RESIDING IN	Brooklyn, New York, United States
YEARS IN THE BUSINESS	13
CURRENT POSITION/FIRM	Partner and creative director, 2x4, Inc.
PREVIOUS EMPLOYMENT	Bethany Johns Design (1990-93)
DESIGN EDUCATION	BFA, Rhode Island School of Design (1989)

As one of the founders of 2x4—along with Susan Sellers and Michael Rock—Georgianna Stout has led the branding, identity, retail and environmental programs for a veritable range of cultural institutions, including the Brooklyn Museum, Dia:Beacon, and the Museum of the Moving Image, as well as packaging for products like the typographi- cally-gifted Malin+Goetz. Before 2x4, Stout was a designer for Bethany Johns Design, where her affinity for sublime solutions for art organizations and cultural institutions was first fostered.

1

2

[1, 2] Identity, publication, merchandising, and signage program for the Brooklyn Museum; design with Michael Rock, Alex Lin, Eddie Opara, Katie Andresen, Dan Michaelson and Albert Lee; photographs by floto+warner (2004).

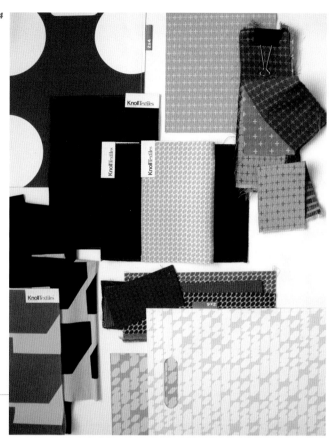

[3] *"Pause" vinyl wall covering and "Plus" upholstery from the Chatter Collection for Knoll Textiles; design with Albert Lee and Dan Michaelson* (2004).*
[4] *Field Theory Collection and Chatter Collections, comprising of woven upholstery fabric, printed technical fabric and printed vinyl wall covering for Knoll Textiles; design with Albert Lee and Dan Michaelson* (2004).* **[5, 6]** *Branding, retail, packaging, web and environmental design for Malin+Goetz; design with Anisa Suthayalai and Kiki Katahira (2004).*

* Images courtesy of Knoll

SUSAN
SELLERS

NATIONALITY	American
YEAR BORN	1967
CURRENTLY RESIDING IN	New York, New York, United States
YEARS IN THE BUSINESS	13
CURRENT POSITION/FIRM	Partner and creative director, 2x4, Inc.
PREVIOUS EMPLOYMENT	Total Design, Amsterdam (1990) UNA, Amsterdam (1991)
DESIGN EDUCATION	MA, American studies, Yale University (1994) BFA, Rhode Island School of Design (1989)

Before founding 2x4 with partners Georgianna Stout and Michael Rock, Susan Sellers spent time in Amsterdam working for renowned firms Total Design and UNA. At 2x4, Sellers oversees identity and branding projects, as well as book design for cultural institutions around the world, including Museo Picasso Málaga in Spain and the Guggenheim Museums in New York and Berlin. She is a visiting critic at the Yale University School of Art, where she received her master's degree and explored, as her faculty bio states, "mid-nineteenth-century labor practices in craft industries of printing and typesetting and the emergence of professionalized design practices." Sellers also writes about design for publications like Eye, Design Issues, *and* Visible Language.

1

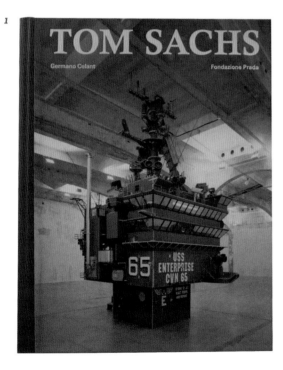

2

[1, 2] Tom Sachs exhibition catalogue for the Fondazione Prada; design with Kiki Katahira and Anisa Suthayalai (2006).

"*Now that I have children I divide my time between my studio life and home life. This is a constant negotiation that changes day by day, week by week.*"

[3, 5] Identity for the Museo Picasso Málaga; design with Sarah Gephardt, Alex Lin, Dan Michaelson, and Michael Rock (2003). [4] Identity for International Women's Health Coalition (2000). [6, 7] Exhibition design of "Saadiyat Island Cultural District Masterplan" for the Guggenheim Foundation; design with Natasha Jen and Martijn Deurloo, Fabienne Hess, Kiki Katahira, Sung Kim, Daniel Koppich, and Abigail Smith (2007). [8, 9] Exhibition design of "Peeping Probing and Porn" of Japanese Shunga, for the Museum of Sex; design with Fabienne Hess and Anisa Suthayalai (2006).

Photo by Tejo Krijgsman

NATIONALITY
Dutch

YEAR BORN
1960

CURRENTLY RESIDING IN
Amsterdam, The Netherlands

YEARS IN THE BUSINESS
23

CURRENT POSITION/FIRM
Principal, Irma Boom Office

PREVIOUS EMPLOYMENT
Dutch government publishing and
printing office in The Hague (1985–91)

DESIGN EDUCATION
AKI School of Fine Art, Enschede

Sculptural, epic, and dramatic are not typical adjectives for the physical presence and design of a book—unless designed by Irma Boom. Unconventional in size, overall volume, printing methods and design structures, her books defy expectations and conventions: running more than 2,000 pages, using eighty spot colors on press, and inventing new paper are only a few of her undertakings. Since 1991, when she opened her own studio, with an impeccable pacing of content and memorable construction of the object itself, Boom's work has garnered awards—including the "Most Beautiful Book in the World" prize at the Leipzig Book Fair—and awe from the industry. She teaches at Yale's MFA graphic design program and at the Van Eyck Academy in Maastricht.

1
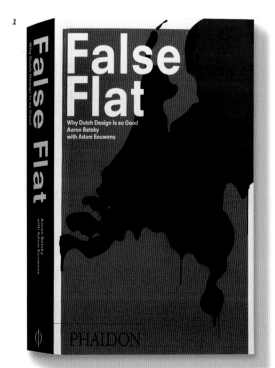

2
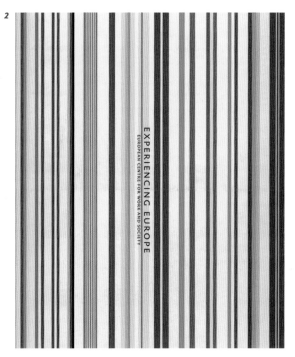

[1] *Book design for* False Flat: Why Dutch Design Is So Good *(2004).* **[2]** *Book design for* Experiencing Europe, *European Centre for Work and Society (2004).*

3

[3] *Book design for Dutch company SHV (1996).*

4

5

[4] Book design for Rotterdams Kookboek *(2004). [5] Book design for* Otto Treumann Graphic Design in The Netherlands *(2001).*

6

7

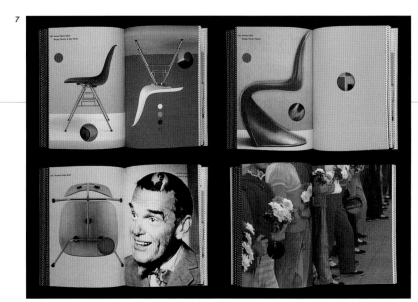

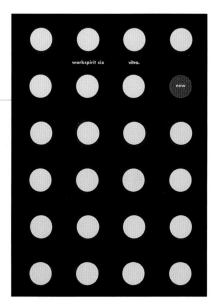

8

[6] Book design for Sheila Hicks: Weaving as Metaphor *(2006). [7] Book design for* Vitra Work Spirit *(1998). [8] Postage stamps for the Royal Dutch PTT (post office) (1993).*

JHOANA
MORA

NATIONALITY	Mexican
YEAR BORN	1975
CURRENTLY RESIDING IN	Tijuana, Mexico
YEARS IN THE BUSINESS	12
CURRENT POSITION/FIRM	Organizer, International Design Conference "Esquina Norte" (secretary, best girl, logistics, public relations, Reiki therapist, assistant, translator, fundraiser, driver, babysitter, gaffer, entertainer, art director, maintenance, operator, media coordinator, promoter, administrator, etc.)
PREVIOUS EMPLOYMENT	PR, event coordinator and project manager
DESIGN EDUCATION	BFA, graphic design, summa cum laude, Universidad Iberoamericana, Mexico City (1998)

Since 2001 some of the world's best graphic designers—April Greiman (U.S.), Neville Brody (UK), Ken Cato (Australia)—have traveled to one of the most intriguing destinations in Mexico to talk about design: Tijuana, and specifically to Esquina Norte, the conference founded and organized independently by Jhoana Mora, a tireless champion of exposing design professionals and students to the best the profession has to offer. Mora was founder of the AIGA Baja Chapter in 1999, and has been involved in event planning and promotion for more than a decade. Resourceful and creative, Mora is sought after by cultural institutions—and even the groundbreaking band Nortec Collective—to coordinate their events and exhibits.

Most internationally acclaimed design conferences are put together by established organizations that count on staff to help manage the details and can leverage partnerships with generous sponsors. You do Esquina Norte by yourself. How?

Well, in the only way you can organize an event in Mexico: without asking others for input, without depending on any institutions or companies, and without looking for support from a community that does not have a culture of sponsoring events of this nature. The big companies that "support" cultural activities will not get involved in a small event that will not give them a significant

Esquina Norte logo; design by Eduardo Escobar (2001).

return in increased sales or will not place their huge logos throughout the city. We never have to wonder about money either, because there never is any! So I try to get things as gifts, on loan, or in exchange; what little support we get in cash allows me to give scholarships and discounts to students with high GPAs or limited income, and to create a venue that serves as inspiration to over 3,000 Mexican, American and Latin American students.

I do several activities on my own, from inviting speakers, to defining logistics, seeking sponsorship, making purchases and even putting up posters all over town. The only thing I don't do directly is create the event image; this is done by several designer friends, under my art direction.

I get help from students from the different universities—they either volunteer or count the experience as their social service requirement. They help me assemble name tags, fill participant goody bags, pick up speakers at the airport and, most importantly, make decisions at critical moments, all of which will no doubt help them in their future profession, and without which Esquina Norte would not be possible.

Many people wonder why I don't have a sizable work team like other events, or why I don't even have an office. The answer is simple and logical: While many people have offered to help, once they discover that there isn't a lot of money to be made, their enthusiasm fades. Fortunately, there are always the few I can count on unconditionally, and to whom I am infinitely grateful. As for my office, it is anywhere I happen to be with my laptop and cell phone.

Esquina Norte is undeniable proof that things can be done the right way, as long as they are done with stewardship, organization and commitment. In 2003, designer Marc English wrote an article about the conference for *Communication Arts* magazine entitled "Esquina Norte Proves MexiCANs."

With a number of other design conferences throughout Mexico, what do you think attracts so many attendees to Esquina Norte?

I believe there are several factors that contribute to Esquina Norte being so well attended. First, the quality and diversity of speakers: graphic, industrial, and fashion designers; plastic and visual artists; photographers; illustrators; architects; and typographers—everyone from international design gurus to young and promising creators, who in many cases had never set foot in Mexico as speakers at a conference.

Another important factor is that from the very beginning I wanted to set us clearly apart from other conferences, being true to the project and doing activities that aren't even being considered by other venues yet, such as having participants enter into direct contact with the speakers, whether to just ask for an autograph or even to go out for a beer on their free time; or giving a better value

to the students by including in the admission price a five-hour workshop with one of the conference speakers, at no additional cost. Furthermore, it is the only event of its kind that includes high school students; starting with the 2005 edition, I implemented a successful special pricing program for high school students, which more than surpassed all my expectations. Its goal: to improve the academic performance and involvement of university freshmen, as well as to expand their career alternatives.

Over the last seven years I have sought to create a special vibe at the event where people can feel at home and have the freedom to ask questions, give their opinion, debate and work as a team.

And, of course, the city that serves as its host, Tijuana, is an enigmatic city with many legends about it, which builds excitement; Esquina Norte is a great excuse to visit it. Known by some for being a cultural melting pot, a good party spot, home to cartels and kitsch, and by others only through the Manu Chao song that says, "...Welcome to Tijuana: tequila, sex and marijuana," which serves as a suggestive invitation for many.

Do you have any ambitions for future editions of this conference?

I once said that the second edition of Esquina Norte would be the last because of all the hard work and time it requires. I have been thinking of putting together a compilation book, to be presented at the 2010 edition of Esquina Norte, which means the conference will last at least until then. I have no book publishing experience, so I think putting it together will take me some time, but I want it to include bios, the works, comments, as well as a special message from all past conference speakers, along with a DVD with excerpts from the most representative presentations and a photo gallery.

After that I will think hard about the future of this conference and decide whether the conference continues or if I want to change its direction, perhaps, or, I don't know, perhaps spend more time on my personal life.

In the meantime, I would love for outstanding designers, film directors, photographers, and creative minds in other disciplines to continue sharing their experiences with us. I'd like Esquina Norte to be, as it has always been, more than a display where we can look at their work as if flipping through a book, but a place where they can continue infusing us with their energy, their ideals, their work, their passion for design, and their dreams.

[1] *Name badges for all Esquina Norte conferences (2001–07).* **[2]** *Esquina Norte 2007 Conference (2007).* **[3]** *Rinzen workshop at Esquina Norte 2007 (2007).*

NATIONALITY
American
YEAR BORN
1963
CURRENTLY RESIDING IN
Brooklyn, New York, United States
YEARS IN THE BUSINESS
22
CURRENT POSITION/MAGAZINE
Editor-in-chief, *Print* magazine
YEARS AT *PRINT*
10 (5 as editor-in-chief, 5 as managing editor)

JOYCE
RUTTER KAYE

Stepping in for Martin Fox, who was editor of Print for more than forty years until 2003, Joyce Rutter Kaye never missed a beat—and, in fact, she has now established her own—in continuing the traditional high standards of critical and provocative writing that have come to define the magazine since it was first published in 1940. Kaye had worked as managing editor for five years at the magazine before taking on the principal editorial position—and prior to Print she was managing editor of the revered U&lc—where she has led it to two National Magazine Awards for General Excellence and, more significantly, to a continued interest from the design community.

1

2

3

[1] Print magazine covers. [2] "Some Like It Ri Nao" by Daniel Elsea, Print magazine (September/October 2006). [3] "Falling Leaves" by Herbert A. Friedman, Print magazine (September/October 2003).

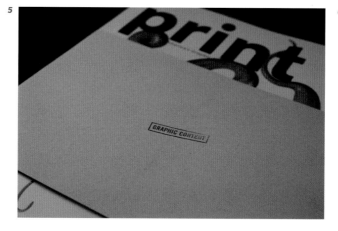

"A typical day could involve any of the following: line editing features and departments; planning future themes and articles; reviewing cover and layout directions; meeting with contributors; planning competition judgings; having status meetings with the staff; dealing with business-side issues related to circulation, advertising, marketing, web traffic and budgets; fielding story pitches; reading news sites, blogs and magazines; reviewing portfolios; maybe attending exhibition openings or talks; then, going home to my other job, as a mom of two boys."

[4] *"It Takes a Village" by Tom Vanderbilt,* Print *magazine (September/October 2003).* [5] Print *magazine cover, "Sex Issue" (July/August 2004).* [6] *Cover detail.* [7] *"For Openers" by Steven Heller,* Print *magazine (January/February 2005).* [8] *"Truth and Reconciliation" by Edward Lovett,* Print *magazine (January/February 2005).* [9] *"Sweet Spot" by Tristan Taormino,* Print *magazine (July/August 2004).* [10] *"Thinking Images" by John Canemaker,* Print *magazine (September/October 2006).*

"*My approach has been to find ways to incorporate the teaching of basic skills into broader, more collaborative contexts. In essence, like many of my colleagues in design education, I'm seeking to double up on instruction.*"

Marcia
Lausen

Detail of: *Proposed Cook County ballot (2000).*

JULIA
HOFFMANN

In ten years, Julia Hoffmann has stretched her design career from Frankfurt, Germany, to Boulder, Colorado, stopping at a handful of design landmarks. Springing from a BFA at the School of Visual Arts and a healthy dose of internships, Hoffman worked at Doyle Partners for nearly a year before joining Paula Scher's team at Pentagram, where her work bloomed over the course of almost four years through posters, packaging, book and identity design. In a considerable change, Hoffmann joined the advertising powerhouse Crispin Porter + Bogusky, where she leads a range of projects, including interactive and advertising. Hoffmann's youthful enthusiasm and design abilities have been rewarded with Young Gun honors from the Art Directors Club and Print magazine's New Visual Artists (under 30).

NATIONALITY

German

YEAR BORN

1977

CURRENTLY RESIDING IN

Boulder, Colorado, United States

YEARS IN THE BUSINESS

5

CURRENT POSITION/FIRM

Creative Director, The Museum of Modern Art (MoMA)

PREVIOUS EMPLOYMENT

Art director and senior interactive designer,
Crispin Porter + Bogusky (2007-08)
Pentagram Design (2003-07)
Doyle Partners (2003)

DESIGN EDUCATION

BFA, School of Visual Arts (2002)

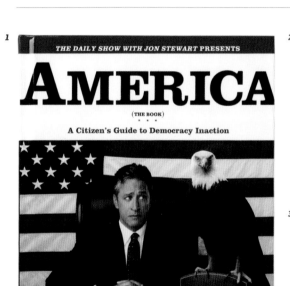

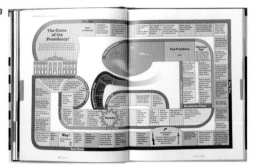

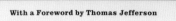

All work created at Pentagram, under Paula Scher's creative direction. **[1, 2, 3]** *Design and illustrations for* The Daily Show with Jon Stewart Presents America (The Book): A Citizen's Guide to Democracy Inaction *by Jon Stewart and the writers of The Daily Show, Warner Books (2004).*

4

24 hours of Julia's life:

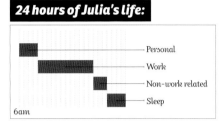

Personal

Work

Non-work related

Sleep

6am

5

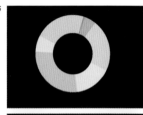

6

7

8

9

[4, 6, 8] Campaign for The Metropolitan Opera (New York) 2006-07 season (2006). [5, 7] Redesign of the Criterion Collection, including an onscreen animation and DVD packaging (2007). [9] Identity and collateral redesign of POV (2005-07).

JULIE
LASKY

NATIONALITY
American

YEAR BORN
1960

CURRENTLY RESIDING IN
New York, New York, United States

YEARS IN THE BUSINESS
25

CURRENT POSITION/FIRM
Editor-in-chief, *I.D.* magazine

YEARS AT I.D.
5

PREVIOUS EMPLOYMENT
Editor-in-chief, *Interiors* magazine (1998–2001)
Managing editor, *Print* magazine

DESIGN EDUCATION
On the job

Structuring a magazine that draws content from almost every area of the broad topic of design requires an endlessly curious and willfully open approach to interpret them—a job perfectly suited for Julie Lasky. As the editor-in-chief of I.D. magazine since 2002, Lasky has guided it to become one of the few publications that equally embraces all forms of design and typically does so in an innovative manner, both in its writing and in its presentation of information. Lasky was previously managing editor of Print magazine and editor-in-chief of Interiors magazine. Her dedication to a journalistic approach has earned her a Columbia University National Arts Journalism Program fellowship and a Richard J. Margolis Award for journalism, and she was a Journalism Scholar in 1995 at Northwestern University.

1

2

3

[1, 2] I.D. magazine cover and spread "Design and Religion" issue (March/April 2006). [3] I.D. magazine recurring feature.

Time well spent at I.D. magazine:

— Reviewing new design projects via post, e-mail, studio visits, trade-show attendance, product launches, site visits, boutique openings, and office meetings
— Managing staff and collaborating with other departments on promotion and marketing of magazine
— Editing and writing magazine content

[4] I.D. magazine cover "Design and Religion" issue (March/April 2006). **[5]** I.D. magazine cover contents detail. **[6]** I.D. magazine cover "Mighty Materials" issue (March/April 2005). **[7]** I.D. magazine ".../n+n" spread (March/April 2005). **[8]** I.D. magazine recurring feature. **[9]** "Ornament Decriminalized" by Steven Holt and Mara Holt Skov, I.D. magazine (March/April 2007). **[10]** I.D. magazine cover "Don't Hate Me Because I'm Beautiful" issue (March/April 2007). **[11]** "Trying To Keep The Sabbath Wholly" by Jon Fasman, I.D. magazine (March/April 2006). **[12]** "The Artists Doth Protest" by Diane Vadino, I.D. magazine (March/April 2007).

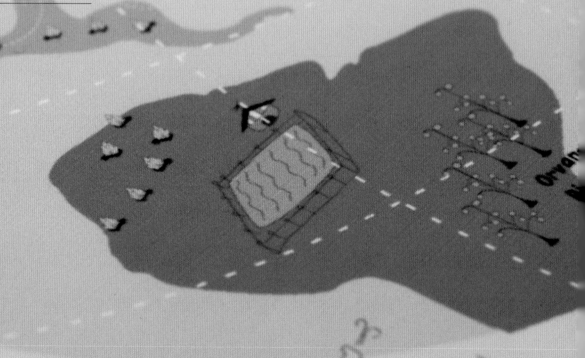

"The root of my interests is questions. I have many questions, and I often meet people who have similar questions. I find it important to put a form around these questions."

Amy
Franceschini

Detail of: F.R.U.I.T. poster for Smart Museum of Art, University of Chicago (2004).

KARIN
FONG

NATIONALITY	American
YEAR BORN	Year of the Pig
CURRENTLY RESIDING IN	New York, New York, United States
YEARS IN THE BUSINESS	14
CURRENT POSITION/FIRM	Director and designer, Imaginary Forces
PREVIOUS EMPLOYMENT	WGBH Boston (1993–94) R/GA (1994–96)
DESIGN EDUCATION	BA, art, Yale University, and collaborating with talented people ever since

Movies with Imaginary Forces-designed opening titles are instantly recognizable—not through mere style and execution (something they excel at, of course), but rather through their recurring playfulness, limitless creativity, and their ability to tell a full story even before the feature film has begun. Since 1994, when she was hired by Kyle Cooper, at then-named RGA/LA, Karin Fong has been producing work spaning film, television and built environments that never ceases to delight through an arsenal of illustrative- and typographic-driven approaches. Fong's work is not limited to movie theaters and living rooms; it's equally engaging in art installations or large-scale stage productions, like the 27'-diameter screen with accompanying 45' × 90' waterfall at Wynn Las Vegas hotel and casino, where she composed two- and three-minute projections.

1

[1] *Herman Miller "Get Real" promotional film; design with Grant Lau and Dan Meehan; edited by Mark Hoffman; for Fairly Painless Advertising Agency; creative direction by Peter Bell; agency art direction by Julie Lasky (2003).*

[2] Zoom, *feature film prologue; designed with Jyoteen Majmudar; illustration by Alex Maleev; animation by Stan Lim, Paul Yeh, Bradley Grosh, Arya Senboutaraj, Ian Kim and Daryn Wakasa; editing by Justine Gerenstein and Danielle White; for Revolution Studios (2006).* **[3]** Dr. Seuss' The Cat in the Hat, *feature film main title; designed with Chun-chien Lien; illustration by Brett Krauss; animation by David Alexander, Chris Pickenpaugh and Brian Castleforte; for Universal Studios, DreamWorks SKG and Imagine Entertainment (2003).* **[4]** Dead Man on Campus, *feature film main title; designed with Adam Bluming; illustration by Wayne Coe; editing by Kurt Mattila and Doron Dor; for MTV Films/Paramount Pictures (1998).*

KATHLEEN
MEANEY

NATIONALITY
American

YEAR BORN
1971

CURRENTLY RESIDING IN
Raleigh, North Carolina, United States

YEARS IN THE BUSINESS
11

CURRENT POSITION/FIRM
Designer, Terms & Conditions
Professor, NCSU College of Design

PREVIOUS EMPLOYMENT
Pentagram Design (1997-2001)
Professor, School of Visual Arts (2002-04)

DESIGN EDUCATION
BA (1993), BFA (1994), University of Notre Dame
MFA, Indiana University (1997)

As a result from an uncompromising sense of humor and a restrained design sensibility, the work of Kathleen Meaney feels jubilant and accessible, without ever sacrificing seriousness. Her writing is an even more convincing example of her traits. After five years working with Michael Bierut at Pentagram in New York, Meaney established North Carolina-based Terms & Conditions with partner Matthew Peterson in 2001 where they produce printed materials for clients like Chronicle Books and the New-York Historical Society. She is adjunct professor at NC State University's College of Design and a former faculty member of the School of Visual Arts in New York.

1

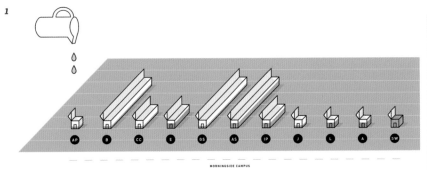

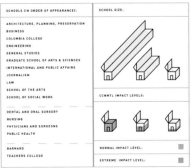

2

[1] *Progress chart for Columbia University, CCNMTL (2003).* **[2]** *Film titles for* Horsefingers *by Kirsten Kearse (2002 and 2008).*

3

4

5

6

7

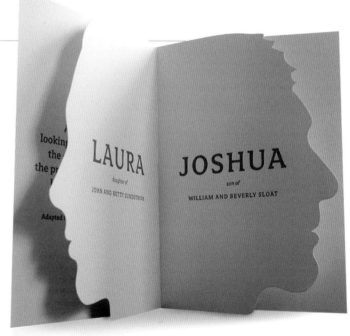

8

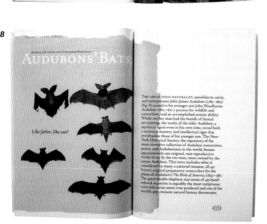

[3, 4, 6, 8] The New-York Journal of American History *by The New-York Historical Society (2001–present).* **[5]** *Clapping Penguin Card (2003).*
[7] *Janus Wedding Invitation for Sloat and Sundstrom (2005).*

KERSTIN
SCHEUCH

NATIONALITY
Austrian

YEAR BORN
1968

CURRENTLY RESIDING IN
Mexico City, Mexico

YEARS IN THE BUSINESS
15

CURRENT POSITION/FIRM
Director, general management,
CENTRO de diseño, cine y televisión

PREVIOUS EMPLOYMENT
Strategic consultant, Art Center College of Design
Executive consultant, ICE Strategy, KPMG Consulting
General Manager, Secession
Marketing and development, coordinator,
25th Council of Europe Exhibition, Künstlerhaus
Department Liaison and PR, Sotheby's Vienna

DESIGN EDUCATION
History of Art, Universities of Vienna
and St. Andrew's, Scotland

In June of 2008, the first generation of students from CENTRO—a new, fully accredited school in Mexico City offering degrees in architecture, film and television, visual communication, industrial design, textile design, and marketing—graduated from their four-year education at this groundbreaking institution. Ensuring that the institution meets its goals, as well as helping shape the experience at CENTRO—where she has been involved in its development since 2001—is Kerstin Scheuch, the school's director, whose wealth of international experience in cultural institutions like Sotheby's in Vienna, as well as consulting expertise for corporations like KPMG in London, assertively informs its growth.

While not a designer by education, your work has constantly revolved around the profession. Where is the magnetism? What has drawn your attention towards the world of design?

My fascination with design beyond an extension of the decorative arts and my collection of shoes developed slowly. It seems to me that the ubiquity of design is such that it is easily overlooked as form, taste, appearance, fashion… something exterior, not intrinsic. Work introduced me to the potential of design, first as a methodological tool and later as a way of thinking and re-thinking things.

During my time at the Secession (Contemporary Exhibition Hall, Vienna) we implemented a whole new graphic design concept by Heimo Zobernig for all printed material. It was very powerful: simple and complex at the same time, bold and sensitive, direct and subtle, independent and connected… It amazed me in terms of the response it generated from both the audience and the artists, and, I feel, it had an incredible impact on the entire institution for quite an extended period of time.

Later at KPMG I worked on a brand study for a major telecommunication company and all the evaluations showed that the design of the brand represented considerable additional value in regard to share price. This was eight years ago and studies by the British Design Council and other institutions have since confirmed this phenomenon: a lot of concretely measurable, financial value is created by design. (I guess this is my MBA fascination with design.)

However, working in education and in the context of Mexico, what currently interests me the most is the potential of design regarding humanitarian and environmental issues: Exhibitions, books and campaigns such as "Design for the other 90%" (Cooper Hewitt), "Design as if you give a damn" (Architecture for Humanity), and *Worldchanging: A User's Guide for the 21st Century* (Alex Steffen, Al Gore, and Stefan Sagmeister), have highlighted the ability of design in attracting attention to social problems, shaping opinions, promoting action and even solving truly pressing issues. I feel very lucky to be part of a structure that is involved in this process.

You recently relocated to Mexico City, where you are helping shape the new school CENTRO, which focuses in all areas of design. (Oh, how we wish the school had been around when we studied in Mexico.)

1

2

Being the first of its kind, what kind of cultural impact do you see the school having within the city? What has been the reaction from the student body and alumni?

Mexico has some very good design programs which are embedded within large, renowned universities. However, these design programs are not what the universities are known for, nor is it their main focus.

CENTRO's approach is different. It has given design, film, communication and creativity center stage. Our energy and all our resources are 100 percent dedicated to inspiring and generating excellence in the creative fields. Everybody and everything at CENTRO—students, faculty, conference speakers, administrative staff, building, equipment, exhibitions, signage, etc.—are part of this effort. We are forming an environment at CENTRO that inspires creativity and learning and that reflects the potential of ideas and their successful implementation.

We also spend a lot of time connecting people from different contexts, nationally and worldwide. We focus on improbable but necessary encounters that generate surprises, exchanges, ideas and collaborations—and thus contribute to opening up for new ways of thinking and doing.

However, the biggest impact will come from the students. In June 2008 the first generation will graduate (all of CENTRO's programs last four years). In this time, we have shaped each other, students have trusted us when we were new and didn't have a track record, and now, it is a lot easier for us to trust them. They will make a difference!

What were some of the challenges of building a school from the ground up? How do you compete against established institutions with reputable design and communication programs in the city?

The main challenge is to have a good idea: to imagine something that does not exist and that—once it exists—seems obvious. The second challenge is to find the key resources (people and money) to make it happen. Gina Diez Barroso de Franklin, the founder of CENTRO, took care of both of these challenges. She created the vision, she found the right people, and she invested her money (against all good advice). But maybe the most important aspect was that she was persistent to the point of stubbornness. She never questioned the idea and she never sacrificed quality.

Luckily, an exciting project like this, a "once in a lifetime" opportunity to truly change things at the roots (education!), manages to tempt and attract extremely talented and experienced people despite the fact that they are also extremely busy and occupied. The program directors are key: they carry the main responsibility, their enthusiasm and vision shapes the institution, but they also need freshness, restlessness, unwillingness to compromise, megalomania, pragmatism, a lot of humility, great relationship skills, and a profound dose of idealism—a tall order.

There is a quote by William Lethaby, which I like a lot: "An art school is generated only by the intensity and heat of a common pressure." I think one of the main challenges in building an educational institution is to open this quote beyond students and faculty and to understand that the administrative staff plays an intrinsic role. Before we opened CENTRO, we visited many design schools and we found that programs/faculty and administration were always treated as two completely separate entities and that this caused a lot of communication problems (at best) and power struggles and conflicts in most other cases. At CENTRO we have tried to form an integrated team; starting with the location of the offices—everybody is mixed together—and going all the way to

[1] *CENTRO de diseño, cine y televisión; architecture by studio F304 (Salvador Arroyo, Alejandro Hernández, Frederico Quiros and Juan Carlos Tello) (2004).*
[2] *CENTRO de diseño, cine y televisión façade; design by Jan Hendrix and Uzyel Karp (2004).*

decision making structures and processes. This is definitely not a comfortable solution (a lot of discussion!), but it is transparent and problems are identified and solved fast and together.

An initial list of goals, developed by the founders and the directors of the school, mentions the priority to raise the level of design education in Mexico City and beyond. We experience that the competition is getting stronger by the day and we consider that one of our achievements so far has been to have raised the bar. There is more intense competition, resulting in more energy and movement, and that that will ultimately benefit the whole profession.

Talking about cultural impact, can you speak to the differences you note between Vienna and Mexico City? The design sensibilities, issues and challenges faced by the profession in Europe and Latin America?

The main difference, I think, lies in the challenges. Mexico City is one of the largest cities in the world with over 20 million people living in the metropolitan zone, and it keeps growing exponentially... The city is both an urban, logistical nightmare and a miracle. Our program director for Visual Communication once made a short list of the context for designers in Mexico which included the following points: 10 percent of the population illiterate; one third of the population with basic reading skills; 4.5 million daily rides on the underground in Mexico City; one telephone line per every ten inhabitants of the country; 6 million with access to the Internet (5.5 percent penetration); US$10 average budget per person spent on books; 64,000 design students: 3,000 graduates of graphic design every year. The numbers might be somewhat outdated but add traffic,

pollution and social issues, and it can be somewhat overwhelming.

How to compare this with Vienna?! One only has to contrast the headlines on the front pages of the newspapers to understand that the problems here are of a different scale and range. Or drive from the airport to the city through the high forest of enormous billboards, or walk down one of the streets with hand painted typography and signage overload. How to communicate with such a diverse audience, in such a filled space? How to design in an environment where the supply of basic skills and materials may be temporary, production consistency the exception, quality control a luxury, and distribution an impossibility? But rather than frustration, this environment has fermented incredible energy and ingenuity that measure up to the challenges. I have found that many successful designers here are resourceful problem solvers on all possible fronts: from production logistics to networking skills to business abilities—the entire value chain of the profession is often integrated in one person.

You are also involved with the Art Center College of Design, Pasadena as a strategic consultant for international initiatives. What does this role entail?

I worked as a consultant for Art Center College of Design from 2005 to early 2007. Art Center played a crucial role in the development of the structure for CENTRO's study plans and they also consulted us on a wide range of other academic and operational aspects.

After the successful opening of CENTRO, Art Center invited me to be part of a team that was investigating the potential of extending the college in a

dynamic, content driven, and pioneering way to Barcelona following an invitation it had received by the city authorities and the government of Catalonia. It was an extremely intense time as Richard Koshalek (president) and Erica Clark (senior vice president international initiatives) are two of the most visionary, inspiring and dedicated people I have met, and simply to keep up with them is a challenge... To be able to contribute by working weekends and late nights became a routine. We interviewed over 200 key figures from different fields related to design, built networks with opinion leaders and important institutions, analyzed ideas, developed possible models and structures, discussed and rethought them with representatives from the Art Center team, fundraised, etc. Seldom in my life have I felt that all my skills and senses were so completely employed and stretched as during this project, it was a period of rapid growth far beyond the professional aspect.

Unfortunately, this time coincided with a personal tragedy in my family and I had to make space and time to attend to it, so I had to pass on my responsibilities at Art Center. The good news is that the project has so many fantastic people involved and thus has managed to achieve impressive results within the last year. In March 2008 the first "Art Center Global Dialogues" will be presented in Barcelona: a series of on-stage conversations with internationally renowned thinkers in many fields whose "disruptive" ideas and actions challenge convention, break current paradigms, and inspire positive changes in the larger world.

And this is only the beginning...

"Ultimately, design—in its many incarnations—is my way of connecting with the world."

Moira
Cullen

MARCIA
LAUSEN

Photo by Kathryn Marchetti, UIC News

NATIONALITY

American

YEAR BORN

1953

CURRENTLY RESIDING IN

Chicago, Illinois, United States

YEARS IN THE BUSINESS

25

CURRENT POSITION/FIRM

Principal, Studio/lab

Director, School of Art and Design,
University of Illinois at Chicago

Professor, graphic design,
University of Illinois at Chicago

PREVIOUS EMPLOYMENT

Various design studios in Boston, San Francisco, and Chicago

DESIGN EDUCATION

MFA, graphic design, Yale University,
School of Art (1985)

BFA, graphic design, Indiana University,
School of Fine Arts (1981)

After the unclear results of the confusing voting ballots in Florida during the U.S. Presidential election of 2000, citizens—designers included—reacted vociferously to the flawed process. Marcia Lausen has been deeply involved in stimulating change in the voting process through design. With a complete redesign for the Cook County ballot in Illinois and with the help of her students at the School of Art and Design at University of Illinois at Chicago, Lausen has built a compelling case—carefully assembled in her book Design for Democracy: Ballot and Election Design—*for its embrace across the nation. Lausen founded the Chicago office of Studio/lab in 1993, she has been solidly involved with the design community through AIGA since the mid-1990s, and she has devoted much energy to solidifying design education.*

You've had a nice professional progression, starting as a designer in the early 1980s, senior designer in the late 1980s, design director in the early 1990s, and segueing into a founder of the Studio/lab Chicago office in 1996. In retrospect, how important was it to have all this previous experience to take on your current role?

Very important. I moved around a lot—to different cities and through different types of design organizations—all on a quest to learn and grow. I would do things that I knew were not in my character (i.e., one year in advertising) just to see what it was like. All I've done in the past adds up to what I'm doing today. I have very specific ideas about how I want to experience and share design processes and outcomes, and these ideas are informed by actual experiences (both good and bad).

One of your most celebrated projects has been the proposed redesign of the voting ballot for Cook County in Chicago after the 2000 election, which in turn led to the creation of Design for Democracy, a non-profit organization devoted to improving the voting experience. What have been the highlights of this process?

The opportunity to demonstrate the potential impact of design to a broad audience that was previously unaware of what we do. I became engaged with this work as an act of advocacy for the profession.

You received an MFA from the Yale University Graduate Program in graphic design in 1985, just as the Macintosh was being introduced. Do you remember this having an effect on your first job?

I graduated one year before the first Yale class received Macintosh computers, so I missed the boat on this. In an educational environment in 1985, I can imagine that there was some fun experimentation. However, in this same time period in the professional world, I can remember that everything designed on a computer had a very specific look. There were very compromised versions of the typical print products, such as highly formatted newsletters. The type controls were nothing like we have now. Those of us concerned about typographic refinements were a bit resistant or uninterested. I didn't have access to a computer in my first few jobs. When I moved to California in 1989, everyone was working on a Mac, so I quickly got up to speed. And, of course, the software was rapidly getting better.

1

2

3

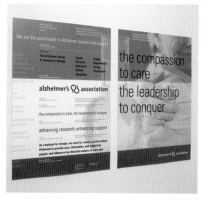

4

5

rar

6

7

Unless otherwise noted art direction by Marcia Lausen. **[1, 2, 3]** *Identity, brand guidelines and posters for Alzheimer's Association; design by Kelly Bjork, Jill Hoffheimer, Tara Kennedy and Jody Work; writing by Wendie Wulff (2004). Photographs by Tim Wilson.* **[4, 5, 6]** *Environmental graphics and wayfinding for the Spertus Insitute; architecture by Krueck & Sexton Architects; design by Jody Work, Hillary Geller and Cheyenne Medina (2007). Photographs by Tim Wilson.* **[7]** *Christina Ramberg Drawings, Gallery 400 University of Illinois at Chicago College of Architecture and the Arts; design by Marcia Lausen; (2000). Photograph by Wes Cleaver.*

8
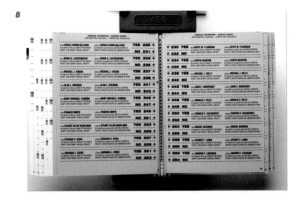

9
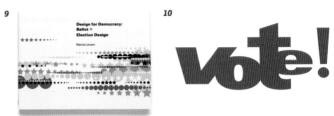

10

11

12
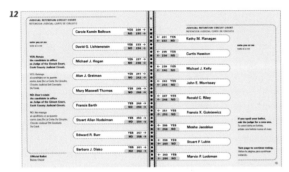

13

Looking back, it is amazing to think about how long it took to make things without a computer... sizing images on a stat camera, using metal or press type and specifying, ordering and waiting for type from typesetters. It's great that we can now do all this quickly and inexpensively. As a result, design processes have become much more fluid and experimental and intuitive.

You have lectured and written about education matters, and you have been teaching at the University of Illinois at Chicago since 1994. How do you see the role of design education changing? How do you approach teaching?

Like the profession itself, the role of design education is becoming more complex. We can only address so much in four years of undergraduate study. Because they are seeking to add a variety of desired skills such as writing, design research, interaction design and interdisciplinary team practice, many programs are greatly reducing their focus on the basics. Immersive study in typography, form-making, visual abstraction—those things that give us our design "chops"—are being sacrificed as we "dive right in" to complex problem definition and solution.

My approach has been to find ways to incorporate the teaching of basic skills into broader, more collaborative contexts. In essence, like many of my colleagues in design education, I'm seeking to double up on instruction.

A natural evolution for our profession is a future in which we recognize the limitations of an undergraduate education and encourage more designers to engage in postgraduate studies. We like to consider ourselves professionals as opposed to service providers. Yet the professions with which we compare ourselves (doctors, lawyers, etc.) require advanced specialized degrees to practice. These areas of study and practice have clearly defined the nature and role of research for their profession, and they have more established forms of publication and peer review. We are an emerging profession that has just begun to head down this path.

You have been a notable member of the Chicago design community since the late 1980s. What has kept you in the city and involved with organizations like AIGA?

Chicago is one of the world's great cities. AIGA is the forum for our professional voice. Life is good.

[8, 12] Cook County Ballot, before and after; design by Marcia Lausen (2000). [9, 11, 13] Design for Democracy: Ballot + Election Design by Marcia Lausen, University Of Chicago Press; design by Marcia Lausen and Cheyenne Medina. (2007). Photographs by Tim Wilson. [10] Logo for the election design initiative of Design for Democracy; design by Veronica Belsuzarri, Thomas Brandenburg, graphic design students at University of Illinois at Chicago with Marcia Lausen as instructor (2001).

MARIAN
BANTJES

NATIONALITY
Canadian

YEAR BORN
1963

CURRENTLY RESIDING IN
Bowen Island, British Columbia, Canada

YEARS IN THE BUSINESS
As what? Either 3 or 13

CURRENT POSITION/FIRM
Graphic artist

PREVIOUS EMPLOYMENT
Graphic designer
Book typesetter

An illustrator, designer, writer and teacher, Marian Bantjes carries the weight of twenty-three years of knowledge, experience and practice in design and typography. From an island off the coast of Vancouver, Bantjes has worked as a book typesetter, run her own design business and now straddles and blurs the line between design, typography and illustration. She has been the Communications Chair on the Board of the Society of Graphic Designers of Canada (GDC), BC Chapter 2003–2006; teaches typography through Emily Carr Institute of Art + Design, in Vancouver, Canada; and is a writer for Speak Up. She collaborates with designers across the world, and her work has been widely published and celebrated.

There is one thing everyone wants to know... Do you keep an army of vectorizing lemmings in your basement that helps you twist and turn the hundreds of thousands of Bézier curves found in your work? If no lemmings are involved, tell us a little about how you produce some of your work.

I wish I had lemmings. Smart lemmings. But, alas, it's just me. I can't say I really understand this fascination people have with my process. It's pretty simple: I draw in pencil, then painstakingly trace in vector, and then adjust, adjust, adjust. If there's any magic involved it's my ability to create a good and natural curve by pencil, and my ability to see where and how it's wrong in vector art, and fix it. I suspect this is an uncommon ability, and I have no idea how I got it or when. To me, it's as natural as dreaming.

Ornamentation in the most unexpected and innovative ways—muscle cars lace, anyone?—is your defining modus operandi. How did you arrive at it? It doesn't seem like something you stumble upon.

I am still learning about myself and finding new clues as to what makes me tick. While most of my work has manifested itself in something of an ornamental nature, the form and visual flavor varies widely. What all my work shares is complexity, and this is what interests me most. I like figuring out how to resolve or even create complex arrangements and forms—not in aid of making them simpler, but in aid of making them more interesting. About twenty years ago I became obsessed with patterns, and that's certainly when both the "figuring things out" and the ornament started to emerge. But, believe it or not, I'm extraordinarily good at writing instructions and structuring logical information, and I would infinitely prefer to spend my time working on something with complex hierarchy, even if it meant working with square boxes, than I would making a single word exist in a swirl of flourishes. So the ornament is a manifestation of a deeper interest, and if the ornament is not creating its own structure or connecting with itself or other elements in some complex way, then it's not interesting to me. I have a deep distaste of the current "barf on the page" manifestation of ornament, where people regurgitate all manner of swirls and graphic ephemera over everything in sight. It has no structure or reason, and its only complexity is abundance. I find it very upsetting and very ugly.

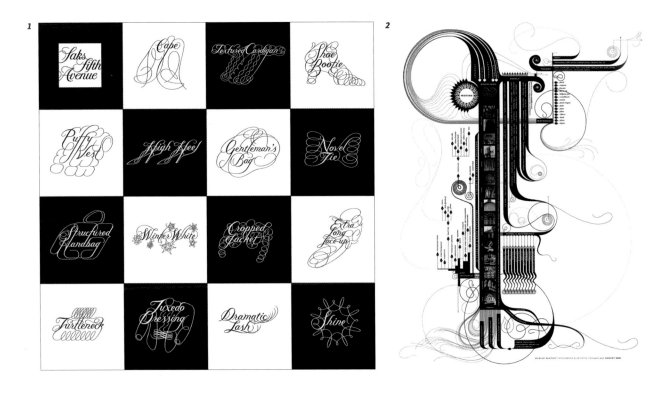

Before doing what you do now, you had a previous life as a graphic designer and even typesetter. How do those experiences influence your current work?

Well, my life as a graphic designer gave me a near phobia about working with people who aren't themselves in the graphic arts. I had a very average experience as a designer producing above average (but not extraordinary) work. And while I must have learned skills while I was a designer, mostly I learned lessons from what was largely a bad experience. I wish that weren't so, because I sometimes have attitude problems that

I need to self-correct with a rolled-up newspaper. My years as a book typesetter were far more positive and influential on my work and on the way I think about type and design. Book typesetting is very rule bound, conservative and "correct," and I like structure and order and systems. I'm deeply influenced by having learned to work with type the "right" way, in all its glorious detail—even if it's to break every damned rule I've always abided by! But the truth is I'm very good with type. Maybe even excellent. I'm extremely proud of my typographic skills, and I know it doesn't go unnoticed. A large part of the respect I've earned is

> **"I'm very good with type. Maybe even excellent. I'm extremely proud of my typographic skills, and I know it doesn't go unnoticed."**

because it's obvious I know what I'm doing, and what may look wacky on the surface has this very solid foundation. Book typesetting gave me that.

In a span of three or four years you went from unemployed, doing free T-shirts for design blogs—us!—to overbooked, creating artwork for dozens of high profile clients—Saks! Other than hard work, what do you attribute this quick success to?

The free T-shirt. As flippant as that may sound, I owe a huge debt to Speak Up. Yes, I was already out there self-promoting, and the quality of my work had not gone completely unnoticed. However, the T-shirt led to *Details* magazine, which was my first paid job; but more importantly it led to Rick Valicenti. Rick and I became friends, and while I'm not aware of him having overtly promoted me (until

[1] *Illustrated "Want it!" items for Saks Fifth Avenue; in collaboration with Terron Schaefer, senior vice president of marketing (2007).* **[2]** *Influence Map created for Milton Glaser's summer class at the School of Visual Arts (2006).*

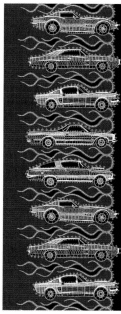

In August of 2003 Speak Up held a T-shirt contest (which would be decided by popular vote), promising neither fame nor fortune to the winner. Of the 39 submitted designs, Marian's T-shirt got the most votes (59 out of 490) and was printed with flashy silver ink on black.

the Fox River Paper portfolio piece on me, which was a wonderful gift that happened after I'd already achieved some notoriety), I have often wondered if my association with him didn't make Stefan Sagmeister and perhaps others give me a more serious look. It was also through Speak Up that I met (in an online sense, and later in person) Michael Bierut, who has hired me for several projects—one of which is for Saks Fifth Avenue. And, of course, there's Debbie Millman, fellow Speak Up author and now a good friend, who *has* overtly promoted me. So it was this

weird thing, through the strength of my work, my writing and the friends I made on the Internet, that suddenly I gained all this attention. Now I am friends with, know and/or have worked with many of the big names in graphic design—and some wonderful, talented people—and it's simply amazing to me because it was never a goal… what has happened in the past three years is so far beyond my goals that I never even imagined it. And it's ironic considering how, in the beginning with Speak Up, I worried about how much time I was "wasting" on this web site. I feel very lucky, like I am one of the alumni that came out of this very special placc, with a great core of people, at just the right time.

Having such a specific and recognizable style, does it worry you that you might

become repetitive? How do you inject new ideas into your work?

Well, I am not worried about myself, but I am very worried about the perception of my work and the kind of work that I am asked to do. My own interests are extensive, and the ideas come thicker and faster than I can ever hope to execute them. They have commonalities but also surprising variation. The problem is that most of the things I am interested in are, well, a little weird or challenging visually, and it takes a while for people to get used to unexpected things. I'm having a real problem with people treating my work like a catalogue from which they pick a style and ask me to create something in that style. This is intensely boring to me, and I'm currently training myself to turn down work of this nature. I really am not

[3, 4] Lace muscle cars created for the Fox River Paper promotion on her work. Promotion designed by Rick Valicenti (2006).

5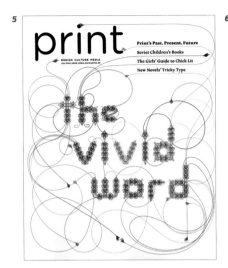

6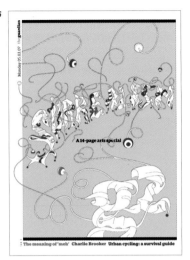

7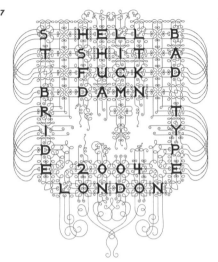

8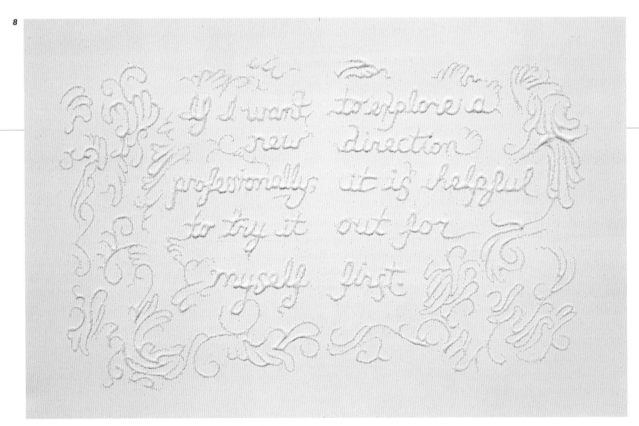

[5] *Magazine cover, "The Vivid Word" for* Print *(2006).* [6] *Cover for* The Guardian's *supplement, G2: Surrealism (2007).* [7] *Poster for the St. Bride Conference, "Bad Type"; ultimately, it was not used (2004). The poster uses a prototype of the typeface Restraint released in 2007.* [8] *From Stefan's "Things I have learned..." series; one of six pieces in sugar (2007).*

9

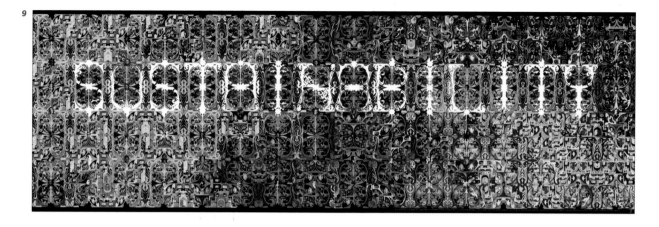

10

"It has occurred to me recently that working 90 percent of my waking hours is not really what you would call a balanced life, nevertheless I'm afraid it's often true. Within this time I would say I spend it:"

- Drawing at a table
- Drawing/working on the computer
- Sitting in a chair thinking
- E-mail, web, writing, mooning over unattainable men, and so-called administration

the go-to girl for flourishes. However, this makes my future uncertain as those people willing to take a leap of faith with me are rare, but those who do are well rewarded. By far my best work has come from people who give me very simple, wide-open design briefs. If I can keep finding those people I am confident my work will continue to evolve and surprise.

You live in a small, 3,500-people island off the coast of Vancouver. What advantages are there to your lifestyle? How do you think it would differ if you lived in a big city?

One of the advantages is my low cost of living. When I left my design company in 2004, my income dropped to zero and stayed at zero for a year and a half. There is no way I could have survived that without having the relatively low overhead

that I have here (plus, no dependents!). Also, I work a lot, but I don't work hard. I putter around, take breaks, go to the beach… all in all I have a very stress-free life. But, also, I'm not constantly interrupted by other people or having to drive here or there to go to meetings. It's very quiet here, and clean and incredibly beautiful. That I can live and work from this semi-remote place is a kind of miracle.

I do get lonely, though. A couple of years ago I was considering moving to New York. I have so many friends there now, and I imagined how we would all get together and have so much fun. But eventually I realized how fuckin' busy people are and how busy I would have to be in order to pay to live there. So I visit, and that works out just fine.

---

[9] *"Sustainability," commissioned by William Drenttel for Stora Enso (2007).* **[10]** *From Stefan Sagmeister's "Things I have learned…," series in six billboards (2006).*

MOIRA
CULLEN

It's hard to imagine how the role of design within a mammoth corporation like Coca-Cola or Hallmark is perceived and valued when it is surrounded by layers of corporate life—for Moira Cullen, it's not a matter of imagination, but her responsibility. In 2000, Cullen first led the Hallmark design team to break through and become an integral part of the business, while also attracting designers from across the nation. After five years, she assumed the role of design director at Coca-Cola, arguably the biggest brand in the world. How is that for responsibility? Cullen also acted as department chair of Communication Arts at Otis College of Art and Design before Hallmark, and has been actively involved with AIGA throughout her career.

You led the Corporate Design Group at Hallmark. What was this experience like? Was it a welcome contrast after working in design firms like Pentagram and Push Pin?

Hallmark is a beloved brand. It was my professional home for five years. After accepting their invitation to help grow an internal design culture, I seized the chance to revive the brand's design legacy and elevate our designers' organizational presence (and power) not just to design product but also to contemporize the brand. What began as an entrepreneurial experiment within the creative department and were later legitimized (and subsidized) by marketing as a valued strategic resource. We unleashed some amazing design thinking and talent that animated the brand's promise to enrich lives. And by crossing over to "the other side" (from creative to corporate with a stint in academia in between), I built a rich 360° perspective of designing—from instruction to ideation, process through production. And I gained an invaluable, unvarnished view of design's role in business (initially humbling), including daily practice in the artful navigation of politics, managing perceptions and the importance of language.

You are currently design director for Coca-Cola North America. It goes without saying that this must be no easy task. What do you expect to achieve in this position? What are some of the greater challenges?

I'm here to develop and lead a strong internal team that partners with brilliant design firms to create the new icons of twenty-first-century refreshment. There are multiple brands across a variety of categories, including bottlers, printers, distributors and retailers; the scope and scale of the enterprise can be daunting. A key challenge is time: It's called FMCG—fast moving consumer goods—for a reason. Another challenge is culture: Promoting design's value in a business led by rational, linear thinkers is not for the faint of heart. While our products are ephemeral, they are also personal: People hold them in their hands, put them to their lips and carry them as they travel through the day. And as brands, they embody ideas and values that have resonance in people's lives. Design plays a significant role in this emotional and functional exchange. The end goal: Integrate design thinking into the mix, drive strategy, build speed and scale, and inspire culture (inside and out).

As department chair of Communication Arts at Otis College of Art and Design from

1996 to 2000, what principles did you look to instill in the program?

I had a strong vision that my role as leader of the graphic design and illustration programs was to inspire and prepare students for twenty-first-century professions. We were educating the next generation of visual thinkers. I challenged them to be curious, courageous collaborators; to transcend traditional boundaries of media and defined disciplines; and to tell stories, shape messages and create experiences that make cultural, emotional connections by giving abstract ideas and information a tangible, visible form. Together with a dedicated faculty team and a terrific roster of visiting lec-

turers and guest speakers, we created a vibrant, open environment—a creative community—that encouraged risk and experimentation and supported the friction of diverse views. We recalibrated a dynamic curriculum to develop conceptual and strategic thinking expressed through strong craft, writing, presentation and technical skills, with a keen understanding of context and empathy for people's diverse desires and needs.

You've been in many leadership positions with AIGA: President of the Los Angeles and Kansas City chapters, president of the Center for Brand Experience and, most recently, a member of the National Board. These go

beyond volunteer positions. What attracts you to these opportunities?

I believe in the transformative power of design. As a process, a way of thinking, interacting and producing, it creates true value. AIGA offers an amazing framework, forum, network and community to animate this potential. Developing conferences and competitions, curating exhibits, producing events, leading and growing local chapters—I love bringing people together to make something happen. It's the ultimate service and a fulfilling way to extend my contribution to the profession. Ultimately, design—in its many incarnations—is my way of connecting with the world.

[1, 2, 3] Hallmark brand strategy; design with Darren Abbott and Amanda Halbrook. [4] Coca-Cola packaging, for Coca-Cola Classic and Coca-Cola Zero; design by Turner Duckworth; and Diet Coke; design by CMA Design (2006-07). [5] Coca-Cola packaging for Coca-Cola Classic, Coca-Cola Zero and Diet Coke; design by Turner Duckworth (2006-07).

"Although I write for civilians—general readers, rather than designers—in my International Herald Tribune columns, I really enjoy the insider discourse around graphic design on blogs like Design Observer and in magazines such as Dot Dot Dot. I look forward to the emergence of a similar debate in multimedia design."

Alice
Rawsthorn

Detail of: *Design Museum identity by Graphic Thought Facility (2003).*

NAGI
NODA

NATIONALITY

Japanese

CURRENTLY RESIDING IN

Tokyo, Japan

YEARS IN THE BUSINESS

12

CURRENT POSITION/FIRM

Freelance director

Art director

Artist

Fashion designer

Dancing eyeballs, fitness-video-exercising poodles, half pandas/half other animals, and singing merchandise in a boutique store are only a few of the vivid, perplexing imaginings of Nagi Noda, the talented, eccentric and boundary-pushing artist, art director and fashion designer from Tokyo. Unfettered from any discipline or industry limits, Noda's work extends from book design and music packaging, to short films, to music videos and commercials—including a hypnotic ad for Coca-Cola, with music by the White Stripes's Jack White, commissioned by London agency Mother—and even to clothing design. Noda is signed with Partizan, a leading agency that represents cutting-edge directors, photographers and artists.

[1] *Television commercial for Coca-Cola world (2006).* **[2]** *Music video for "She's My Man" by Scissor Sisters (2007).* **[3]** *Music video for "Far From Home" by Tiga (2006).*

hanPanda

©2004 nagi noda/uchu-country

[4, 5, 9] *Advertising campaign for Laforet (2006–07).* **[6, 7]** *Logo and products for Hanpanda (2005).* **[8]** *"Ex-Fat Girl" short film for Panasonic (2004).*

[10] Advertising campaign for Nike (2002). [11] Advertising campaign for Laforet (2003). [12] "Sentimental Journey" (YUKI) music video for Epic Records (2003). [13] Relax magazine (2006). [14, 15] Advertising campaign for IT company (2008).

PAULINA
REYES

Energetic, cheerful and colorful sums up the work and personality of Paulina Reyes, a Mexican-born designer and illustrator who has been working in the U.S. since 1999, first in Minneapolis with Laurie DeMartino, whom she met as an exchange student at Minneapolis College of Art and Design, and then at Duffy & Partners. In 2003 she moved to New York to work with Louise Fili, and soon after joined Kate Spade—where her exuberantly minimalist style has adorned many of their products, including handbags, knit hats, umbrellas and adorable baby china. Reyes has been named a Young Gun by the Art Directors Club and one of the New Visual Artists (under 30) by Print magazine.

NATIONALITY
Mexican

YEAR BORN
1976

CURRENTLY RESIDING IN
New York, New York, United States

YEARS IN THE BUSINESS
9

CURRENT POSITION/FIRM
Art director, Kate Spade

PREVIOUS EMPLOYMENT
Louise Fili Ltd. (2003)
Duffy & Partners (2001-03)
Laurie DeMartino Design (1999-2000)
Artes de Mexico (1998)
Freelance illustration in Mexico City (1998-99)

DESIGN EDUCATION
BA, Universidad Iberoamericana, Mexico City (1998)
Minneapolis College of Art and Design (1997)

1

2

[1] *Proposed illustration for a Kate Spade agenda (2005).* [2] *Fish totes for Kate Spade (2006).*

[3] *Illustration for Kate Spade's baby paper line, for Kate Spade and Crane & Co. (2006).* **[4]** *Illustration of cafeteria cups for Target stores (1998).*
[5] *Baby china for Kate Spade (2005).* **[6]** *Proposed illustration for a Kate Spade agenda (2005).*

SARA
DE BONDT

NATIONALITY

Belgian

YEAR BORN

1977

CURRENTLY RESIDING IN

London, United Kingdom

YEARS IN THE BUSINESS

10

CURRENT POSITION/FIRM

Director, Sara De Bondt

PREVIOUS EMPLOYMENT

Printer Imperialiste (1996)
Koninklijke Musea voor Kunst en Geschiedenis (1999)
Foundation 33 (2001-03)

DESIGN EDUCATION

BFA, Sint-Lukas, Brussels (1997)
MFA, graphic design, Sint-Lukas, Brussels (1999)
Erasmus exchange programme, graphic design,
Universidad de Bellas Artes, Granada (1998)
Postgraduate research residency, Jan van Eyck Akademie,
Maastricht (2001)

Somewhere between the formal and experimental use and execution of typography lies the work of Belgian-born Sara De Bondt—strictly refined and carefully deployed, yet subtly different and unmisakably out of the ordinary. After working with Daniel Eatock at Foundation 33 for two years, De Bondt opened her London studio in 2003, where she designs books, identities and exhibit graphics (among other projects) for cultural institutions and, every so often, for herself, where she is prone to a little sense of humor— whether it's a postcard with two mailing sides, or a T-shirt with a single, wandering "hair" silk-screened on the lower torso. De Bondt teaches at Central Saint Martins College of Art & Design and leads workshops across Europe.

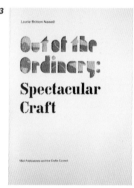

[1, 2, 4] Corporate identity, printed matter and book for Wiels, Centre for Contemporary Art, Brussels; typeface developed with Jo De Baerdemaeker; booklet cover image developed with Benoit Platéus (ongoing). [3, 5] Out of the Ordinary: Spectacular Craft by Laurie Britton-Newell, Glenn Adamson and Tanya Herrod, catalogue for V&A Museum (2007).

6

7

8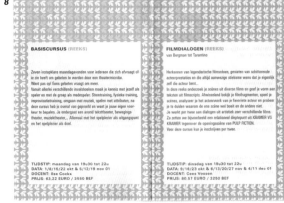

9

DESIGN AND ARCHITECTURE

Autumn 2005

●● BRITISH
●● COUNCIL

10

11

12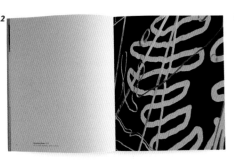

13

[6, 7, 8] Program brochures for Theaterwerkgroep Kopspel (2001–04). *[9, 10]* Illustrations and layout of the Design & Architecture *newsletter for the British Council, Design & Architecture department (2005).* *[11, 12, 13]* DJ Simpson: Selected Works 2000–5 *for Mead Gallery and DJ Simpson; in collaboration with James Goggin (2006).*

TAMYE
RIGGS

For more than a decade, Tamye Riggs has been intimately involved with type in different, enriching capacities. In the mid- to late 1990s she was creative director for Phil's Fonts and GarageFonts, and later she was general manager for the bustling, digital foundry FontShop International. Riggs's reputation, though, has come from her incessant display of poise, patience and perseverance since 2002 as the executive director and overall enabler of TypeCon, a yearly conference that has grown since 1998 into one of the most engaging events of the year. Concurrent with that activity, Riggs is executive director of the Society of Typographic Aficionados, which is responsible for the conference as well as other initiatives. Riggs also writes for publications like HOW and has co-edited the popular Indie Fonts book series.

NATIONALITY
American

YEAR BORN
1960s

CURRENTLY RESIDING IN
Alameda, California, United States

YEARS IN THE BUSINESS
20ish

CURRENT POSITION/FIRM
Freelance writer/editor/designer/typographer, TypeLife
Executive Director,
Society of Typographic Aficionados/TypeCon

PREVIOUS EMPLOYMENT
FontShop International (2004–05)
GarageFonts (1996–2001)
Fossil (1993–94)
DDB Needham Dallas (1989–93)
Tracy-Locke (1989–93)

1
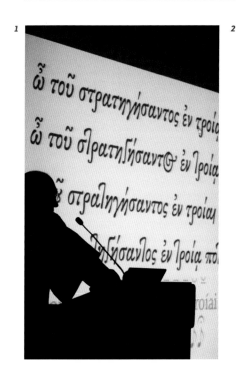

2

[1] *TypeCon2007 presentation by Robert Bringhurst. (2007). Photo by Eben Sorkin; copyright The Society of Typographic Aficionados.* **[2]** *Gabriel Martínez Meave at TypeCon2007 closing night (2007). Photo by Stephen Coles.*

3

4

5

"How do I divide my time? I'm a bit schizophrenic, bouncing around between all projects at a given time. It sometimes takes more time to get things done, but the resultant cross-project inspiration is essential. Working from home cuts out the time suck and frustration of a daily commute. The downside is that it tends to blur the lines between work and non-work life—I end up being "on call" a lot more than I should; I try to involve my family in my work so that there is more togetherness. I travel frequently and whenever possible I combine trips, packing in tons of meetings and socializing so that the time away from home is spent fruitfully. The closer I get to a major deadline or event, the more I multitask— I thrive on the intensity and adrenaline surge that comes with impending chaos."

[3] Book series Indie Fonts *co-authored with Richard Kegler and James Grieshaber (2003-07).* **[4]** *Type specimen for Akira Kobayashi's online showcase for Monotype Imaging (2007).* **[5]** *Interpretation of Utopia in collaboration with Corp.Unit for Transmission: Utopia (2001).*

"For me, there is little difference between working and non-working. I love everything that I do (well, almost everything), so what I do does not really feel like work, so to speak. It is all part of the life I have always dreamed of living."

Debbie
Millman

CONTRIBUTORS

ALICE RAWSTHORNE
INTERNATIONAL HERALD TRIBUNE
IHT.COM

ALICE TWEMLOW
SCHOOL OF VISUAL ARTS
DESIGNCRITICISM.SVA.EDU

ALLYSON LACK
PRINCIPLE
DESIGNBYPRINCIPLE.COM

AMY FRANCESCHINI
FUTUREFARMERS
FUTUREFARMERS.COM

ANN WILLOUGHBY
WILLOUGHBY DESIGN GROUP
WILLOUGHBYDESIGN.COM

ANNE BURDICK
THE OFFICES OF ANNE BURDICK
BURDICKOFFICES.COM

APRIL GREIMAN
MADE IN SPACE
MADEINSPACE.LA

BARBARA DEWILDE
DEWILDE DESIGN
KNOPF PUBLISHING GROUP
RANDOMHOUSE.COM/KNOPF

BARBARA KRUGER

BONNIE SIEGLER
NUMBER 17
NUMBER17.COM

BRYN MOOTH
HOW MAGAZINE
HOWDESIGN.COM

CARIN GOLDBERG
CARIN GOLDBERG DESIGN
CARINGOLDBERG.COM

CATELIJNE VAN MIDDELKOOP
STRANGE ATTRACTORS DESIGN
STRANGEATTRACTORS.COM

CATHERINE ZASK
CATHERINE ZASK
CATHERINEZASK.COM

CHEE PEARLMAN
CHEE COMPMANY
CHEECOMPANY.COM

DEBORAH ADLER
MILTON GLASER, INC.
MILTONGLASER.COM

DEBORAH SUSSMAN
SUSSMAN/PREJZA & COMPANY, INC.
SUSSMANPREJZA.COM

DITI KATONA
CONCRETE DESIGN COMMUNICATIONS INC.
CONCRETE.CA

ELAINE LUSTIG COHEN

ELLEN LUPTON
ELUPTON.COM

DEBBIE MILLMAN
STERLING BRANDS
STERLINGBRANDS.COM
DEBBIEMILLMAN.BLOGSPOT.COM

EMILY KING

EMILY OBERMAN
NUMBER 17
NUMBER17.COM

EMILY POTTS
ROCKPORT PUBLISHERS
ROCKPUB.COM

ESTHER MUN
LITTLE FURY
LITTLEFURY.COM

FANETTE MELLIER
FANETTEMELLIER.COM

GAEL TOWEY
MARTHAS TEWART LIVING OMNIMEDIA
MARTHASTEWART.COM

GAIL ANDERSON
SPOTCO
SPOTNYC.COM

GEORGIANNA STOUT
2X4
2X4.ORG

IRMA BOOM
IRMA BOOM OFFICE
IRMABOOM.NL

JANET FROELICH
THE NEW YORK TIMES
NYTIMES.COM

JENNIFER MORLA
MORLA DESIGN
MORLADESIGN.COM

JENNIFER STERLING

JENNIFER SUKIS
PRINCIPLE
DESIGNBYPRINCIPLE.COM

JESSICA HELFAND
WINTERHOUSE STUDIO
WINTERHOUSE.COM
DESIGN OBSERVER
DESIGNOBSERVER.COM

JHOANA MORA
ESQUINA NORTE
ESQUINANORTE.COM

JOYCE RUTTER KAYE
PRINT MAGAZINE
PRINTMAG.COM

JULIA HOFFMANN
CRISPIN PORTER + BOGUSKY
CPBGROUP.COM

JULIE LASKY
I.D. MAGAZINE
ID-MAG.COM

KARIN FONG
IMAGINARY FORCES
IMAGINARYFORCES.COM

KATHERINE MCCOY
MCCOY & MCCOY ASSOCIATES
HIGH GROUND TOOLS AND STRATEGIES
 FOR DESIGN
HIGHGROUNDDESIGN.COM

KATHLEEN MEANEY
TERMS & CONDITIONS
TERMSCONDITIONS.COM

KERSTIN SCHEUCH
CENTRO DE DISEÑO, CINE Y TELEVISIÓN
CENTRO.ORG.MX

LAURIE DEMARTINO
LAURIE DEMARTINO DESIGN CO.
LAURIEDEMARTINODESIGN.COM

LAURIE HAYCOCK MAKELA
O-B-O-K

LOUISE FILI
LOUISE FILI LTD
LOUISEFILI.COM

LOUISE SANDHAUS
CALIFORNIA INSTITUTE OF THE ARTS
CALARTS.EDU
LSD (LOUISE SANDHAUS DESIGN)
LSD-STUDIO.NET

LUBA LUKOVA
LUKOVA.NET

MARCIA LAUSEN
STUDIO/LAB
STUDIOLAB.COM

MARGO CHASE
CHASE DESIGN GROUP
CHASEDESIGNGROUP.COM

MARIAN BANTJES
BANTJES.COM

MEREDITH DAVIS
NORTH CAROLINA STATE UNIVERSITY
NCSU.EDU

MOIRA CULLEN
THE COCA-COLA COMPANY
THECOCA-COLACOMPANY.COM

MÓNICA PEÓN
IGLOO DESIGN
IGLOODESIGN.NET

NAGI NODA
UCHU-COUNTRY.COM

NOREEN MORIOKA
ADAMSMORIOKA, INC.
ADAMSMORIOKA.COM

PAMELA ZUCCKER
PRINCIPLE
DESIGNBYPRINCIPLE.COM

PAOLA ANTONELLI
THE MUSEUM OF MODERN ART (MOMA),
  DEPARTMENT OF ARCHITECTURE AND DESIGN
MOMA.ORG

PAULA SCHER
PENTAGRAM DESIGN
PENTAGRAM.COM

PAULINA REYES
KATE SPADE
KATESPADE.COM

PETRULA VRONTIKIS
VRONTIKIS DESIGN OFFICE
35K.COM
ART CENTER COLLEGE OF DESIGN
ARTCENTER.EDU

REBECA MÉNDEZ
REBECA MÉNDEZ DESIGN
REBECAMENDEZ.COM
UNIVERSITY OF CALIFORNIA
UCLA.EDU

ROBYNNE RAYE
MODERN DOG DESIGN CO.
MODERNDOG.COM

RUTH ANSEL
RUTH ANSEL DESIGN
RUTHANSEL.COM

SARA DE BONDT
SARA DE BONDT
SARADEBONDT.COM

SHARON WERNER
WERNER DESIGN WERKS, INC.
WDW.COM

SHEILA LEVRANT DE BRETTEVILLE
THE SHEILA STUDIO
YALE UNIVERSITY SCHOOL OF ART
ART.YALE.EDU

SUSAN KARE
KARE.COM

SUSAN SELLERS
2X4
2X4.ORG

TAMYE RIGGS
SOCIETY OF TYPOGRAPHIC AFICIONADOS
TYPESOCIETY.ORG

TINA CHANG
LITTLE FURY
LITTLEFURY.COM

VÉRONIQUE VIENNE

INDEX

MORE GREAT TITLES FROM HOW BOOKS

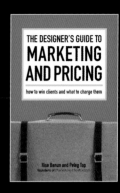

COLOR INDEX 2
By Jim Krause

This companion to Jim Krause's best-selling *Color Index* provides a new system for combining colors and features over 1500 new color combinations for print and web media. Includes CMYK and RGB formulas.

ISBN: 978-1-58180-938-1, 360 pages, #Z0670

BEYOND TREND
How to Innovate in an Over-Designed World
By Matt Mattus

Now that marketers have discovered the value that design brings to their brands, the pressure is on for creative people to continually deliver the newest looks and ideas. It's a whole new world for creatives, and big business is inviting you in. But the design world is becoming less predictable. Now that everything has been designed, what's next?

ISBN: 978-1-58180-961-9, 224 pages, #Z0682

THE WORD IT BOOK
Speak Up Presents a Gallery of Interpreted Words
By Bryony Gomez-Palacio and Armin Vit

Based on the poular online design community Speak Up (www.underconsideration.com/speakup), this fun and inspiring design gallery provides 30 simple words—accompanied by 8-10 thought-provoking visual interpretations—to inspire you to think about ordinary things in fresh ways.

ISBN: 978-1-58180-925-1, 224 pages, #Z0677

THE DESIGNER'S GUIDE TO MARKETING AND PRICING
How to Win Clients and What to Charge Them
By Ilise Benun and Peleg Top

From learning which marketing tools are most effective to discovering how to establish contact with potential clients, you'll learn how to achieve design success with this must-have guide for navigating the design business world.

ISBN: 978-1-60061-008-0, 256 pages, #Z1042

These and other great HOW Books titles are available at your local bookstore or from www.howbookstore.com.
www.howdesign.com

Odile

The body text is set in Odile, a family of eight fonts designed by Sibylle Hagmann in 2006 and available through the type co-op Village. Odile's upright italic functions delightfully as a display typeface throughout the book as well.

Ronnia

For display, as well as some of the book's tiny details, text is set in Ronnia, a family of twenty fonts designed by Veronika Burian and José Scaglione of Type-Together. Despite the extensive options provided by Ronnia, only the extra bold weight and its italic counterpart are utilized.